Ultrapreneuring

Ultrapreneuring

Taking a Venture from Start-up to Harvest
in Three Years or Less

James B. Arkebauer

McGraw-Hill, Inc.
New York   San Francisco   Washington, D.C.   Auckland   Bogotá
Caracas   Lisbon   London   Madrid   Mexico City   Milan
Montreal   New Delhi   San Juan   Singapore
Sydney   Tokyo   Toronto

Library of Congress Cataloging-in-Publication Data

Arkebauer, James B., date.
   Ultrapreneuring : taking a venture from start-up to harvest in
three years or less / James B. Arkebauer.
      p.   cm.
   Includes bibliographical references and index.
   ISBN 0-07-002508-8 (hard)—ISBN 0-07-002509-6 (pbk)
   1. New business enterprises—Management. 2. Entrepreneurship.
I. Title.
HD62.5.A74   1993
658'.041—dc20   93-19901
                                                    CIP

1 2 3 4 5 6 7 8 9 0 DOC/DOC 9 9 8 7 6 5 4 3

ISBN 0-07-002508-8 (hc)
ISBN 0-07-002509-6 (pbk)

*The sponsoring editor for this book was James H. Bessent, Jr. and the
production supervisor was Pamela A. Pelton. It was set in Baskerville by
North Market Street Graphics.*

Printed and bound by R. R. Donnelley & Sons Company.

This book is dedicated to
Geraldine C. Wenzel-Arkebauer

Contents

3. What It Takes to Be an Ultrapreneur   53

4. Building the Inside Ultrapreneurial Team   83

7. Securing Ultrapreneurial *Debt* Financing   **137**

8. Securing Ultrapreneurial *Equity* Financing   **157**

9. Making It Happen—Ultrapreneurial Style   193

Acknowledgments

Authors, not unlike Ultrapreneurs, have to choose an opportunity (a book's subject), assess the opportunity (identify the contents), put together a business plan (a book proposal), search for financing (find a publisher), and then execute the plan (write the book). Also like Ultrapreneurs, authors have to wait patiently, maybe even more so than Ultrapreneurs, for the harvest (will the book sell?).

All this, for both Ultrapreneurs and authors, requires a team effort. Although I identified the opportunity for this book, my editor, Jim Bessent of McGraw-Hill, focused the subject matter. He also helped by implementing the plan, leading the way in marketing the concept to his editorial board, and then leading the charge in shaping the final results. My thanks to an Ultrapreneurial team leader and to the rest of his team.

I also thank A. David Silver for yet another successful publisher contact. And I thank Maita Lester for Ultrapreneurial-type encouragement, and Ella Lester for her prowess in reading and spotting numerous author errors.

This book is dedicated to my mother. She spent decades correcting my English and I'm sure if she were capable today, she would have a field day with this manuscript and its contents. I miss that love.

James B. Arkebauer

Introduction

This book explains how to conceive and successfully execute a focused plan of starting a company, with the goal of selling the company at a predetermined stage for a predetermined price, to a predetermined buyer.

Even though entrepreneurship has been around a long time, its performance and execution evolves with the prevalent economic conditions of the day. This is even more prevalent as we prepare to enter the next century. Entrepreneurs have always been thought of as different, as independent spirits who are persistent, self-reliant, bootstrapping system buckers. Entrepreneurs have learned to be flexible within business cycles and aware of cyclical booms and crashes.

It is no different today. The '90s entrepreneurs are a different breed than their immediate predecessors from the '80s. The path to successful entrepreneurship is ever-changing as the art and science of entrepreneuring is taking on a new chameleon color. This new breed of entrepreneur is challenging the old notion that entrepreneurs are born, not made. There are several parts to this change.

Teaching Skills

One stems from the fact that universities across the country are now teaching entrepreneuring. This itself has come about because students see little opportunity, appeal, or security in conventional corporate jobs.

These courses emphasize development of analytical skills while at the same time imparting practical knowledge. They study anticipatory growth stages and the problems that accompany growth. This includes team building, persuasion, negotiating, and networking. The university premise is that entrepreneurship isn't about business; it's about solution strategies—ways

1

of solving problems in business or politics, the arts or philanthropy. Pick your entrepreneurial field.

With the spread of free markets, other countries are now encompassing entrepreneuring and cultivating entrepreneurs in business-school programs. Universities from Canada, Singapore, Bangkok, Spain, Italy, France, the United Kingdom, and the Pacific Rim countries are creating incubator programs that are designed to incubate and teach entrepreneurship. Many governmental bodies are also providing government financing, offering tax advantages, and special enterprise and trade zones to entrepreneurs. They have recognized that entrepreneurship is a potent force and will become more so in the coming decades. The growth of these programs worldwide shows that a fundamental change in the international business environment is afoot. This is creating a new breed of entrepreneur and is taking with it a change in political and economic philosophies in countries around the world. The results are leading to major advances in business practices and methods. Additionally, many governmental bodies, especially state and local, have developed special educational programs and financial incentives to encourage small business.

Global Competitiveness

Another part of the change is being dictated by our globally competitive, tight-financing, unforgiving business environment. Entrepreneurs no longer have the luxury of long development and product-proving timespans. Windows of market opportunity open and close rapidly. Consequently, new products and services are conceived, created, tested, produced, and marketed quickly. Besides, with speed they are done worldwide. You may be conceiving a product from your Fargo, North Dakota, United States location, while simultaneously an entrepreneur in Brussels, Belgium is also working on your same concept for the European market.

Add in just-in-time manufacturing capability, concurrent engineering, and electronic self-design, and it's easy to see that today's entrepreneur needs to have a different basic mindset about establishing and operating a company. That mindset is what I term *Ultrapreneuring.*

The Age of the Ultrapreneur

Summed up, *the Ultrapreneuring concept is to identify a business opportunity, determine its viability, and form a company. It requires assembling a supercompetent management team who then develop, produce, and market-prove the product or service. They then sell the majority interest in the com-*

pany. All of this with maximum resource leverage of both talent and money in the shortest, optimum time period.

Gone are the days of developing a company to die with—no more cradle-to-grave management thinking. Ultragrowth companies aren't made to pass on to the next generation. Ultrapreneurs create them and then sell out, merge, or combine. Their lifelong challenge is to do it again and again.

This presents new problems and challenges to entrepreneuring. Gone is the lonely gunslinger, replaced by a determined team. A team-developed Ultrapreneurial mindset is employed throughout all the organizational thinking. It must infiltrate all aspects of business planning and goal setting. The watch word is *harvest*. The sole intent is to build a company to sell out, to exit, to harvest. The challenge is to fashion a business strategy in such a way as to be able to leverage the investment dollars, the management team, the product or service niche to be attractive to a predetermined, designated purchaser.

It means that you predefine who that purchaser will be when you start the company. At the least, you have identified a narrow range of prospective buyers or the methods to sell your company. You have a feel for and continually analyze the industry, keeping your exit target in focus. *Everything you do is aimed at adding value to your exit plan.* Ultrapreneuring infiltrates all aspects of your planning, execution, and goal reassessment as you proceed.

This requires that from day one, conception, to day end, selling out, that all management disciplines are narrowly focused. It means that you analyze the initial product or service to be sure that it fits predetermined criteria, that you have the talents to guide an Ultragrowth company, that you assemble a management team that agrees with the ultimate goal, that you fashion an exit financing plan, and that production and marketing supports the harvest strategy. The Ultrapreneurial strategy itself dictates that one person can't do it all. It takes an Ultrapreneurial team to replace the single entrepreneur. The team has to design a business plan that focuses on growing the company quickly and effectively. The financing has to be flexible and the early stages of growth have to be tightly scheduled. All aspects of the company have to be aimed at the harvest.

Combining all these important parts is a distinct challenge. *Ultrapreneuring* guides you through these challenges.

Ultrapreneurial Qualifiers

This book is not written for small thinkers. A lot of studies have indicated that the failure rate for small companies is much greater than for those conceived to grow to midmarket size, i.e., $20 to $100 million in annual revenues. Consequently, two primary Ultragrowth qualifiers show up.

The first is that start-ups have a lot better chance of success if the first- to second-year sales revenues are a minimum of $500,000. $1 million in sales seems to be the better threshold.

Second, there appears to be a threshold size of at least ten employees, and more is better. This translates to a rule of thumb of $50,000 of sales per employee yearly, although this figure can vary considerably from industry to industry. Ultrapreneurs need to keep these figures in mind; their survival odds improve greatly when they can meet these types of minimums.

Preview of What You'll Learn

The entrepreneurs of the 1990s will be different from their predecessors; this book addresses many distinct ways that entrepreneurship has been and is changing to Ultrapreneurship.

Mary Anne Devanna of Columbia Business School said, "In the '80s, people learned they must take control of their careers and destinies."[1]

Ultrapreneuring addresses this point; it shows how people are taking control, by Ultrapreneuring. It's also chock-full of tried and tested how-to-do-its. It leads the reader through the details of specific company building techniques as it introduces the "Ultrapreneurial" approach.

This approach suggests that entrepreneurs can successfully conceive or identify a product or service around which they can create an Ultrapreneurial company. The management focus is toward growing that company quickly to a point that best achieves the highest investment return on the efforts and financing committed. This book addresses topics that Ultrapreneurs must incorporate into their thinking when building their company.

You, as a business reader, are short on time; consequently you want fast, specific, useful information presented in an easy-to-follow and comprehensible format. You want to quickly grasp the overall picture, but you also want to know that the details are there as needed. The promise is made and kept. Specific techniques are spelled out in each chapter, and plans for attacking, customizing, and implementing programs are provided. The how-to material is useful.

Interwoven in each chapter are reflections that illuminate the character and spirit of the Ultrapreneur. Examples include such diverse subjects as:

Ambition—the will to succeed

Creative Problem Solving—how to make business use of it

---

[1] Eleanor Siegel, "Doing Business Books," *Publishers Weekly,* August 17, 1990.

Fear of Success—does it hold one back?

Left/Right-Brain Thinking—pocketbooks versus emotions

Persuasion—ten tips

Planning—it's important, important, important

Risk—the psychological need to control our destiny

Success—tips on how to achieve and maintain it

Success Forces—steer you toward success or failure

All of these factors are aimed at Ultrapreneurship, part of the spirit of Ultrapreneuring.

Having had both success and failure in my personal entrepreneurial activities—as well as hundreds of venture capital entrepreneurial investing decisions—I have watched the evolution that is currently taking place. *Ultrapreneuring* is written as a guidebook for entrepreneurs and those associated with them.

The Opportunity

The first chapter of the book sets out the important guidelines for determining ripe, capitalistic opportunities. It discusses how the times are changing and how small companies have become the heartbeat of our free enterprise system. It notes the ingredients needed for a start-up, highlights a diverse group of opportunity areas to get your creative opportunity juices flowing, and points out some trendsetting statistics. This chapter also sets out the stages of growth of a company, noting some distinctive characteristics and warning signals.

The Ultragrowth Opportunity

The second chapter continues the opportunity search with an emphasis on the marketing side. It explores the marketing challenges to be considered, and gives you some marketing qualifiers to use in sorting through opportunities. One Ultrapreneuring trend is strategic partnering; cited are what to look for, how to qualify strategic partners, and how to be sure your emotions don't overrule your pocketbook when analyzing potential opportunities. Additionally, this chapter takes up the important subject of business goals and why they're needed. This is presented with a new twist that shows the importance of balanced goal setting. Finally, a checklist is provided for the initial analysis of any opportunity. Ultrapreneurs are being presented new challenges for Ultrapreneuring in the nineties, and this chapter leads you through these challenges.

What It Takes to Be an Ultrapreneur

As a student of the personal characteristics and nature of entrepreneurial success, I've had many discussions about entrepreneurs with other entrepreneurs, venture capitalists, investment bankers, human-resource people, academicians, and other support professionals. Generally speaking, entrepreneurs are hardy, ambitious, goal-achieving dreamers. They spend their lives in stressful environments working with stress-producing problems. While many succeed, many others fail, again and again. Still others merely survive. However, a few create entire new industries! Their common bond is hard work, dedication, perseverance, and spirit. This third chapter briefly looks at entrepreneurial history and then details the twelve basic characteristics of successful Ultrapreneurs. This is taken from many studies, sources, and personal observations. It goes on to note how Ultrapreneurs differ from entrepreneurs in their outlook toward failure, how they learn from it and use it to their benefit. This is tied back into success points which brings up an age-old debate of youth-versus-experience as well as female-versus-male Ultrapreneurs.

Building the Inside Ultrapreneurial Team

Eagles don't flock and Ultrapreneurs need eagles on their management team. The fourth chapter discusses the process of selecting and building a business team, starting with the definitions of the requirements needed for all management disciplines. It carries on into the valuable subjects of identifying, interviewing, and hiring tips. It also includes detailed pointers for assembling a working board of directors and advisors.

Assembling the Outside Ultrapreneurial Team

Unlike many entrepreneurial efforts, Ultrapreneurs recognize that their inside team members don't necessarily complete the picture. They know they need and depend on some outside players that must be integrated into and support the Ultrapreneurial concept. These outside team members are always highly qualified, very knowledgeable in their areas of specialization, and motivated to assuring that the Ultrapreneurial effort succeeds. They are consultants, advisors, accountants, and attorneys. The fifth chapter shows you how to identify, qualify, and retain these special outside team members.

Planning the Ultrapreneurial Venture

Chapter 6 establishes the premise that, for Ultrapreneurs, their business plan is like running the company on paper. The text reviews the two primary purposes of any business plan and notes the basic guidelines. It then outlines the fifteen key points that need to be covered in an Ultrapreneurial plan. Also addressed are how to structure and value an Ultrapreneurial company, as well as the key ratios that are used upfront to be sure that the Ultrapreneurial opportunity will be suitable for creating an Ultragrowth company.

Securing Ultrapreneurial Debt Financing

All companies have two primary financing choices: debt and equity. The key to successful Ultrapreneurial financing is how these choices are made. Chapter 7 talks about the choosing process, and explains the subtle differences in choices. It sets out the accepted stages of growth for Ultrapreneuring companies and then proceeds to explain the various types of debt financing as well as identifying the many sources of debt financing.

Securing Ultrapreneurial Equity Financing

The subject of equity financing, from identifying dollar-fund-providing angels, to finding, qualifying, approaching, and presenting your project to traditional venture capital funds is discussed in Chapter 8. Additionally, a major section discusses the most prevalent form of initial fundraising, the private placement, as well as other vehicles that are exemptions for the selling of Ultrapreneurial financing. Finally, the life-sustaining subject of cashflow is highlighted, and the Ultrapreneur's secret to financing is restated.

Making It Happen— Ultrapreneurial Style

After identifying the opportunity, assembling the team, and obtaining the financing, the Ultrapreneur's challenge is to make all the pieces fit, to be sure the business plan is executed flawlessly, and to assure that the company reaches its harvest goals. Chapter 9 concentrates on these challenges by discussing the importance of operational planning and the ongoing necessity of changes. The success philosophies and success forces that Ultrapreneurs need to possess and implement are noted, and the chapter concludes with a large group of Ultrapreneurial edicts, proclamations, and claims to live by to ensure a profitable Ultrapreneurial harvest.

The Ultrapreneurial Harvest

For Ultrapreneurs, the harvest is what most separates them from their entrepreneurial counterparts. While large companies and a lot of entrepreneurs are concerned with asset protection, the Ultrapreneur is driven toward wealth creation. Whereas some are concerned with preserving the here and now, the Ultrapreneur is more gain-driven. The harvest is the realization of the Ultrapreneurial planning and years of concentrated effort. Chapter 10 discusses the pricing and terms of a successful harvest and how to manage the "you name the price and I'll set the terms" method of making a deal. Seventeen categories of pricing are discussed and five considerations for terms are presented. Finally, each of the six primary methods for harvest are explained with both pros and cons.

Building and harvesting a company results in a recycle of talent, money, and knowledge that, in turn, spurs on the Ultrapreneurial cycle. The Epilogue presents *the* ultimate Ultrapreneurial opportunity for the upcoming decades. It points out what has been the United States' most driving Ultrapreneurial influence for the past thirty to forty years and *the* general area that will offer the greatest number of opportunities for Ultragrowth well into the 21st century.

Entrepreneurs have been a major force in the business environment for centuries. During the last decade, they have led many new business developments around the world. This book sets out the process that will lead entrepreneuring into the next decade, the time of the ultimate entrepreneur—the Ultrapreneur.

1
Analyzing the Ultrapreneurial Opportunity

Four things come not back: the spoken word; the sped arrow; time past; the neglected opportunity.

OMAR IBN-HALIF

Scenario One: As a venture capitalist and investment banker, I frequently have prospective entrepreneurs tell me: "There is no other product like ours on the market; we don't have any competition." My thought and common reply is "This means you have designed the perfect product for a market that doesn't exist." Every product or service has competition.

Scenario Two: By the turn of the century, there will be something like twenty highly qualified candidates for every single upper level management position in corporate America. This seems to me a compelling reason to consider entrepreneurship and, even better, to take an Ultrapreneurial approach.

Times Are Changing

The above opposite scenarios are more true today than ever before in entrepreneurial history. On one hand, it's getting tougher and tougher to determine valid markets and opportunities; on the other hand, the oppor-

9

tunities for entrepreneuring are rising at unprecedentcd rates. Although the challenges remain daunting, it's the nature of the beast. The challenge becomes how to select a product or service for which there is a valid market and then capitalize on your concept within a timetable that results in your having sufficient dollars in your jeans to repeat the Ultrapreneurial scenario again and again.

The United States has always been a sucker for speculative economic booms and spectacular busts. We went from the roaring '20s to the depression '30s, from the austerity of the World War II '40s to the unprecedented national progress of the '50s and '60s. Then we beat up on ourselves in the '70s and rewarded ourselves in self-indulgence in the '80s. This historical push/pull of the United States economy, which is always changing, is good reason for carefully scrutinizing entrepreneurial opportunities.

Today We're Globalized

Today's impetus for change is the globalization of *everything*. We now deal with a global world in all areas of life: economically in the dollar versus the yen versus the ruble versus Europe's new monetary standard, politically in democracy versus socialism versus the last vestiges of communism, morally in birthrates versus abortion versus starvation versus AIDS. Where our primary concern in this book is economic, discussions about Ultrapreneuring can't totally ignore political, moral, and ethical factors. The monetary causes are numerous and include recessions (notice how fast they come and go, how fast they roll across regions); the binges in the financial markets of the eighties (undersaving, overinvestment, overleveraging, overspending, mounting debt); steady rises and steep declines in the stock markets (both United States and the rest of the world); and the list goes on. Added to these monetary changes are a host of marketing challenges.

For 200 years, the United States has been a market unto itself. Our resources so rich, our dollar so strong, our onshore markets so big that as entrepreneurs, we could easily afford to ignore the rest of the globe. Now we have rapid technology changes, a whole new European market, the turmoil in determining the economical future of the eastern bloc countries, and what's really happening in the Pacific Rim countries? But that's just the start.

Typically, in the past, when entrepreneurs have come up with a new idea or concept for the marketplace, they could count on taking their time in developing it. They could afford to tweak the improvements, carefully control the manufacturing and testing, introduce it locally, and then expand marketing on an easy-to-manage scale from regional to national. All the time knowing they were building a company that could last them a lifetime, provide security, pile up equity, and then, at some far distant point in the future, they could cash out and live a life of leisure.

The Windows Are Closing

Today, entrepreneurs just don't have the invention, conception, financing, and market windows that allow for this. The technology change is just too rapid. If it's an invention, it costs a small fortune to get the patents and it also takes an abnormal amount of time. It was the near final nail in the coffin when Congress in November of 1990 raised patent fees 69 percent. It now costs $395 for a basic filing fee, up from $185. Maintaining a patent over its 17-year life now costs $2770 instead of $1480. None of this includes any legal, agent, or special fees.

To further complicate the patent scene, even though a lot of financing people still hold patents in high regard, a lot of others just view them as an excuse for a weak management team. A patented product with worldwide market potential has a lessening value because many countries' patent laws—if they have any—don't have the teeth that provide the shield of protection we know here in the United States. That's just the patent window.

Market windows just kill entrepreneurs who dally in the process of getting their product into the users' hands. We used to worry that somebody else was burning the midnight oil in their garage and might get to market before us. Today, the worry is how many garages are going to beat us to the market, what distribution tactics are they taking, and how deep are their financial pockets.

Because our lives have become so complicated, we have developed a lot of specialties. Consequently, to be proficient in new product conception, entrepreneurs have to be "operable" in their products base technology—at minimum, at least industry knowledgeable.

Further, the opportunities today are not for new products as much as they are to obsolete existing products. This has to be done with a product that offers more efficiency, usually costs less to purchase and maintain, and is probably environmentally disposable when we wear it out and buy a new one.

The financing window has always been a tough window to estimate. Coming out of a recession makes it even tougher. Recessions are about correcting imbalances. The binges of the eighties left entrepreneurs and the country with some whoppers: undersaving, overinvestment in real estate, overleveraging of corporations, overpadding of payrolls, overspending by government, and mounting consumer debt.

But You Still Have Choices

All of these recession factors affect entrepreneurial opportunities with regard to the two basic financing choices, debt and equity. Do I want to hock everything I own and then some, or do I want to sell a part of my soul? It would seem that in the eighties, we had lots of choices. The gunslinger type of financing gave us such vehicles as: partnerships, both limited and research and development; enhanced capital gains tax breaks, both corporate and individual; and accelerated depreciation and amortization. Add to these the more sophisticated areas such as leveraged buyouts, mergers and acquisitions, and the now infamous junk bonds.

A veritable potpourri of financing choices, now gone, is stashed in the same closet with 8-track tapes and war bonds. Times, they are a-changing. Fortunately, money is like water—it always seeks its own level. And while it might rush to what appears to be a better exit, sound financial fundamentals always work, even better when packaged into the investment choice of the day. What's also true is that for every overreaction—like stiffer financial regulations—society's pendulum does swing back with experience and reason. New twists of old financing methods are conceived and they then become today's most logical vehicle. We'll explore a lot of these in the financing chapter. Suffice it to say that an Ultrapreneurial team needs to be equipped and qualified to assess the best method to use in obtaining dollars for their particular type of enterprise.

It Gets Even More Complicated

We're not done complicating the challenges in the analytical process yet. There are many more points to consider, such as:

Can small companies compete with giants?

How does the strength of the dollar affect foreign markets?

Do we need to test the products before putting them out for consumer use?

Can we preserve profit margins with competition sure to come?

How much time do we have before we're forced to introduce a second-generation product or an improved version of a service?

Does this mean that the old truism of being in the right place at the right time applies? You bet; however, it's been added to—it also depends on how you capitalize on the opportunity.

The challenge then becomes what factors have to be observed and what points need to be taken into account when we analyze the Ultrapreneurial opportunity.

In the entrepreneur's world, products don't make a business; successful business creates and develops successful products. This becomes a key to analyzing the myriad opportunities for Ultrapreneurs to make their mark.

In this chapter, we'll discuss the opportunity discovery process. Sections are devoted to establishing the characteristics of opportunity analysis, what should be considered when judging an opportunity, and then what qualifiers need to be present to make the opportunity be Ultrapreneurial in nature.

Small Is Best—Again

For America, small was beautiful well into this century. We were a country built on individual proprietorships, small shop owners, small family-owned businesses and farms. Then we turned to worship big—big business, big corporations, big farms, and big problems.

Between 1980 and 1990 the Fortune 500 companies shed some 3.5 million jobs. At the same time, our economy created some 23 million jobs. So while big was shedding, small was gaining in a big way. In a closed economy in which smaller companies depend on larger companies as customers, the decline of large businesses could be serious. But America is no longer a closed economy. Small companies are now just as likely to be exporters and more likely to be innovators than large ones.

The eighties saw a return to entrepreneurship. There has been a continuing increase of new incorporations. Where many small companies used to be founded because the entrepreneur had a long-term vision of what might be, today a large number of companies are started out of frustration, by people who are frustrated with their current jobs because the big companies are downsizing, restructuring, and putting new initiatives on hold.

This opens up a lot of opportunities. When big companies have trouble fighting foreign competition or keeping pace with rapid product innovation and technology change, their difficulties create a vacuum into which a lot of smaller companies can enter with a rush.

We've come back again to entrepreneurship, to people starting their own businesses. We're more willing to take risks because so many of the big companies are not as stable as was supposed. For large companies, their biggest fixed investment has become people instead of fixed assets. Downsizing is prevalent, and starting a company has become a more viable career path.

This trend has opened the door for Ultrapreneurs. The big companies have discovered that small companies can adapt to change faster, grab market share faster, create new products and services faster, bring them to market faster, start selling faster, cut fat, trim overhead, go lean and mean with growth-oriented management that is more alert and better equipped to capitalize on opportunities. Small companies thrive best where the rest of the globe hasn't yet dared to venture. Growth companies can plow income back into operations because the larger reward is the ultimate buyout by the biggies.

Two things are happening. The size of economic units that do things is getting smaller, and the number of these units is increasing. It's a fundamental shift in the economic structure which is irreversible for the foreseeable future. Big companies will never look like they did in the 1960s and '70s. Their profitability and market share will come not because of hiring more people but because they use fewer people and use them smarter.

Venturing Capital Changes

Traditional venture capital—those funds fueled by institutional investment—has also changed. It blossomed, bloomed, and then got pressed between the pages during the late 1970s and through the '80s. Its big push came from deregulation and more lenient tax laws in the late '70s. Millions of institutional dollars flooded the coffers, and the environment was ripe to invest. Invest they did, into new computer-oriented firms, into gobs of supposedly leading-edge biotechnology-driven companies. Their lemons ripened fast. After investing in hundreds of computer hardware companies in the early eighties, only a handful survived. They bought into a lot of biotech projects when no one fully realized how long the development window would be. And by the mid-eighties, the initial public offering market collapsed and the venture capital firms lost their best exit. Along with their ill-advised investments, they couldn't turn over their investment dollars and get any reinvestment monies out of the good ones they had. This caused an aversion to funding start-up company risk and they became progressive bankers—investing in lower-risk projects with a considerably lower rate of return. They sought the safer returns of bridge financing and go-go leveraged buyouts.

Meantime, in the late 1980s, the young innovative startup companies, starved for cash, died out or just limped along with limited progress.

The entrepreneurial financing problem was compounded by the banking and lending scene. The bank and S&L failures—which we're still working out and will be for years—placed an emphasis on borrowing based on premium tangible assets such as Class A real estate. This bias favors large, mature companies at the expense of small ones. Small companies' key resources are locked up inside people's heads; they walk out the door every night and travel in airplanes. They're not invested in hard-dollar, fixed-capital assets.

This same scenario held true for the largest pool of start-up financing we have, that of angels—those well-heeled investors who hold a special place in their hearts for high-risk, high-return, innovative and inventive entrepreneurs. Their pool of investment dollars, although illusive in nature, is believed to be many times larger than traditional venture capital. They finance a lot of start-ups and they really went under the rocks when the rain came. Angels lost all their traditional exits—the ways they got their investments back out—which were venture capital for second round, banking for growth, going public, and selling out for harvest. They didn't have anyone left to hand their startup investments off to. Consequently, by the late '80s, they went to the sidelines, just plain quit investing.

Changing Times Means Greater Opportunity

The dawn of the 1990s saw the pendulum swing back again. The initial public offering markets opened up. That doesn't mean they will stay open forever, but the windows have reappeared, just as they always do. This gives everyone the opportunity to have some exits. This is coupled with the fact that big business is looking for opportunities and there are a lot of them out there.

Small companies have always had the potential to be more effectively and efficiently managed. Now we are finding ways to create operating and strategic partnerships that enhance these operating efficiencies. Two trends are important. First, the shift from manufacturing to services has created a huge number of smaller suppliers to larger companies. Second, the globalization of the economy has forced us in the United States to produce higher quality with fewer, better-trained employees. This causes large companies to break into smaller units with less indecisive middle management. This gives the privately owned smaller enterprises more access to decision makers; that, coupled with the smaller company's fast flexibility to respond, reinforces strategic partnerships.

Small now becomes beautiful because it can stay small and lean. It has access to affordable computer technology, a competitive advantage that a few short years ago was the exclusive domain of large companies. Small companies can leverage this computer advance with results and without bureaucracy.

All these factors, and more to come in this chapter as well as throughout this book, lead one to the conclusion that there are even more opportunities for Ultrapreneurs than ever before: big corporate downsizing, rapid technology change, increasing global markets, new environmental concerns: the list goes on. These prove conclusively that there are a lot of viable opportunities waiting to be snatched up.

How we discover them, how we balance the pros and cons, what we do with them, and ways to qualify them are the subjects for the rest of this chapter.

What You Need for Ultrapreneurial Start-up

From those who have studied the subject, the general conclusion seems to be that there is no ideal way to find venture opportunities. They seem to pop up in a variety of ways. Most commonly, they are uncovered by recognizing an opportunity as a result of being active in a particular industry.

The Ultrapreneur spots a need and determines to start a company to fill it. This may start by moonlighting after hours and on weekends and develop into full-time businesses. The Ultrapreneur ofttimes plans a venture during employment in preparation for resignation and start-up thereafter. What points should be considered in this initial planning process?

Acquire These Five Ingredients

Just like setting out to accomplish any task, one should assess what's needed to initiate the project. For the Ultrapreneur, there are some basic ingredients.

1. *Product or service idea.* A thoughtful concept for what the product or service is going to be has to be clearly in place. The company may start with one idea and modify it into something entirely different than what was originally imagined.

2. *Technical know-how.* Preferably, Ultrapreneurs should possess the professional skill and knowledge to generate the company's product or service. If you don't have it, you must be able to hire or acquire the knowledge.

3. *Personal contacts.* Ultrapreneurial ventures are not started by persons living in isolation. The Ultrapreneur and the team must have connections with other people regarding virtually all of the requisites of start-up and company operations. This includes professionals such as attorneys and accountants, but also includes business connections such as people involved in sales or distribution and others involved in production or materials acquisition.

4. *Physical resources.* Many types of physical resources are needed to start a company. These include capital and assets; some of them may be substantial. Pulling them together is the primary early role of the Ultrapreneur.

5. *Customer orders.* Prior to start-up, the Ultrapreneur must have strong indications and commitments for sales. Without sales, obviously no venture will succeed.

Even though each of these seems elementary, it often happens that entrepreneurs concentrate on some and ignore others. The results are usually very negative. Ultrapreneurs know that the sequence doesn't matter, simply that all the ingredients need to be in place.

Anticipate These Main Hurdles

There are needed ingredients and there are hurdles, three main ones, and the most devastating one might surprise you. One is a failure to obtain operational financing. This probably isn't too surprising. Many entrepreneurs can put the money together to get started, some even to get going on a small scale. It's their personal financing along with some help from close family and friends. But gaining operational financing is another matter. This is the larger amount of money needed to expand production, sales, inventory, and receivables. It has to be anticipated right from the start, and we'll help you determine how and where to get it in the chapters on Ultrapreneurial financing.

A second hurdle is sales. If the company is not generating revenues, it needs to at least substantiate that sales *can* be generated. A new product or service idea is not enough. There has to be genuine proof that not only can the product be sold, but that there is substantial customer interest, proof solid that customers will order and reorder. That word of mouth says "hey, it works," and customers will tell others.

But the most important hurdle is to identify a venture with a product or service that has sufficient profit margins. First, there has to be margin to make a profit. Second, there has to be margin to provide for the unforeseen, which always arises. And third, there has to be enough margin to cope with competition, entering the market, most likely with lower prices. As an Ultrapreneur, you don't go into a venture without high profit margins. That's your reason for existing.

With the basic ingredients in mind, and knowing the hurdles to overcome, let's examine some opportunity areas.

Examining Opportunity Areas

Just like people, Ultrapreneurial business opportunities come in a veritable potpourri of sizes, shapes, personalities, and intricacies. Some opportunities are local, others regional and reaching out for national. Ultrapreneurs should be on the lookout for international opportunities. Since a beginning point in the process should be *not* to exclude any area, let's look at a few general areas regarding what they are doing today, for what the future promises, and what some trends may be.

Biotechnology

A decade ago, biotechnology was a sexy investment idea gone bad. A lot of original investors lost patience and money because they had not realized how long a timeframe was involved and that a whole industry substructure needed to be developed. Biotechnology is now an acknowledged growth industry and it presents a lot of opportunities. Piece by piece we are learning more about the human body as well as other living things at the molecular level. Through biotechnology, new drugs and therapies are evolving, extending life, improving health care, and providing accomplishments and hope to those with illness and disease. We can't help but notice the impact on our lives. However, some biotech developments are very quiet, some are ones we don't necessarily want to know about or just aren't quite ready to accept.

For instance, biotechnology developments in food and agriculture are appearing with tangible benefits to the food industry and the customer. This is causing a dichotomy in forces: one, our obsession with truth in labeling, and the other, our resistance to the unknown or unproven. Biotech is doing what some may term strange things. How do customers tell if their tomato sauce was made from biotech high-solids tomatoes that require less water removal (a relatively expensive manufacturing process)? How do consumers know that the fresh asparagus they buy in the fresh vegetable section was produced from seed-based systems developed from tissue-cultured plants (all male, so no volunteer plants develop as weeds)? How do consumers know that the potatoes they buy were produced from virus-free stock that have demonstrated greater yields? They don't, because they just don't want to associate "exotic" technology with something as personal as food.

There are two main reasons that these types of biotech applications in food products remain silent. First, a biotech tomato that doesn't spoil for weeks still looks and tastes like a homegrown tomato except that it just doesn't spoil as fast. Second, the industry knows that the consumer prefers to associate food with friendly Farmer Bill Brown and not Dr. Bio Weirdly. The biotechnology revolution in our food products is essential to the development of the food industry, but for now it's best done quietly. These could be typed as "consumer-silent" technologies.

Genetic engineers have perfected gene-splicing practices to work on a variety of other crops. The following are some of the more exotic splices.

The crop	The genes added	For what purpose
Potato	Chicken	Increase disease resistance.
Corn	Firefly	Serve as an identifiable marker.
Tomato	Flounder	Reduce freeze damage.
Soybean	Petunia	Greater herbicide tolerance.
Sunflower	Brazil nut	Store more proteins.
Potato	Insect	Reduce bruising.
Tobacco	Mouse	Reduce metals accumulation.
Rice	Bacteria	Resistance to antibiotic.

This small selection of biotech crop developments indicates that Ultrapreneurs are having a field day with leading-edge product development. Opportunities in biotechnology will continue to stack up well into the next century, and Ultrapreneurs are there to meet the challenges, whether they be in research, development, new marketing methods, or creating new service techniques surrounding biotech.

Computing Tomorrow

The changes in computer hardware and software over the next decade can be compared to the change that the PC has brought to our lives in the past decade. It will be an astonishing experience as we learn to function with hand-held computers, watch video images on flat panel screens, and use lightweight optical disks. The Apples and IBM PCs we now know will become relics. Computing will be cheap, it will be omnipresent, and the power of your processor won't be nearly as important as the quality of your connections to other computers and every manner of data from text to live video. Today's personal computer will go the way of 8-tracks and records. The fork in the computing road will on one hand move upward into workstations and on the other downward into information appliances. The new word is *picocomputing*, from the digital devices that will bring us into the era of personal computing anytime, anywhere, everywhere. These will combine computers, communications, and consumer electronics—many opportunities for Ultrapreneurs.

Electronic Publishing

For years, technologists have been predicting a paperless electronic future. So far, it appears they have been wrong—industry consumption of paper has increased every year since World War II. However, electronics has permeated every corner of the publishing industry. Newspapers are written and edited on the computer screen. Stock tables, sports scores, words and pictures from wire services all over the world are transmitted to newspaper computers. The computers edit the information, set the type, and usually transmit it to an electronic database for storage. The completed editions are then bounced off satellites to remote printing plants all over the country. The process is virtually paperless until the presses begin to roll.

Fax machines and copiers use paper, as do laser printers from desktop publishing. Paper has become an interface—an increasingly transient, disposable medium for the actual viewing of electronically compiled information. Many times we read it and then promptly throw it away, safe in the knowledge that if we should ever need to read it again, it's tucked away in a computer database.

Electronic newspapers will be digitally transmitted to the reader's portable computer via cable television networks, direct broadcast satellite, high-speed digital telephone, or digital cellular telephone transmission. Ultrapreneurs will present these opportunities sooner than you think.

Bits and Pieces for Ultrapreneurial Consideration

Cable Television. Here's what has happened in this industry in just twenty years.

	1970	1990
Subscribers	5 million	55 million
Revenues	$1 billion	$20 billion
Number of systems	2,000	10,000
Monthly rate	$5	$18

Ultrapreneurs will easily surpass these growth rates in the next decade.

Computer Chips. IBM's first PC/AT, introduced in 1983—behind a lot of other manufacturers—incorporated Intel's 80286 computer chip. It was expensive, powerful, but bulky. It resided on one large circuit board about the size of a dinner plate. Since then, the 80286 has become almost generic and is simply referred to as the 286. In less than ten years, Advanced Micro Devices has shrunk the 286—to also include all the other AT control circuitry—onto a chip the size of a thumbnail. And we can be sure that Ultrapreneurs will get these chips even smaller.

Japan Consumer Electronics. In Japan, most consumer goods have a shorter life cycle than in the United States. The average is six months compared to our one year. They already have modem, cellular, and satellite systems in place. When looking at new portable or mobile equipment, they insist on very portable, lightweight products requiring minimum power inputs. Quality, product design, and costs must constantly be improved if a company is to maintain a competitive edge. Because in Japan a higher price does not necessarily equate to quality, the United States producers find the Japanese markets very difficult to enter. Japanese companies spend 15 percent more time planning new products than United States companies. As a result, they suffer 21 percent fewer development setbacks and spend 15 percent less time debugging finished products. They invest 10 percent more managerial time in new products and receive 16 percent more in revenues from new products. Planning obviously pays.

What We Own.   U.S. percent of households with:

	1951	1971	1991
Answering machine	0	0	42%
Cable TV service	0	7%	53%
Car	60%	83%	87%
Cars	4%	35%	53%
Microwave oven	0	N/A	86%
PC	0	0	26%
Television	23%	94%	98%
Televisions	0	28%	71%
Telephone service	62%	91%	93%

What Things Cost

	1951	1971	1991
University of North Carolina (tuition, room, board)	$3,625	$4,264	$4,948
Harvard	$7,424	$14,170	$22,080
Car (most popular model)	$7,623 Chevrolet	$11,741 Chevrolet	$12,725 Honda Accord
Gallon of gasoline	$1.39 Full-serve	$1.15	$1.15 Self-serve
Converse sneakers	$53.78	$66.57	$31.95
Television (Sears)	$1,740 20″ B&W	$1,436 21″ color	$270 20" color
Physician office call	$20.48	$28.63	$43.00
Dozen eggs	$3.91	$2.03	$0.94

How We're Changing Jobs

	1950	1990
Manufacturing	38.9%	21.6%
Transportation/Utilities	10.3%	6.3%
Wholesale/Retail Trade	24.0%	28.4%
Finance/Insurance, Real estate	4.8%	7.5%
Services	13.7%	29.6%
Mining	2.3%	0.8%
Construction	6.0%	5.8%

SOURCE: Bureau of Labor Statistics.

Could This Be the Ultimate Marketing Tool?   Let's say you want to open a doughnut shop. You don't want it near any competitors; you want it in a neighborhood with plenty of teenagers, but not in a high-crime area. How do you find the ideal location, on a map, quickly and without a lot of personal reconnaissance expense?

Maybe you want to target-market a new upscale combination auto/home alarm system. First you access a digital database of homes with valuations of over $250,000. Next, you combine that with a digital record of licenses for high-end autos. Then, with a third database, you identify which roads in the area carry the most traffic. Based on this information, you can then target specific billboards that will be seen by the highest percentage of potential customers. How do you execute both of these complicated but valuable market research projects?

You query your *GIS* on your computer. GIS (Geographic Information System) is the marriage between computer maps and digital data. A GIS system has five components: hardware, software, data, applications, and people. Except for the people part, a system can be assembled for less than $20,000, down from $100,000 just a few years ago.

It takes a 486 PC with a small digitizing tablet and color plotter for the hardware. Add a standard software operating system (DOS, UNIX) and one of the hundreds of GIS application software packages available. Then fuel the system with data, usually a landbase database (maps) and attribute (describes the mapped features) database. Finally, you hook in applications, which are the programs or specific instructions that tell the computer what data to get, how to combine or otherwise manipulate it, and how to display it. When you add the people that make it work, you're off and running with a map that pictorially shows your marketing data—the ultimate marketing tool.

New Discoveries. When President John F. Kennedy declared that we were going to the moon, the result was not only one small step for mankind, but multiple major influences in our present daily life. We spend vast sums of hard-pressed taxpayer dollars to attempt huge leaps in our knowledge. The spinoffs from this type of advanced research result in many high-tech products that filter down into our factories, offices, and homes. The following list indicates some of the massive projects underway now and through the turn of the century that will spark numerous Ultrapreneurial companies.

Category	Project	Expected completion	Cost to build
Space station	Orbiting outpost to Mars	1999	$30 billion
Human genome	Largest basic biology ever	2005	$3 billion

Planetary exploration	Probe 3 planets	1992–96	$2.1 billion
Earth observation	Orbiting satellites	1992–2000	$18.2 billion
Astrophysics	X-ray ultraviolet telescopes	1991–2000	$1.4 billion
Physics	Supercollider and Accelerator	1994–99	$8.4 billion
Materials science	Advanced photon and light source	20–30 years	$665 million

SOURCES: NASA, Dept. of Energy, National Science Foundation.

For many in the Baby Boomer generation, their teenage alphabet consisted of GM and GTO, of DMZ, VD, and U-2. Their adult alphabet is made up of the FAX, the VCR, the VDT, the BMW, and AIDS. This shows the changes that take place in just twenty years. Whole new industries are conceived, born, raised, matured, and in some cases discarded. New problems and concerns arise, get lots of attention, and then quietly disappear. A lot of this is influenced by societal changes, many of which are tremendously influenced by the media. This alphabet change is indicative of societal changes which always spell opportunity for Ultrapreneurs.

Conclusion

After looking at this small selection of industries and some additional data, it's easy to see that there are a lot of opportunities available. I'm sure you know of several in your particular area of expertise. The point here has been to get the opportunity thought process stimulated.

From here, we can examine more specific issues in opportunity identification. Whether your project is service- or no-tech-oriented, for it to be a bonafide Ultrapreneurial project, it must have Ultragrowth potential. Since high-tech product-oriented projects are the standard for Ultragrowth, they make the natural guideline for studying what's needed for Ultragrowth Ultrapreneurial opportunities.

Ultrapreneurial Company Life Cycles

Strategic concerns to the Ultrapreneur when examining opportunities are the timeframes and stages of a project's development. The focus is at what time period or in which stage can they best harvest their opportunity, cash in, and move on to the next challenge. In some business industries, it may be a relatively short period, say one or two years. Perhaps the Ultrapreneur just buys a different bunch of the same types of businesses located in different parts of the country. The stages are simple: Consolidate operations, centralize management offices and systems, fill in some holes, and capitalize on the synergy. In other types of industries, there may be a long product development cycle that means the company may not even begin to market product until the fourth or fifth year. What's the case for Ultrapreneurial companies? Can we define a life cycle? The short answer is yes, qualified by the fact that there are many different interpretations of high tech and high growth. However, each high-growth endeavor has certain characteristics in its life cycle that are typical and that we can apply to our individual situations. Let's look at six stages.

First Stage—The Seed Stage

This is the idea conception, testing, and proving stage. The Ultrapreneur and probably several initial team members are filled with a "can do" attitude backed by a lot of determination and tenacity. They are most likely seeking dollars, which means they are or should be preoccupied with producing a business plan. They should be assembling a team of outside advisors, experienced attorneys, accountants, angels, venture capital connections, and more eagles for the management team. The project is very dependent on not having weak management or a poor business plan.

Second Stage—Organization and Product Development

Concentration here is on developing a working prototype and establishing a corporate structure to secure the next round of financing. Actions are focused on superutilization and control of resources. Tasks are identifying initial marketing channels and targeting markets, which includes identifying an outstanding marketing director. This person is needed to provide input on product development and to help plot market strategies. The top management focus is to worry about cash, to be sure it doesn't run out prior to the next step. This is a natural stage at which to develop a manufacturing strategic alliance.

Third Stage—Production and Market Ramp-up

The primary concentration here is to achieve volume production along with opening market penetration. The tasks are to add middle management, revise the business plan for the next level of financing, and develop strategy for a second and follow-up products. Additionally, the company needs to explore foreign markets (not necessarily selling to them yet), and pay particular attention to customer service. The company is evolving from engineering or service concept-proving to marketing concentration. It needs good financial controls by having budgets and monthly financial statements, and it needs to watch the flow and fill of distribution channels and instigate tight inventory controls. It's a natural stage at which to develop a marketing strategic alliance.

Fourth Stage—Major Financing

This is the natural stage for a public offering, selling out to a larger company, or merging for the longer run. This is the stage of a high-tech company that the Ultrapreneurial team is driving for. This is their harvest point, usually the point of greatest leverage for selling out.

Fifth Stage—Rapid Expansion

The first product is firmly in place and the second and additional products are coming on-line. International expansion is now appropriate along with new compensation plans built around cash for new employees instead of equity. The risks at this stage are delays in delivering new products on time which are capable of performing as promised, and price erosion from competitive market forces, i.e., maintaining leadership.

Sixth Stage—Maturity

At this stage, most likely the original team is gone or comfortably settled into mature company operating patterns. The former middle management is moving into the corporate hierarchy and the company is evolving into a caretaker mode over assessing risk, but still it may be a cash cow.

Distinctive Characteristics

Along with having defined stages, Ultragrowth companies, especially high-tech companies, have two distinctive characteristics.

First, they take advantage of advanced knowledge and information that is more tightly and economically bundled than that of their competition. This advanced knowledge comes from being involved in their industries' state-of-the-art research and development.

Second, their product or service has a distinguished level of high-technology knowledge or information built in, which can be repeated consistently and economically and which cannot be accurately or too quickly duplicated by others.

These distinctive characteristics are what open the window of opportunity. It is likely to be superseded in short order by more advanced applications, hopefully by the original company. These types of opportunities represent the cutting edge of commerce and science and the ultimate Ultragrowth high-tech opportunities.

Warning Signals

Watch for the following when examining high-tech opportunities.

"There is no other product like ours on the market." It may mean that it's the perfect product for a market that doesn't exist. Be sure the product can be sold—profitably.

"We only have a very small window, timewise, to do this." Be very wary of projects that are trying to beat a known and verifiable time clock; too many things can go wrong.

"I've got ten super products." It's hard enough to develop one product to success without trying to do multiple products simultaneously.

"We can't lay these employees off." Don't try to keep all employees while business is "picking up" or there is a delay in bringing out a new product.

In many high-tech projects, the failure rate is high because the technology is so new, and may be so radically different, that it is very hard to test the market. In many cases, the market doesn't even exist yet—you can't be sure your product is needed, let alone identify customers to buy it. The best an Ultrapreneur can do is attempt to uncover every bit of evidence and justification, and then take a calculated Ultrapreneurial risk.

In this chapter, we've looked at the effects of rapid change in the process of analyzing an opportunity, how globalization affects the process, and the fact that small companies are once again in the spotlight. We reviewed the ingredients and the hurdles of a start-up and then looked at a sampling of opportunity areas. This background, along with examining the life cycles of a company, naturally leads us to taking a look at the all-important area of marketing. Every Ultrapreneurial effort, whether product or service, has to be marketed. Simply building a better mousetrap and waiting for the crush of buyers doesn't work. The world's too complex and moves too fast to ignore the marketing process when analyzing an Ultrapreneurial opportunity.

2
The Ultragrowth Opportunity

Ultragrowth can best be described as very high growth. It's difficult to quantify in dollars, percentages, or people. However, some general statements can be made. A 100%-per-annum, compounded growth rate, over a five-year period, is entry level for Ultragrowth companies. This means that a company with initial first-year revenues of $500,000 would grow to fifth-year revenues of $8,000,000. Or a company with ten original employees would have 160 people in its fifth year.

More typical of Ultragrowth would be these examples:

Apple Computer's first formal investor put in $91,000, and three years later the company's sales exceeded $100 million.

Apollo Computer, Inc., founded in 1980, saw an increase in corporate value by 1984 to over $600 million with 500 employees.

Daisy Systems Corporation, a manufacturer of computer-assisted engineering (CAE) systems was founded in 1980 and reached a corporate value in excess of $400 million four years later.

People Express Airline, Inc. reached both sales revenues and a corporate value of over $400 million in four years with 4000 employees. Mismanagement of Ultragrowth was the demise of Peoples.

Software Publishing Company had a corporate value of $67 million in its fourth year with 169 employees.

TOYS R US, Inc. was revived from bankruptcy and six years later had achieved a corporate value of $2.2 billion.

A typical traditional venture capital firm qualifies a potential high-growth investment as a company where they can achieve a minimal ten-times return on their initial investment over a three- to seven-year period. Naturally, they all wish this was their norm; however, this type of growth is only achieved approximately ten percent of the time. Regardless of what type of growth others achieve, Ultrapreneurs only seek opportunities that have the potential to achieve very high growth rates that will allow them to harvest their investment with outrageous returns. This always means they have to closely scrutinize the market in which their prospective company operates. This chapter addresses marketing challenges and choices and presents tips on how to achieve Ultragrowth.

Ultragrowth—The Marketing Challenge

While the most important aspect of the Ultrapreneurial company is management, a most important challenge is marketing. Consequently, analyzing any opportunity requires analyzing the market into which the prospective product or service is going to be placed. It is the most factual way to qualify a prospective opportunity. Because marketing is so strategically important to many aspects of a company, it is discussed in various chapters of this book when it is subject-applicable. In this section, some of the more important facts are brought out with regard to high-growth marketing problems. These are points that can become very significant or that especially apply when a company is faced with very high growth rates— Ultragrowth—or when they must enter the market under unusual timeframes or tight market windows.

Ultragrowth occurs in markets that are unsaturated, in markets where a clear leader is not yet present, or when the product or service is so new that it doesn't have an established customer following. In an Ultragrowth environment there are no real competitors; market share is there for the taking, becoming a leader is almost a piece of cake—that is, assuming the company has the rest of its act together so it can properly support market Ultragrowth. The ideal thing to do in an Ultragrowth environment is to strive for good profit and high sales volume rather than market share. Getting the product into the users' hands generates word-of-mouth advertising, still the best form of advertising any company can develop.

Seek Maximum Gross Profits

Whereas the Ultragrowth market may appear to be an Ultrapreneur's dream, in truth its unique complexities make it a very difficult environment in which to operate successfully. The key to Ultragrowth success is for a new company to achieve a very high growth rate very early in its product cycle—

momentum builds momentum. This task becomes increasingly difficult as a product niche becomes more mature, as more companies enter a new market, and as initial high-profit pricing structures begin to break down. But the most important and frequently missed goal in any company, entrepreneurial or Ultrapreneurial, whether or not it operates in a hypergrowth environment, is to seek maximum gross profit for its new products. Anyone can rack up huge sales selling a hundred-dollar product or service for $99.50. But huge unit sales and high revenues don't do a company any good if every sale translates into a net dollar loss. That should be self-evident. What is not self-evident is that simply making a profit on each sale is not good enough either. Sales strategy must aim at making the maximum gross profit for the maximum time while maximizing market share. It's a tough strategy to contend with. It takes keen market awareness to assess both competitive pricing, product qualities, and optimum distribution methods.

Assess the Time Window

If the Ultrapreneuring company is dependent upon market time-windows, additional cautions appear. Finite market time-windows open for participants in every area of high technology on a continual basis. The window opens quickly, remains open for a while, then closes. Then the "me-toos" come on, fast and furious. They bring product improvements, sometimes quality upgrades, usually gross margin cuts. Once the window closes, opportunities for the start-ups end.

When the Ultrapreneuring time-window opens on a new area of high technology, the first companies enter a very forgiving market. This is one where demand is so high that an amazing level of corporate mismanagement sins are forgiven, buried deep under a huge number of orders and back orders.

The tendency is to release poor-quality, incompletely tested or user-proven product. Management can get away with a lot of inefficiencies including inferior personnel, insufficient policies, and inadequate procedures. Marketing and customer service departments are forgiven for inattention and below-par service response. All these things are ignored or overlooked by the customers because they badly want or need the product. To them, the price is right and, supposedly, the product represents good value for the money. The economic imperative is there. Bottom line: They don't have any other choice; there's nowhere else to buy from. As the time-window matures, competition enters, full steam ahead. They usually enter with higher-quality product, better management systems, attentive and appreciative marketing, and customer service. In short, the market becomes steadily less forgiving.

Become Sinless

The early Ultrapreneurial companies that do well are invariably the companies who set the pace by sinning less. These are seldom the companies that are at the forefront of the technology. The technology frontrunners never seem to have the rest of the management in place. They're usually too technology-driven, always overengineering, never pushing the product out the door because they want to build perfection into a product that can only approach perfection after customer use. Techie products don't come out on top. In the early stages of Ultragrowth, newer and better products are unimportant, providing the existing product is perceived by customers as adequate. With fast growth that is supported by high profit margins, a substantial competitive lead can be built by creative advertising and ingenious public relations.

The survivors of hot new product introductions, once the time-window closes on any area of high technology, are the largest companies and the niche companies. The large ones do well because they have built a financial cushion by maintaining profit margins that are kept in line by instigating production and manufacturing efficiencies which then allow them to offer the best prices and top-quality customer support. The niche companies succeed by addressing specialized markets that are too small to interest the big guys. Without the big guys as competition, there is a lot less price sensitivity, and high profit margins can be maintained. For Ultrapreneurial companies, the secret to gaining and maintaining a general market leadership is fast growth. The later in the time-window that you enter the market, the faster you must grow—again, Ultragrowth. The caution is to keep in mind that you are doing so in a steadily less forgiving environment.

Building Market Leadership

There are some keys to being an Ultrapreneurial leader. Marketing, sales, and public relations programs comprise one. They must be outstanding.

Advertising has to have a super storyline that captures readers.

Marketing has to be positioned to motivate the execution by buyers.

Public relations has to be on the constant lookout for unique ways to position the company and its products.

Another key to maintaining Ultrapreneurial leadership is that there must be a strong engineering department to generate new products. Improvements have to be coming out in a continuous stream. Upgrades should be designed and offered, preferably without obsoleting initial product lines. Developing and building generational product lines is the secret. Computer software companies may be the best model for this type of effort. They have become master executers of releasing new versions; with each version, they conduct lots of prerelease public relations, do extensive advertising upon release, and are continually engineering the next version.

Analyze the Manufacturing Dilemma

In Ultragrowth situations, there are differing opinions about the subcontract versus manufacturing in-house subject. The school that favors in-house manufacturing contends that they don't have to include subcontractors' profits in their own cost of goods. They contend that this enables them to make greater gross margins while offering a less expensive product; consequently they can take a greater market share. The subcontractor school contends that by using subcontract manufacturing, they can be more flexible in product offerings because they don't have as large a continuing overhead burden; their side benefit is a greater return on equity. This is where the Ultrapreneuring team comes into play. A top production person coupled with a sharp accountant can run the numbers on both scenarios using the input from savvy marketing people.

There Are No Shortcuts

New product introductions pose another problem for Ultrapreneuring companies. This applies both to the first product as well as second and further generation products. There's no room for mistakes. It takes intense focus to stay on the leading edge of the new product curve. If the Ultrapreneuring team falls off, it's extremely difficult to catch up. The Ultrapreneuring challenge then becomes to bring out a new product, most likely every year, and it has to be right. Management can't seem to accept a simple truth. There are no shortcuts when bringing out a new product! Ultrapreneurial companies typically are under unbearable economic pressure to make premature product introductions. Even after the first product is successfully introduced and sales are booming, a one-product, Ultragrowth, high-tech company cannot last one month without sales. And any number of uncontrollable contingencies can cause manufacturing or sales to come to a screeching halt. When this happens to management, as it inevitably will, ever-greater pressure is applied to engineering, manufacturing, and product quality control teams who then tend to resort to all kinds of shortcuts that consequently lead to even more premature product introductions. Careful planning with built-in flexibility and predetermined alternatives goes a long way in coping with this challenge. We'll fully address the Ultrapreneurial business plan in Chapter 6.

Foreign Marketing Challenges

Many American Ultrapreneurial manufacturers with an Ultragrowth product face another marketing dilemma: foreign markets. Word spreads fast in high-tech circles, and foreign users are just as eager to have the latest items or technology as Americans. The caution for American producers is that they must establish their own European markets—and quickly—otherwise the "grey market" will take over. There are always the select few American dealers or distributors, while protesting their integrity, that just can't help responding to cash waved under their noses and selling to anyone. The cash wavers are a proportionately small group of aggressive European merchants who dump product all over Europe without addressing the need for customer service and support. This problem emerges quickly. Many times the result is that the product then develops a bad reputation, making later legitimate European market distribution, with properly set-up customer service, very difficult if not impossible to accomplish.

Consumer Products

For manufacturers of consumer retail products, sold in a number of different types of retail outlets, the scene has also changed. The days of customer brand loyalty have almost completely disappeared. Because of the highly competitive nature of retailing, brought about by discounters, bargain outlets, specialty bulk resellers, and direct mail catalog operations, most retailers only stock products for which there is a demonstrable customer demand. As a manufacturer, the Ultrapreneur can't assume that just gaining shelf space will create sales. Retailers today are a different breed of cat. They don't spend much time or money creating demand for the products they carry. Creating this ultimate end-user retail customer demand is the manufacturers' responsibility. Retail outlets only carry products for which someone else has created demand—and this with one proviso: Profit margins must exceed some minimum threshold. Hot retail dealers only stock the Ultrapreneur's product as long as the retail consumer demand remains. Dealers have no brand loyalty either. It's only there as long as there is independent consumer demand. They just can't afford the altruism of any such loyalty. Therefore, the Ultrapreneuring manufacturers must base their advertising, public relations, and marketing strategies on creating a high level of consumer awareness and demand for the product. Dealers run only "me too" advertising, the theme of which is: "Hey buying public, I have the hot product." Their shelves will remain stocked only as long as the product is hot and then it's removed only to be replaced with the next hot item, hopefully the Ultrapreneur's second-generation product. Retail dealers drop a product with as much speed as when consumer demand disappears, irrespective of whether or not the manufacturer treated them well.

Trends

The trend in high technology for Ultragrowth companies is simple. Products are getting smaller, cheaper, lighter, easier to use, more powerful, and more reliable.

The marketplace has its own trends that intersect the technological trends. The marketplace trends include:

The demand for tight inventory control

Quick order turnarounds

Higher quality at an increasingly low price

Easy, clean environmentally safe disposal

Interchangeability between systems or generations of products

Upward and downward compatibility

Ease of use

Better service

More responsive customer support response

The issues become rather exaggerated in areas where Ultragrowth is occurring and the Ultrapreneurial marketing challenge is to get a grasp of and stay ahead of these trends.

Opportunity Testing
Marketing Guides

Even for established companies, the process of putting a new product on the market is a high-risk adventure. This is doubly true with a new company, and even more important with an Ultrapreneuring endeavor. The following are some areas that should be carefully examined.

Be First

Being first is important for Ultrapreneurs. There is a need to ascertain, sometimes called guessing, the customers' wants and needs. Ultrapreneurs try to gather validated market research that supports their ability to create and sell a product or service that fits buyer demands and to do so at a price that the buyer is more than willing to pay. This customer-pleasing product/service needs to be on the market before the competition. Getting to the market with just what's needed doesn't do any good if you're second.

Product development is a lengthy, time- and dollar-consuming process. By validating the following points, the Ultraprencur can save on all of these areas:

1. Is the product wanted and/or needed?
2. Can the market segment be tapped?
3. Can the company produce what is needed?
4. Should the product be manufactured internally or contracted out?
5. Can it be sold competitively and profitably?

Ultrapreneuring marketing involves not only sales skills, but also distribution, consumer testing, pricing, packaging, promotion, and everything else that gets the product or service to the consumer. Simply put, Ultrapreneurial marketing is the process of discovering and translating consumer needs and wants into products or services, creating demands for them and then expanding the demand. Marketing is the performance of various business activities that direct the flow of goods and services from producer to consumer. Many manufacturing companies are manufacturing oriented instead of being Ultrapreneuring marketers who manufacture in order to have something to market. Preferably, to be the first one into the market.

Four Quick Ultrapreneuring Marketing Tips

1. Target the buyers and develop a product/service especially designed to appeal to them.
2. Determine the distribution network that most effectively gets the most product/service out to the greatest number of consumers at the highest profit levels.
3. Develop unique advertising, promotion, and pricing strategies.
4. Modify what doesn't work.

Three Quick Ultrapreneuring Competitive Strategy Tips

Businesses don't choose the kind of competition they face. It's determined for them by laws, regulations, finance, technology, and the structure of their particular industry. However, what sets the Ultrapreneurs apart is that they realize that they can determine the product/service market niche. They do this by reviewing:

1. What is the competition offering? Is there a market niche for a specialty offering? Something that is cheaper? That lasts longer? Has a longer warranty? Is of better quality? To edge out a competitor, create a market niche.

2. In Ultrapreneuring marketing, develop advertising, promotion, distribution, and a sales force to create more efficient selling methods.

3. For Ultrapreneurs, market timing is the secret, when to make the move. The larger the company, the less likely its product will continue to be a marketing target. Aggressive Ultrapreneurs get shot with arrows in their backsides. Followers get fatal arrows in the front. Lead, don't follow; it's safer.

Finally, Ultrapreneurs don't get caught with what Theodore Levitt, a professor of marketing at Harvard Business School, calls Marketing Myopia. This is where companies do not offer customers what they need but only what the company wants to sell. This is what happened to the railroads when they didn't recognize that they were in the transportation industry. Or more recently, when IBM stayed in mainframes and didn't offer workstations fast enough. Ultrapreneurs know instinctively that they have to lead, to be first.

And one way of assuring that they have a leading opportunity, that they can gain the lead and maintain it, is by judging the opportunity against the Ultrapreneurial marketing techniques that we have just discussed.

High-tech Qualifiers

Identifying and qualifying an Ultrapreneurial idea is a complex and arduous task. This is even more true if the opportunity is classified as high-tech. Biotechnology is probably the epitome of the high-tech fields today. Because biotech is so powerful, the potential for new products is practically unlimited. On the other hand, because the technology is so complex, the risk factor is a lot higher.

Two Approaches

While there are many approaches to developing viable high-tech business strategies, there are always two criteria that need to be balanced. One is the need to reduce risk; the other is the need to be able to enhance company value.

One approach is to start with newly developed unique technology and then seek market opportunities that may be exploited using the technology. This approach is best used with leading-edge, state-of-the-art technology when the life cycle of the opportunity is very early and because few companies are involved. As the technology is developed and as it matures, many competitors get involved and commit a lot of resources to the technology. This then makes it a lot more difficult to identify large, fast-growing markets.

Another approach is to first identify the market opportunity and then seek out the technology (or skills for a service area) that are required to enter the market. The anticipation is to capture a significant market share, hopefully the leading position. Having a solid and basic understanding of the market and, more specifically, the target market requirements, allows the Ultrapreneur to be able to push development a lot faster and with much less risk. This is considered a more sophisticated approach since it begins with an envisioned product or service in mind and proceeds with a definition of the market opportunity. Some venture capital firms purposely cultivate this type of approach by providing seed financing to a prospective Ultrapreneur to back the process of writing a business plan to explore technical and market viability.

Market Opportunity

Since markets are made up of buying customers, a market profile is simply a customer profile. Therefore, good market definition can only come about and prove meaningful if there is a thorough understanding of the potential customers. This means that good opportunity assessment must include addressing product market issues. The key points in defining a market opportunity include:

- A determination of the potential customers' needs. The best product or service is one that solves a problem.
- A determination of the potential value by analyzing the financial impact the proposed product or service will have on the customer. Will they make or save money because of the product or service you envision?
- A determination of the very important ingredient called distribution. Using what channel, how, and from whom do the customers purchase your intended product or service? Where do they learn about new ideas?
- An essential point, if applicable, is a clear understanding of the regulatory environment. What is the impact on you and your potential customers? This is becoming extremely important in today's "greening" of our society.
- A determination of the competitive scene, both current and potential. "Me too" products result in a lot of business failures if they don't have a distinct competitive edge.

A lot of good product or service ideas fail because they haven't been judged according to these key points. Overlooking or misjudging them means that even the best technology will not succeed if the customer cannot assess the product or service or it does not fill their needs at an economic advantage.

Once the Ultrapreneur has a firm grasp of the customer needs, a superior product or service definition can be developed. This can include detailed technical performance criteria, customer expectations, and solid pricing definitions. The latter helps with production pricing and determining production costing targets.

Technical Approach

With customer needs determined and a product or service definition in hand, the Ultrapreneurs can proceed with selecting the best technical approach. In doing so, they should consider the following:

- Having a versatile "core" technology that can be used in a number of ways or in different markets. This gives the Ultrapreneur the opportunity to change directions, to broaden the commercial potential, and to identify other applications.

- Using technologies that are well defined and understood by decision makers and the particular industry scientific community can be critical to reducing risk.

Basically, there are three sources of technology from which the Ultrapreneur may choose; they can be ranked by degree of risk.

- The least risky is using technology that is already in existence—one that is owned and well understood by the potential customers.

- The second choice is using existing technology that the Ultrapreneur does not own (but may license) and that is well understood by the customer.

- The third, and most risky, is to develop or acquire a new technology that requires a lot of customer education or further development.

Although these qualifiers are especially pertinent to high technologies, they have broad applications in any high-tech arena. Ultrapreneurs considering any opportunities should judge their project against these known and proven successful qualifiers.

Partnering Strategically

When seeking and examining opportunities, the Ultrapreneur should examine the strategic partnering or strategic alliance possibilities. They can add leverage and value to the Ultrapreneurial endeavor. With mean, lean, focused flexibility, small companies are attractive to large companies as they strive to develop networks of suppliers. Large companies, while able to throw large amounts of money at research and development, are not entrepreneurial environments, in that they just can't hold onto a primary

entrepreneurial characteristic called "in touch with the market." They
don't know how to innovate and cash in on their innovation effectively.

Big companies have an increasing need to acquire, form joint ventures,
and cast strategic partnerships with small companies. There are two primary
reasons. First, the rapid pace of technological change confronts large companies with an increasing number of technologies to be mastered. The most
practical way for them to do that is to engage the skills of small, technology-
based companies that focus on niche markets.

Second, large companies in a competitive global economy realize they
must return their focus to what they do best—marketing and distribution.
This heightens their need to rely on small suppliers. In turn, this helps the
small companies as they gain access to capital and channels of distribution
which are global in scope. Big companies need small companies for one
basic reason: Small is more innovative.

Acquisitions Make Them Larger

Big companies are seeking large growth potential, large market-size potential, and synergism related to their mainstream business activities. They
accomplish new business market entry in two ways: internal development
and acquisition. Internal development is usually marked by major time consumption in product research and development. It requires large dollar
expenditures because of the big business "cover your backside" attitude,
and it is normally used only if the new product or service is similar to their
existing lines. Acquisitions are often used to diversify into foreign product
areas. This is where the acquirer is less familiar with the business but
believes it is a growing area.

Strategic partnerships, also called strategic alliances, increased substan-
tially during the 1980s. They weren't limited to the United States; witness
Chrysler-Mitsubishi and Ford-Jaguar among the better-known auto mergers. During the 1990s, the partnering parade will strut even taller and
faster. This trend is being driven by the fact that for big companies, product
development is less important than the ability to compete. The focus is on
yield per employee, the time to market, and return on capital. Increased
worldwide competition means it's no longer possible to rely solely on in-
house resources and the traditional research and development mecha-
nisms. Licensing and acquisitions are a new key—a key that can be very
attractive for Ultrapreneurs. Big corporations excel in mass manufacturing,
distribution, and marketing. Ultrapreneurs excel in fast-paced innovation.

Ultrapreneurs Do It Faster
and Cheaper

If the Ultrapreneurial team can identify a niche product or service, they
can better afford to develop and market-test it than can a large company.

They can do it faster, cheaper, and with a lot more flexibility. Their challenge is to start the process and then seek out a strategic partner who can bring a variety of resources to the table. Large companies are constrained by their bureaucracy that tends to retard the process of innovation. By entering into strategic alliances with an Ultrapreneurial company, larger firms can "jump start" their innovative process to gain new technologies that otherwise may take them years to develop in-house.

Most commonly, this means the large company finances the growth of the Ultrapreneurial company. They make systematic investments and gain a window on the technology or process to integrate into their market applications of the future. For the Ultrapreneurs, they get to exercise their bold new idea, and probably realize partnership economies of scale in manufacturing, marketing, and distribution.

The biggest problem with strategic partnerships is negotiating the initial agreement. It requires a keen focus on the integration of planning with a lot of attention, at the outset, on what the partners expect to achieve and what each will need to put into it to make it work. A lot of issues arise. Who will lead the effort? Who is responsible for maintaining open lines of communication? At what stages do which experts get involved? Does this change the leadership? What financial returns are expected? Are there limits on other joint partners? What risks may arise for both parties? The list is almost endless.

Large companies aren't very good at being partners; they're more accustomed to operate as owners. They have a tendency to treat their acquisitions as buyout candidates. Obviously this can be good for the small company long-range; however, it can cause problems in the short run. Generally, the large company doesn't spend enough time with the smaller company after the initial agreements are signed. Attempts to avoid this should be negotiated upfront. Clear definitions need to be established as to which party is to do what, by when, with an airing of expectations brought forth.

Confirm Two Points

Two additional points stand out. First is that from the very beginning, it must be agreed that an arbitration clause or completely acceptable mechanism for coping with disagreements can be cast. Second, there have to be strong feelings of trust on both sides. This has to include "I like you and I know you like me" attitudes and beliefs. Strategic partnerships are like marriages; loss of trust or faith easily results in divorce.

The natural aim is that both partners achieve their mutual end results as initially anticipated. For the Ultrapreneurs, this may even be the ultimate reward of being bought out, when the major kinks in the product or service have been ironed out. For the large company, their reward may be that they have a product or service that now needs their boast of big-time marketing and distribution. In a way, strategic partnerships can be likened to marriages of convenience.

Qualifying a potential strategic partner is another one of the tools used in analyzing an Ultrapreneuring opportunity. The partner almost always brings financial assistance, but if strategically chosen may provide a major bonus to credibility. That's one way Ultrapreneurs gain added value for their companies.

Using Your Whole Brain to Make Ultrapreneurial Decisions

"The human mind, once stretched to a new idea, never goes back to its original dimensions."   OLIVER WENDELL HOLMES

Picking the right business opportunity encompasses many areas. It's not just identifying strategic partners and it's not just validating Ultragrowth marketing. For the Ultrapreneurs, it means choosing an opportunity that suits their capabilities and provides an enjoyable, challenging, and fulfilling work environment, as well as a meaningful return on the risk investment. Then the work will seem like fun and will lead to success. If you enjoy and find fulfillment in your work, you are more likely to do an outstanding job. And if you do an outstanding job, you are more likely to succeed. These points are also important to the Ultrapreneurial investors. They need to be excited about their investment, which in turn helps energize the Ultrapreneur.

Many people choose business opportunities the wrong way. They don't attempt to match their capabilities and desires with the business they select. They only see the imagined financial rewards. Maybe they don't properly investigate the income potential and the strengths of their competitors. Too often they rely on hot business tips or on recommendations of a friend or relative. More often than not, these poorly thought-out business ventures end up in failure.

The Ultrapreneur needs to maintain consistent thought patterns when analyzing opportunities. Understanding and utilizing both right- and left-brain thinking assures that the proposed opportunity fits your personality and is not just a solution seeking a problem. Right/left-brain thinking helps track emotional-versus-intellectual thought patterns and issues to be sure that the heart doesn't overrule the pocketbook. It helps confirm that viable markets will develop. It provides keys to be sure the financial person analyzing an Ultrapreneurial investment opportunity stays on the right track in assessing the amount of risk-taking inherent in the opportunity.

The premise of this section is that all persons surrounding an Ultrapreneurial project—be they the Ultrapreneur, the top management team, the financiers, or the whole implementation group—need to work from both sides of their collective brains to accomplish the peak performance necessary to achieve the Ultrapreneurial goal. They need to learn the checks and balances of the emotional issues versus reality.

Left/Right Brain Simplified

The following are simplistic comparisons of the functions of the left versus the right side of one's brain.

Left	Right
Analytical	Intuitive
Verbal	Visual
Sensible	Emotional
Organized	Sensory
Scheduled	Spontaneous
Logical	Nonrational
Occupations	
Lawyers–Accountants	Artists–Musicians

Left-brain thinking dominates our society because it is oriented toward technology, power, and money. It's also why over 85 percent of us are right-handed. With computers performing more left-brain functions, work skills are shifting to right-brain jobs. An Ultrapreneurial lesson in right/left-brain thinking can be learned here by studying lower socioeconomic classes. They tend to use language with more right-brain characteristics, depicting situations with rhythm and pictorial images. They tend to solve problems by looking at the whole situation, a trait that Ultrapreneurs should cultivate.

A further study of right/left-brain thinking shows some interesting comparisons between male and female. Men tend to shift further to the left or right than do women. All of us, male or female, tend to prefer one hemisphere to the other, which in turn affects our approach to life. But baby girls have a larger connector between the two hemispheres which allows them to integrate information more skillfully. They usually develop speech earlier and are then encouraged to communicate more. This accelerates verbal learning and leaves less time to develop spatial skills. Boys, on the other hand, develop spatial skills because they are not as involved in communicating verbally.

Determining Your Pattern

When it comes to "lateralization," which is the degree to which brain functions are preferred in the appropriate hemisphere, there is also a male/female difference. Highly lateralized individuals, usually males, move into the task-appropriate hemisphere more easily, while females are usually less lateralized and tend to perform in both hemispheres.

If you're an Ultrapreneur, you should determine your dominant brain pattern and think carefully about assembling key team members to complement your style. If you're a prospective Ultrapreneurial management team member, you should carefully look at the Ultrapreneurial leader and determine their ability to interact with your style. By the way, opposites attract. If you're considering investing in an Ultrapreneurial endeavor, you might spend some time analyzing the situation from both the left and right perspectives.

When analyzing your thinking patterns, remember to do the left brainwork first. Research, accumulate facts, and analyze. Then let the right brain go to work; put things aside and you'll *discover* the overview/strategy pattern.

Two Left-Right Quizzes

Use the following "most likely" and "least likely" industry factors to access a prospective opportunity while incorporating left/right-brain thinking. There's no scoring involved; just assess your proposed endeavor with the following in mind:

Most likely	Less likely
High growth industry	Slow growth industry
Small number of employees	Large number of employees
Recruit capable, ambitious people	Needs average technical people
Rapid technological change	Slow technological change
Low capital investment	Heavy capital investment
Afflicted with periodic crises	Relatively well managed
Located in high start-up area	Located where few start-ups occur

Here's another exercise in left/right-brain Ultrapreneurial thinking that looks at high-versus-low payoff opportunities.[1]

---

[1] Karl H. Vesper, *New Venture Strategies,* Prentice-Hall, 1980, p. 161.

High payoffs	Low payoffs
Hard to find and enter	Easy to think of and enter
Small number of small competitors	Lots of small competitors
Higher capital investment	Low capital investment
High skill needs	Low skills required
Has patents, trademarks, secrets	Nothing proprietary
Established, respected reputation	Not well known
Strong customer ties	Easily formed relationships
Leadership-positive	Not a leader
Innovative but not radical	Ordinary or highly eccentric
High tech, high skill	Single outlet/operator service

The challenge for both of these exercises is to accumulate the left-brain facts for each of the above points and then let the right brain do some further analyzing during the decision/comparison making process. Using both sides of the brain will help the Ultrapreneur choose the most likely opportunity with the highest payoff.

Business Goals

After examining the market opportunity side of a potential Ultrapreneurial opportunity, and after assuring ourselves that we have effectively applied whole-brain thinking with the results that our emotions haven't overruled our checkbook, yet another test is needed. A further refinement to ensure the potential opportunity will fit the Ultrapreneurial approach. This test is the business goal test.

Business goal setting is just as important as personal goal setting. The business management team must decide exactly what they want, and most importantly they must determine the price they will have to pay to get it.

Why People and Businesses Don't Set Goals

There are four common reasons why unsuccessful businesses don't set goals. All of these reflect top management's attitudes toward goal setting as they permeate down through the company's ranks.

First—Top management, and thus the company collectively, just doesn't understand the importance of goal setting.

Second—Top management just doesn't know how to set goals. Think about it: Goal setting is not formally taught in school; we can't take a course on the subject.

Third—Our basic fear of rejection. If we're fortunate enough to read about goal setting, or unless some other caring, mentoring person chooses to clue us in, we pick up goal-setting parameters on our own. Many times we're taught not to share goals but to keep them to ourselves (unless the person we are telling also shares the same goals).

Fourth—A fear of failure. Along with not being taught about goal setting, our natural instinct is preservation coupled with a fear of failure. Proper goal-setting instruction teaches us that sometimes we must fail to succeed. And that the secret to long-term goal achievement is to pick ourselves up and go for it again.

It's primarily through experience that we learn to embrace the concept of failure, that we learn that failure is to break out of the commonplace. In our personal game of life, we are our own umpire and we shouldn't fear change. Goals enable us to control change in our lives, especially the pace of change.

Personal Balanced Goal Setting

For Ultrapreneurs, the idea of having balanced goals is very difficult to accept. The tendency is to sharply focus on just the business goals and give short shrift to others. This is a mistake, as all people need to have three to five goals in each area of their life. The trick is to realize that it's okay to reprioritize them at different times as these various areas change, but to recognize that, long term, we need balanced goals. Here are some examples of balanced goal setting:

Family—Set out both tangible (more frequent contact) and intangible (more loving contact or with deeper emotional feeling).

Business and Career—In these areas, we need to set both dollar and quality-of-life goals.

Health—This may be short-term (weight loss, get in shape) or long-term goals (maintain weight, stay in shape).

Social—Make more friends. Vary between business and social.

Self-improvement—Read for inspiration, business, or pleasure. Take courses or instructions for the same reasons.

It's well established that there can be all sorts of goal categories, but several very important points need to be made. All goals have to be set in harmony with each other, and you need to be realistic about the amount of time that you set aside for pursuing all the various goals you establish.

Method to Program Ultrapreneurial Goal Achievement

The following steps apply to both business and personal goal achievement. By testing a business opportunity against each of these steps, the entrepreneur can gain a better grasp of the reality of successfully executing an Ultrapreneurial business opportunity.

Step 1   *Desire or needs.* Goals should be determined based upon what a company or a person desires or needs.

Step 2   *Belief.* A person or the top management of a company *must* believe that they can achieve the goal. This must be based on a realistic assessment, yet the goal must make one stretch.

Step 3   *Write it down.* Goals must be written and rewritten in as much detail as possible. Writing it down crystallizes it, creates a memory impression, and makes it clear. This helps people commit goals to their subconscious. Writing goals down causes us to think, and the hardest work of all is the art of thinking.

Step 4   *How you will benefit.* This must be written down for each goal. This includes noting what differences will result from achieving the goal. The more reasons, the better.

Step 5   *Analyze the current position.* Whether personal or company, current positions must be analyzed in relation to the individual goals. How much money are you making now? Is there room in the market for another similar product?

Step 6   *Set deadlines.* In setting deadlines, always use the latest outside date. Setting deadlines helps make goal attainment measurable. Deadlines set direction, keep you moving, and help monitor success. Setting goals will give you more time, but no one ever met a demanding goal without devoting time to it.

Step 7   *Identify obstacles.* It's always very helpful to draw up a list of identifiable obstacles to goal attainment. Large obstacles tend to become smaller when written down. When identifying obstacles, high standards should be set—this increases concentration, and, at a minimum, you'll at least hit an intermediate goal.

Step 8   *Identify knowledge.* This is especially helpful. It doesn't matter if it's a personal or a company goal, there is always additional knowledge that must be acquired. You will have to learn something or add to the team someone who has the knowledge.

Step 9   *Identify people.* For both personal or business, people, groups, and their cooperation are needed to obtain goals. Three laws apply:
    a. *The law of return.* Whatever you sow, so shall you reap. You must put in or give before you receive.
    b. *The law of compensation.* Every action has a reaction. Determine what you can put in.

                c. *The law of service.* You can only achieve by serving or filling a need. Today in business it's called customer service. Go the extra mile; do more than you're paid for.

Step 10   Make a plan of the last three steps (7, 8, and 9) and then itemize, prioritize, and list the activities. Review, rewrite, revise; do this as you go along. It's called thinking on paper.

Step 11   Get a clear mental picture. You do this as if your goal is already in existence. By doing this visualization, you can achieve the goal to the degree of seeing the details. Remember, the more you concentrate your gaze on a distant goal, the more apt you are to stumble over something right under your feet. Visualizing in detail helps prevent stumbling.

Step 12   Back up goal setting with determination. With all goals, they must be backed with the determination and resolve to never, never give up. Persistence counts. Realistically, there will be setbacks and failures, but these are signs to alter the goal-achieving strategy. Pick yourself up and go on. Keep on keeping on!

Remember, self-discipline is simply persistence in action and persistence is the measurement of self-belief. *In goal attainment, obstacles are what you see when you take your mind off the goal.*

What Goals Look Like

A goal is long-range. Objectives are the intermediate targets with shorter timeframes. Both have a predetermined end result. The attributes of effective goals are:

Must be demanding

Must be achievable

Should be specific and measurable

Must have a deadline

Should be agreed to by those who must achieve it

Should be written down

Should be flexible

The goal-setting sequence starts with a long-range goal, a specific target. Then work carefully down to today with successively shorter-range targets, called objectives. This makes breaking long-range goals into smaller, more do-able, and mentally achievable pieces. The business goal test is yet another tool in Ultrapreneurial opportunity testing.

Basic Questions Checklist

Long-term viability needs to be considered for any project; this screening process gets grounded in looking at the project's goals. Ultrapreneurs have this long-term concern in mind whether they are intending to sell off to someone else or harvest via a public offering. But along with assessing the longer-term viability, one needs to assess the immediate prospects of getting the company off the ground. The following checklist of questions should prove helpful as an overview for initial analysis.[2]

Basic Feasibility

1. Can the product/service actually work?
2. Will it be legal?

Competitive Advantages

1. What will be the specific competitive advantages?
2. What are those of the existing competitors?
3. How will the advantages be maintained?

Buyer Decisions

1. Who will decide to buy, and why?
2. How much will each buy, and how many people are there?
3. Where are these people located, and how will they be sold?

Marketing

1. How much will be spent on advertising, packaging, selling?
2. What share of market can be obtained by when?
3. Who will personally perform the selling functions?
4. How will prices be set, and how will they compare to competition?
5. How important is location, and how will it be determined?
6. What channels will be used—wholesale, retail, agents, etc.?
7. What specific sales targets should be met?
8. Can orders be obtained before starting the business? How soon?
9. How will returns and service be handled?
10. How will pilferage, waste, spoilage, and scraps be handled?

[2] Karl Vesper, *New Venture Strategies,* Prentice-Hall, 1980, p. 159.

People

1. How will competence in each area of the business be ensured?
2. Who will have to be hired, and when?
3. How will they be found and recruited?
4. How will replacements be obtained if key people leave?
5. How will attorneys, accountants, and other advisers be chosen?
6. Will special benefit plans have to be arranged?

Control

1. What records will be needed for development of product/service?
2. Will any special controls be needed?
3. Who will take care of it?

Finance

1. How much will be needed for development of product/service?
2. How much will be needed for setting up operations?
3. How much will be needed for working capital?
4. Where will money come from? What if more is needed?
5. To which assumptions are profits most sensitive?
6. Which assumptions in projections are most uncertain?
7. What will be the return on equity and sales, compared to industry?
8. When and how will investors get their money back?
9. What will be needed from a bank, and how will they feel about it?

Benefit from This Checklist

An Ultrapreneur can really benefit by addressing all the points in the above checklist. Answers and comments will provide the basis for a lot of the information that will be needed in assembling the prospective company business plan which is discussed in more detail in Chapter 6.

Taking Aim at the Future

Entrepreneurs, mostly acting on their own—but some within established businesses (called Intrapreneurs)—have done more to shake up American business in the past decade than at any other time in United States history.

Entrepreneurs in small businesses have also acted as an important economic shock absorber by making an unexpectedly significant contribution to new job creation. Several decades ago, scholars and forecasters were predicting that the more than 20 million baby boomers who would enter the work force in the 1970s might compel the government to become the employer of the last resort. Almost no one suspected that small business, which for many years had been a far less conspicuous job creator than government and big business, would be the major producer of new employment. But that is what has happened. The facts are well documented: job creation in the United States by small business has continued unabated through regional, national, and international rolling recessions. Employment in Western Europe, by striking comparison, has been stagnant during most of the same period.

To be competitive in a global economy, America is learning to pare the size of its manufacturing labor force and substitute more competitive factory automation. It's estimated that less than ten percent of the labor force will be engaged in manufacturing by the turn of the century. The reality, which is continuing to become more accepted, is that the productivity gains that are being put into place by automation are extracting a painful cost in employment displacement. Small business is taking up a lot of the slack.

People today want to become entrepreneurs. Lots of new ideas are being tried out, touching off a creative entrepreneurial boom, a lot of it driven by women. A great deal of former big company executives are now getting their piece of the rock by participating in stock ownership plans. In other cases, management buyouts have created a new group of employee-owned companies.

While many basic industries have disappeared and others are struggling, America's creation of wealth has faltered under the hardship of economic transition. The emphasis has shifted back to basic wealth generation based on the simple fact that a society must first generate wealth to be able to distribute it equitably. The United States is the epitome of this ability.

The trend of privatization of public enterprises is now firmly in place all over Europe and is spreading into the Eastern European countries. This is a long-term process whereby the world is recognizing that industry deregulation and the contracting out of local, state, and federal public services can be accomplished with greater efficiency and at less cost. It's a broad shift in intellectual sentiment toward private-sector solutions and away from big public project solutions to economic growth. This is occurring not only in the major developed countries but also throughout the developing world. There is a new emphasis on small labor-intensive industry and agricultural self-sufficiency as a means to get development back on track.

The Age of the Entrepreneur Is Here

Former President Ronald Reagan, speaking at St John's University in Queens, New York, in 1985 said, "We have lived through the age of big industry and the age of the giant corporation, but I believe that this is the age of the entrepreneur, the age of the individual." Ultrapreneurs are proving to be the catalyst of high-technology development. Innovation is a process to which they contribute. Many times their job creation is not long-term, but it provides the foundation for the large companies to acquire new products and services that then drive the bigger companies in their international presence.

In many instances of new technology, competitive efficiency depends more on design of a product or service process than on sheer size, speed, or delivery. This is where Ultrapreneurs excel. A lot of these design efficiencies and innovations can be made with a minimum of capital. This is a secret to the kind of contribution Ultrapreneurs can make. Even though it continues to be a tough Ultrapreneurial challenge to innovate in an increasingly complex global environment, a secret is to explore the service areas or exploit market niches. With the speeded-up pace with which both consumer markets and industry markets change, just the ability to respond quickly favors smaller, more adaptive companies.

Today's reprogrammable computer-driven machines are making small-batch production runs more economically feasible. Ingenuity and skill can overcome sheer size. Computer-aided-engineering, computer-aided-manufacturing and computer-aided-ad infinitum really lowers entry barrier costs for smaller enterprises to be competitive. Simple but highly capable low-cost PC systems enable many companies to instigate sophisticated management systems to assist them in staying on top of what's happening in their companies. They can track hundreds of thousands of inventory items, all of their production, management, and sales costs. They can intimately track sales orders to assist in keeping inventories low and receivables current, which in turn eases cashflow. "What if" scenarios are simply run on a variety of readily available spreadsheets, and large databases store gigabits of marketing information many times gleaned by tapping into a variety of modem-accessible sources.

On the negative side, Ultrapreneurs who operate in international markets are often affected by constant currency changes. This problem is being addressed by the banking industry and specialists who assist small business in hedging their transactions. Because the United States has always been its own huge market, we collectively have not developed a sophisticated international marketing sense. Time and circumstances are curing this fairly quickly, but if a sizeable portion of an Ultrapreneurial company's revenues or business involves international exchanges, it's a red flag to be sure currency fluctuations are more than adequately covered.

Financing

The biggest problem faced by most small companies is financing. While a full chapter is devoted to this subject, it bears some mention while examining opportunities. Initial financing is the hardest to come by, and as such it is a major roadblock to many entrepreneurs. Unfortunately, the old saying of "them that got's the gold, rules" still applies. This is the toughest hurdle for many minorities and poorer or less educated entrepreneurs. Hopefully, various community and government-funded programs will continue to be developed. Maybe we can even get our government to back a French scheme that encourages prospective entrepreneurs to build savings in a special bank account which the government supplements with soft loans. This long-term saving incentive almost forces the entrepreneur to invest some time in management thinking, while they're saving, which could be enhanced by business training assistance. Why not devise such an equity scheme for the United States?

By far, the most important thing we could do is to develop good public education programs. These programs need to teach entrepreneurial skills, build good business ethics, and instill confidence. This in turn provides competent employees. It will be critical as future years roll around that our competitiveness be gained and maintained in the new knowledge- and technology-intensive industries. Access to knowledge is as important in the information age as access to financing.

Business incubators, a phenomenon of the 1980s, have proven that assistance provided in a group atmosphere drastically increases small business success. Technical assistance from universities, government technology transfer programs, formal classes in management, and access to a variety of funding sources have enabled a lot of communities to regain valuable jobs. This same "grouping" of industrial centers like Boston's Route 128, The Carolina research triangle, California's well-known Silicon Valley, and many lesser-known regional efforts have proven to be worth their weight in gold. The synergism that develops when entrepreneurs are surrounded on a daily basis with their peers to exchange information, share trials and tribulations, as well as get problem-solving input, has been the secret to many an Ultrapreneurial success story.

Reviewing the Opportunity

We've covered a lot of ground in the process of determining and qualifying valid Ultrapreneurial opportunities. Guidelines and checklists have been furnished to help quantify the process; what at first glance appears to be off-the-wall thinking has been explained to show the Ultrapreneur, the Ultrapreneurial team members, and those that finance Ultrapreneurial projects some new insights to uncover and analyze Ultra-preneurial opportunities.

When all is said and done about analyzing business opportunities, when all the numbers have been gathered and the assumptions confirmed; when the due diligence is close to being completed, there are still some bottom-line feelings that will tell you "go or no-go."

These come from the gut, and ofttimes it's hard to remove the emotion involved. But that's the point. Emotion is what makes successful Ultra-preneurs. If you *feel,* and your research seemingly justifies that the opportunity is a good one, then check your enthusiasm level. Ultrapreneurs use this all the time. Do you *feel* enthusiastic about the choice you're making? Are you excited about its potential? Do you have a *feeling* that its success is intricately woven into your existence? Do you *feel* that the opportunity is an extension of yourself? Do you *feel* that you will be excited every morning when you face the daily challenges? Are you sure you can retain an interest in learning, improving, and changing? Will the opportunity keep you motivated?

Motivation is more than just another capability. It is *the* single capacity that can, and will, help you overcome a lack of capabilities in other areas. It's what makes your potential opportunity valid, keeps you fascinated, pre-occupied, and yes, even obsessed.

These are the "gut" questions that need to be answered. A long stream of "gut-level yesses" will confirm your *feelings* about the validity of this being your Ultrapreneurial opportunity.

3

What It Takes to Be an Ultrapreneur

*America makes a promise to Ultrapreneurs.
It is that every person has a chance and is
presented with an opportunity. It is that
every person, regardless of sex, heritage,
birth place or economic status, has the right
to live, work, play, to be yourself and
become whatever you and your vision can
combine to accomplish.*

I'm going to give you the secret right up front, right here in the first paragraph. *There is no definitive set of characteristics to describe an Ultrapreneur.*

In fact, there doesn't seem to be a definitive set of characteristics to describe an *entrepreneur* either. However, as you'll learn, there are some very subtle but all-important differences between entrepreneurs and Ultrapreneurs. Just having a business idea may qualify one to be an entrepreneur, but as you'll continue to learn, that isn't what makes an Ultrapreneur.

Fifteen years ago, when I first started studying the possibility, I felt that a significant set of characteristics could be developed. A number of studies, both formal and informal, have been conducted over the years, and a lot of books, articles, and papers have been written. They have approached entrepreneurial characteristics from many angles. A. David Silver in his book, *The Entrepreneurial Life—How to Go for It and Get It* (John Wiley & Sons, 1986), took the approach of selecting 100 entrepreneurs who had each achieved personal wealth of $20 million. His mail survey resulted in 54 replies and, although he carefully stated that the results were suggestive rather than definitive, the results did track many other surveys and studies.

Silver conducted another landmark survey for his book, *Entrepreneurial Megabucks* (John Wiley & Sons, 1985). This book provides individual profiles of his selection of the 100 greatest entrepreneurs of the last twenty-five years. Although I'm sure there would be some changes should he update his list from 1985, I'm more positive that he would expand it. His books give one the ability to test some of the characteristics that others have set forth. I admit, his comments have influenced my thoughts for many years and have colored many of my speeches and articles on the subject.

What Do Venture Capitalists Think?

If you ask a venture capitalist or investment banker what is *the* most important ingredient in the success of a company, they'll immediately reply: the people, the management team. If further pressed as to which team member is the most valued, regardless of industry, product, or service, they'll tell you the entrepreneur, the founder, the guiding light. This even applies in high-tech projects where the invention or conception of a new product is commonly brought to life by an engineer or scientist. Even an Ultrapreneurial company has to be assembled and then guided by an entrepreneur.

Having had both success and failure in my personal entrepreneurial activities—as well as tracking hundreds of investment opportunities of other entrepreneurs—I have been a continuing student of trying to determine if I can qualify the personal characteristics of entrepreneurial success.

I've had many discussions with venture capitalists, investment bankers, human resource people, academicians, and other support professionals to entrepreneurs. We've kicked around how to identify and assess personal motivation, greed, personality background, levels and degrees of education, and personal and professional life experiences. My conclusions to date are presented in this chapter.

Hardy, Ambitious Goal Achievers

Entrepreneurs are hardy, ambitious, goal-achieving dreamers. They spend their lives in stressful environments working to solve stressful problems. Some fail all their lives. Others just survive. A few are Ultrapreneurs and create entire new industries—like Henry Block of Block Brothers, who revolutionized tax reporting, or Mary Kay Ash of Mary Kay Cosmetics, who opened the entrepreneurial door to women and created thousands of two-income families. Their one common bond is hard work.

The United States was not only founded on the devotion to hard work that is epitomized in entrepreneurs, it has thrived on the major risks inherent in new enterprise development. This underlying fact *is* America. The persistence and involvement of entrepreneurs has led to the creation of many new industries, new technologies, and even new ways of living. All of these were and are promoted by the boundless energy, boldness, imagination, and striving of entrepreneurs. If our country is going to nurture these traditions and lead the world into the next century, the practice of entrepreneurship must be encouraged, supported, and taught.

So can we qualify a number of the success characteristics of a typical entrepreneur? Is there a definitive set of characteristics?

The answer is yes—and no. There is no single all-important set of personality characteristics or psychological profile of a typical entrepreneur. However, there are many areas of commonality, traits that can be identified and learned, abilities that can be cultivated, mindsets that can be adopted. In the end, you'll recognize that there is a great variety among types of entrepreneurs, that they have a diverse psychological makeup, but yet how they achieve success defies the use of any single profile.

Based on this background, we'll explore a number of mental, physical, and environmental characteristics. These will give us a basis of understanding to look at how these traits are certainly changing in light of today's business environment. Then we'll explore how we best adapt our thinking for Ultrapreneurs.

Entrepreneur—The Word and Its History

We best start with a short history lesson. The word *entrepreneur* first appeared in the early French language, referring to persons who were involved in leading military expeditions. The word continued to evolve and expand into economic language.

Joseph A. Schumpeter (1883–1950), born in Austria and educated in Vienna, advisor to a princess in Egypt and eventually a Harvard professor, added the modern-day concept of *innovation* to the criteria of entrepreneur. He suggested that entrepreneurship is a process, and described entrepreneurs as innovators who use the process to shatter the status quo. To his way of thinking, they do this by innovating new combinations of resources and new methods of commerce. He suggested that entrepreneurs and their innovating activity are thus the source of profit in the capitalistic system. He further suggested that entrepreneurship is not a profession or a position that can be handed down from person to person or from one generation to another. It is a special kind of leadership. Schumpeter wrote

> . . . we do not observe (in the entrepreneur's position) the emergence of all those affective traits which are the glory of all other kinds of social leadership. Add to this the precariousness of the economic position both of the individual entrepreneur and of the group, and the fact that when his economic success raises him up socially he has no cultural tradition or attitude to fall back on, but moves about in society as an upstart, whose ways are readily laughed at . . . we shall understand why this type has never been popular . . .

In Schumpeter's time, if the populace laughed at entrepreneurs, it might have caused one to question, "Why strive for that type of indignation?" Schumpeter's reply was:

> First, there is the dream and the will to found a private kingdom . . . Then there is the will to conquer: the impulse to fight, to prove oneself superior to others, to succeed for the sake, not of the fruits of success, but of succeass itself . . . Finally, there is the joy of creating, of getting things done, or simply of exercising one's energy and imagination.

It is difficult to put it better, even a half-century later. However, we can add some new insight that broadens our understanding of today's entrepreneur and indicates society's growing acceptance and respect for them.

Robert L. Heilbroner wrote in his book, *The Worldly Philosophers,*

> Economics (or for our purposes, entrepreneurship) deals with the complex outcomes of social processes, including the act of exchange, the drive for economic expansion, and still other behaviors . . . But these behaviors themselves reflect the historical—or human—setting in which they are found. At the root of the matter lies man, but it is not man the "economic" being, but man the psychological and social being, whom we understand only imperfectly.

For those with a serious bent toward more definitive knowledge of entrepreneurs, a comprehensive compendia of entrepreneurship research continues to flow from the Center for Entrepreneurial Studies at Babson College, Babson Park, Massachusetts 02157. Complete proceedings from annual conferences held since 1981 are available, titled *Frontiers of Entrepreneurship Research,* edited by J. Hornaday, J. Timmons, and K. Vesper.

As this and other studies are carried forward, many tried-and-true characteristics are confirmed. However, as business methods evolve, new characteristics are identified and defined which become the bedrock for examining entrepreneurs. The next section is an assemblage of many of the traits currently used to define an entrepreneur. I have broadened and rearranged them to define the Ultrapreneur.

Characteristics—The Basics

The "perfect entrepreneur" has yet to be invented. It's impossible to arrive at a set of characteristics that are ideal for all situations. It all depends on the fit and mix-or-match of a given opportunity. It depends on the strengths, weaknesses, and mindset of the founder and people chosen to be part of the team. However, the collective team will most likely have almost all the perfect characteristics woven into the fabric of the whole. From all the various studies that have been conducted, both formal and informal, we know there are many characteristics that are proven, both desirable and acquirable. They can be set out in the following baker's dozen traits. If they were contained in one single individual, you would have the ultimate Ultrapreneur. I have listed them alphabetically since it would seem that they are equally important.

Achievement	Honesty
Action orientation	Innovation
Commitment	Intelligence
Communication	Leadership
Energy	Risk tolerance
Goal setting	Self-confidence
Growth orientation	

Achievement

Achievement is generally considered the act of accomplishing or finishing something. For the Ultrapreneur, one would tend to add "successfully." They recognize that success occurs when preparation and opportunity meet. Preparation is up to them, opportunity ofttimes is not. They realize that by means of exertion, skill, practice, and with much perseverance, they will achieve success.

Achievement would also include the component of assessment: that there is a strong desire to accomplish goals that have been established in a carefully determined and thoughtful manner. This assessment comes from reviewing previous records of expanding, of successful goal accomplishment—accomplishment that can be measured, and where most frequently the measurement is money. Not for greed or money itself, but for innovation, sales, market share, capital gains, and profits. Money becomes a tool and a convenient way to keep score instead of the object of the game.

Ultrapreneurs have a strong internally driven desire to compete, a desire for independence. They are self-starters who don't need direction and who pursue and attain goals that are self-imposed. They strive to outperform their own previous records and standards rather than what someone else has imposed.

Their drive is for achievement, not for power or status. Ultrapreneurs realize that if they are successful, if they achieve their company and personal goals, then power and status will follow. Achievement comes from the execution of success plans that are acted upon and that achieve positive results, from seeking ever-larger, more-defined challenges. The people that back Ultrapreneurs, from team members to employees, to financiers to suppliers and customers, need to believe that the leader is an achiever.

Action Orientation

There is one Ultrapreneurial trait that underlies all the other entrepreneurial characteristics. This trait is that successful Ultrapreneurs are action based, always taking action. No matter what the movement, it must move. Sometimes this doesn't prove positive, but in the long run, taking action sure beats standing still. Occasionally, one has to take a step backward to move forward two steps. Ultrapreneurs realize—no—deeply believe and feel this. They know that even if their immediate action proves to have some faults, they're confident they will learn from a mistake, benefit from some new knowledge (not consider it a failure) and then will take corrective action.

This action orientation frequently comes naturally with Ultrapreneurial types. They seem to have a sixth sense about if and when actions should commence. Maybe it's street smarts. Then again, maybe it's from a thoughtful process. Regardless, the decision process to take action (which is the foundation of Ultrapreneurial characteristics) can be broken into a step-by-step Ultrapreneurial action sequence.

Commitment

To this characteristic, Ultrapreneurs add dedication, determination, and persistence. These are the points an Ultrapreneur needs to overcome the incredible odds, setbacks, and obstacles they face in securing their success. These qualities, perhaps more important than the rest, assist the Ultrapreneur in succeeding where entrepreneurs and others fail. They are the goal-attaining supplements to many other weaknesses. They are part and parcel of Ultrapreneurial commitment. Commitment is the willingness to take a stand for what one believes in. It requires that the Ultrapreneur generate a passion for success and a hatred for failure.

The commitment to long-term involvement has to be backed by patience—patience to retain the visionary approach required to keep the ultimate goals in mind, to maintain a continuing awareness of the big picture while fighting the battles of day-to-day Ultrapreneurial warfare. Patience and persistence go hand in hand.

Persistence was once described by Ray Kroc, who was the driving force of the international McDonald's fast-food chain. He said:

> Nothing in the world can take the place of persistence. Talent will not . . . Genius will not . . . Education will not . . . Persistence and determination are omnipotent.

These qualities are what drives an Ultrapreneur to work so hard.

Ultrapreneurs burn with a deep competitive desire to excel and win, to control their destiny, to shape their future by being deeply committed.

Communication

The greatest illusion about communication is that it has been accomplished. A difference between an entrepreneur and an Ultrapreneur is the Ultrapreneur's continuing questioning of the effectiveness of their communication processes. It's called *feedback:* How do we know if what we're communicating is getting across? The answer is positive affirmation, or questions.

An Ultrapreneur must master the basic communication skills of speaking and writing in a forceful, polite, effective way. They must integrate human awareness and relations while seeking feedback and digesting the results before recommunicating. This means that quality Ultrapreneuring involves becoming an excellent listener.

A good listener ignores personal prejudices and listens with an open mind, not prejudging. Further, they listen for key points, ignore trivia, get important facts and relate them to the main points. They avoid distractions, detect and interpret body language, read between the lines for what isn't being said, and avoid the temptation to interrupt.

When the listening session is over (which it never really is for Ultrapreneurs), they organize their thoughts into clear, concise statements and disseminate them via the spoken word, written instructions, and most importantly, positive-reinforcing actions. This is Ultrapreneurial communication.

Energy

Energy is a positive quality—a desire to get things accomplished, to get them done in the right way. It's an active quality, an urgent need to move from one position to another, to advance to a new goal, to accomplish a given task. Energy is never static, and Ultrapreneurs enjoy using it and get excited when they're put to an energizing task.

Energy gives Ultrapreneurs the drive that makes them challenge-takers. It assists their natural tendency to be positive about setbacks and supports their tolerance for stress and the continuing uncertainty that they live with.

Ultrapreneurs must have high energy levels and large energy reserves. Their jobs invariably require long hours for extended periods of time, often with small amounts of sleep. These abilities are frequently thought to be genetic, but can be enhanced and supported through a conscious effort. Good health and emotional stability, together with good eating patterns— which are hard to maintain when one is going ninety miles an hour and every day is four hours too short—are important for providing high energy levels. Also exercise, in consistent, moderate amounts, contributes to a healthy body that can withstand great stress and uncertainty levels. And emotional stability can be learned by careful, inwardly directed study and drive. These enhanced traits feed Ultrapreneurial energy.

Goal Setting

For Ultrapreneurs, goal setting is an obsession. Their goals are their dreams—dreams with a deadline, dreams being acted on. They realize that goals assist them in controlling their lives. They know that their goals have to be positive, have to be definite, have to be emotionally stimulating— something that turns them on, gets them excited, something that they really want to work for.

To them, goal setting is simply the long-term version of keeping track of time. Ultrapreneurs, more so than entrepreneurs, divide their goals into a lot of different areas, compartmentalize them into both small and large objectives. The goals are long-range, while the objectives are intermediate targets with shorter timeframes.

Ultrapreneurs have a keen awareness that goal setting must be in place throughout their company. They know that realistic goals must be established by unified decisions. They have a gut feel for bringing the goal achievers into the process of identifying the goals to begin with. They recognize that building support for defining priorities and establishing measurement standards makes the process of obtaining goals much easier and palatable.

Finally, they have a deep and firm recognition that goals are attained by action.

Growth Orientation

Very frequently, Ultrapreneurs have worked for large companies. Put another way, they have functioned in aging, mature companies that tend to stifle growth. It is for this reason, coupled with many of their other inherent traits, that they strike out on their own. They see the opposites of growth and aging business traits. They know that success comes from embracing risk, as opposed to avoiding it, that growth power comes from the sales and marketing that drives new companies and not from the controls of finance and legal departments inherent in large established companies. They appreciate value-added profit goals but not political game playing. To them, problems are opportunities.

Growth-oriented Ultrapreneurs are into quality—quality of people, of product, of service, of old-fashioned craftsmanship and caring. They understand that growth results from team building, hero making, by giving responsibility and sharing credit with others. Unlike yesterday's entrepreneurial lone wolf, today's Ultrapreneur is growth-oriented via people and establishing a growth-oriented organization.

Honesty

Today's buzzword for honesty is *ethics*. Ethics is simply a code of behavior that is governed by morality and law. It is based on a sense of right and wrong that is not dependent on what the law says one can or cannot get away with. Unfortunately, a lot of supposed business leaders and entrepreneurs lost track of many old-fashioned values in the eighties. Was the cause a reflection of lost values in our society? Or, in some cases, the integration of global practices of many different cultures? The answer lies in the practical reality that humankind best functions when operating under some basic principles. Some things just aren't for sale at any price. Ethical, honest societies, by definition, have high value orientation, high personal standards of integrity, and an orientation toward reliability. They must avoid pursuing a lot of short term gains in place of long-term successes.

A mere century ago, "honor" was defined to the point that men fought duels because of it. Yet today, with impersonal corporations replacing personal entities, it's easy to shirk responsibility for commitments. Honesty, ethics, and honor mean taking responsibility that can be costly. You can lose a job, a customer, a supplier, even a lawsuit. But respect goes to those that stand up to their commitments or mistakes. Since Ultrapreneurs don't pass the buck; you know where they stand and you know you can count on them in the crunch to do the right thing—to be honest.

Innovation

Ultrapreneurs are innovative because they are individuals or are part of small teams, as opposed to bureaucratic, massive projects. Innovation and bureaucracy just don't mix. Bureaucracies seek to minimize and control risk, where true innovation encourages risk. Entrepreneurs, although open to risk, want to hold tight rein over the innovation process and employees who may contribute. Ultrapreneurs manage risks by taking risks on a small scale, encouraging experimentation, and dedicating energy to fixing mistakes instead of finding fault.

Since innovation is making ideas happen, creativity is thinking up new ideas. Without new ideas there can be no great leaps in innovation, and without purposeful execution there can be no innovation. It used to be thought that a person who was creative or innovative had definite inherited or genetic traits. Now it's believed that these qualities can be learned, or at least encouraged.

Once, when Alexander the Great visited his famed teacher, Diogenes, he asked if he could do anything for him. Diogenes's reply was, "Only stand out of my light." Ultrapreneurs know that you shouldn't spoil anyone else's joy of creativity, that often the secret is to simply stand out of the light.

The ability to create or innovate is not necessarily rare, just generally uncultivated. Creativity is simply thinking and making new discoveries; it is a matter of having reasoning processes and, for most Ultrapreneurs, having the right encyclopedic knowledge. Creativity when combined with innovation is the essence of successful Ultrapreneurship.

Intelligence

While there are many manifestations of intelligence, from advanced degrees to Mensa level IQs, entrepreneurial intelligence is often thought of as coming from a rational, logical person, one who has the ability to recognize, understand, and analyze complex situations or problems. Often, these situations arise in areas where the Ultrapreneur has a large amount of technical knowledge and expertise or, at minimum, in-depth experience.

This expertise is then coupled with conceptual ability, gut feel, and a major dose of curiosity. Sometimes the creativity or innovation comes quickly, but usually it develops over an extended period of time. This Ultrapreneurial intelligence, blended with many other traits, as well as a recognition of one's own limits, combined with instincts and cunning, come together to create not only a new company, but sometimes whole new industries.

This Ultrapreneurial intelligence needs to be bound with an ability to assess the areas of expertise where one is lacking. Know your own limits and then surround yourself with other intelligent experts. Entrepreneurs often guard their intelligence, while Ultrapreneurs encourage its development. Today, it is also very helpful if a majority of these experts have both experience and a large awareness of international business activities and the intelligence to deal on a global basis.

The last Ultrapreneurial intelligence component needs to be a keen sense of humor. The pace is too fast, the hours too long, and the stakes too high not to be able to laugh along the way. Summed up, perhaps it's "street-smart intelligence."

Leadership

An Ultrapreneurial leader is one who commits people to action. An Ultra-preneurial leader must convert followers into leaders and agents of change. The traits for Ultrapreneurial leadership are:

Foresight, so you can judge how your vision fits the way your organization, and the environment in which it operates, evolves.

Hindsight, so your vision doesn't ignore past traditions, business cultures, and mistakes, but still isn't afraid to take major new strides.

Global view, so you can interpret the impact of new trends and potential developments.

Depth perception, so you can peer into the details without losing sight of the whole.

Peripheral perception, so you can track the responses of competitors to your new directions.

Re-vision, so you can review your past visions to adapt to current and changing environments.

Ultrapreneurial leadership requires the ability to be a persistent problem solver, to be patient and decisive—to be a motivator by actions and having a temperament to deal with failure. Yesterday's domineering, adversarial leadership style won't fly. Today, good team players can't be attracted with a dictatorial demeanor. Ultrapreneurial leaders, as opposed to yesterday's entrepreneurs, need to be good at conflict resolution, with keenly honed mediator/negotiator skills. Entrepreneurs dictate where Ultrapreneurs lead. Leaders learn to listen with the intent to understand, not to reply. They learn to lead people and manage things, to seek solutions, not just point to problems. "Lead, follow, or get out of the way is their battle cry with a major emphasis on leadership and building and supporting co-leaders in their organization.

Risk Tolerance

Risk is exciting—it stimulates "aliveness" in the person or people who are taking the chance. The willingness to take a risk means you are willing to go beyond a familiar niche. It's a necessary element in Ultrapreneurial self-development, and it's absolutely necessary if a company is to realize its full potential.

To even think about eliminating risk in high-growth businesses is wishful thinking. Risk is inherent in the processes of commitment of existing resources to future expectations. For these companies, the monthly financial bottom line is a summation of dozens of different types of risks that are taken on a daily basis. Winning today only means you get yet one more chance to stay in the game. It's a never-ending season.

Studies have shown that successful entrepreneurial risk-takers have a high level of self-confidence, a fierce need to be in control. For Ultrapreneurs, this includes a realistic vision of how to achieve objectives. Taking risks is the Ultrapreneurs' psychological mechanism that fulfills their control need. They perceive and make meaningful connections between seemingly unrelated variables and are better able to relate the risk to a specific achievement. They don't enter into risks unless their internal perceptions have told them they can win. Ultrapreneurs don't like risk. The difference is that they understand it, they know how to make it work for them, and instead of intimidating them, it energizes them.

Ultrapreneurs learn from failure, seek criticism and feedback, thrive on ambiguity, stress, and uncertainty. They function very well with a lack of organizational structure and rigid order. Ultrapreneurs take things in stride, they like risk excitement and aren't concerned with job security and retirement. Risk to them is more than money—it's their reputation that is at stake. They take the plunge in a very calculated, carefully thought-out manner, planning the odds in their favor with carefully defined strategies that include laying onto others as many of the risks as possible. This is accomplished by finding coworkers, investors, suppliers, and customers who are also willing to share in the risks. Sharing in areas and at levels that they are comfortable with, although most of these shared risk-takers are also personalities that are seeking to stretch their personal development. All of these points come down to a highly developed, keenly honed level of risk tolerance.

Self-confidence

Ultrapreneuring is not for the timid. It's for those with a deep belief in their ability to succeed over a seemingly endless stream of difficulties. It takes an internal focus of control, an ability to compete with one's self and self-imposed standards, to seek and take initiative, a self-reliance to know that you can impact and solve problems, and a willingness to be measured. It is to believe that you can accomplish, and that setbacks lie within your own control and influence.

Top Ultrapreneurs have a well-developed concept of self; in other words, they know who they are, they know where they came from, and they have a very good idea of where they are going. Many have suffered some type of identity crisis in their lives. While similar to entrepreneurs, Ultrapreneurs also encounter their share of hardship, but have learned to smooth out the kinks, pound out the rough spots, and become comfortable with the self into which they have evolved. However, they also have a self-awareness that keeps them from falling into the traps of arrogance, overconfidence, and lack of humility. Their aim is to achieve a level of self-knowledge that works well for them.

Self-confidence is the trait of envisioning victory from situations where others see only defeat, to find promise where others find grounds for pessimism, to see opportunity where others see obstacles. Ultrapreneurs have confidence in themselves and believe that they can personally make a major difference in shaping the final outcome of their project and consequently their lives.

The Ultrapreneurial Action Decision Sequence

Ultrapreneurs understand the need to take action, and they develop the confidence to take action because they have also developed an action-decision making sequence process that supports their confidence. This process is as follows:

Is Action Needed or Not?

The first question is: "Does the situation really call out for attention or a need for action?" But if we say that Ultrapreneurs take action, how can the first point be taking no action? Perhaps it's a situation that should be addressed with "stay cool." No real need to get excited, just "lay back and trust me on this one." Maturity and lots of past experience can be very beneficial in this case. Many decisions stop right here. No action is needed.

Is There a Choice of Actions to Be Taken?

Here the Ultrapreneur works on the importance of selected values or evaluating options as they conclude there is no choice but to take a specific action or *not* to take it. They ask themselves and others, "Is there only one action or do we have others to consider?" In other words, is it an offer that can't be refused? Maybe we're better off seeking and considering alternatives. Usually, comparisons result in all alternatives being easily rejected. The offer suits the situation and they decide that they have no other choice; however, they recognize they can easily adjust to the action.

Will a Habitual Course of Action Suffice?

Habits make our life more simple, a lot easier, and a lot more comfortable. This also applies to the action-decision process. Habits enable us to make fewer decisions. The Ultrapreneur asks, "Is what I usually do (by habit) the best now, or am I better off doing something else?" They question if they can rely on the past, or is this a case where they should get out of the rut, engage in the fact that variety is the spice of life, and do something differ-ent? The choice is between habit or a new alternative.

Reduction of Alternatives

This is used when there are a lot of complicated facts or unfamiliar situa-tions—too many things to choose from. Here the Ultrapreneur doesn't let the alternatives be eliminated or eliminate those not immediately favorable to them. In each case, they specifically question if they should consider the choice or not. This way they can narrow the choices down to a few serious objective contenders.

Choice of Preferred Course of Action

With the alternatives narrowed down to a limited number, each is approached on the basis of: Is this what I ought to do or not? This raises the attractiveness of each of the final alternatives.

Decision to Take Action

This is the last step. The Ultrapreneur asks, "Should I actually do this or *not?*" The stress is now on the rewards of quick action or the penalties of delay.

If the decision still isn't comfortable, the Ultrapreneur proceeds back through the steps. Sometimes it helps to question the rewards and penalties of the contemplated action by adding them to the decision making process as follows:

Question reward—What do I have to gain?

Question penalty—What do I have to lose?

Question positive values—What says it's the right thing to do?

Question negative values—What says it's the wrong thing to do?

Using a learned action-decision sequence helps improve Ultrapreneur-ship. It's another key to understanding what makes a successful Ultra-preneur and differentiates them from entrepreneurs. It helps our quest to understand Ultrapreneurs by studying their basic characteristics. It also helps us understand them by reviewing their positive attitude toward action and to have reviewed their action-decision making sequence. Another key is to examine how they view failures, learn from mistakes, and embrace success.

Entrepreneurial Failures

There is a continuing school of study that attempts to analyze entrepreneurial companies that fail. They do post-mortems on dead deals. What went wrong? Was it a single prevailing factor or a combination? Could the outcome have been altered to prevent the death? Was a key decision made that proved to be a turning point? Was it a team decision made in unison? Was it outside forces like a fickle, rapid market change? Or was it *fear of success* on the part of the entrepreneur?

Fear of Success

The entrepreneurial world is littered with failures; Ultrapreneurs learn from them—from the little Mom-and-Pop shops to multimillion dollar venture capital endeavors. They happen daily all over the country. The Small Business Administration continually points to mismanagement, entrepreneurs that were not prepared to properly run a company. Insufficient financing is often the whipping boy, but the truth usually goes deeper. Top-rated management anticipates financing needs by good business planning. There is a growing school of thought that is pointing to one key area in the more sophisticated failures. It's a fear of success on the part of the lead entrepreneur. Fear of success has become the determined cause when all other factors, such as a good team or a defined market niche, can't be identified as the reason(s) for failure.

Because an entrepreneurial characteristic is "try, try again," we often don't fault a person with another new idea if they failed in attempting to implement a previous one. In fact, our society encourages getting up, dusting off, and trying again. However, prospective Ultrapreneurs—key members of the management team and prospective investors—should look at this fear of success when analyzing a prospective opportunity. Is it a factor in the Ultrapreneur? Is it present in any of the team members?

Definition. Simply, the fear of success is not getting what we want because we don't feel we deserve it, aren't entitled to it. Fear of success occurs because you're afraid your inadequacies will be revealed. You're not afraid of failing because you already have a fear of succeeding. This acceptance of failure is a sure sign of the fear of success, as losers are people who fear winning. Question Ultrapreneurs about past failures. Do they simply express remorse (a fear-of-success sign), or are they adamantly disgusted with a failure? Are they excited about what they learned from the failure? This indicates they are anxious to get on with it and prove that they are capable.

Another sign is anxiety. Entrepreneurs prone to fear of success are always anxious about how well they are doing or how well they may do. Rather than becoming more self-confident and self-assured with successes, they become more nervous and unsure. For many female entrepreneurs, it takes the form of the *impostor syndrome*. They may feel like an impostor, someone who's not really this good. They fear others may find out and expose them as being ordinary or mediocre. Heaven forbid, a pretender to the throne rather than the genuine article.

Yet another fear-of-success sign is goal nonachieving. An entrepreneur may claim to want a goal with great success and may daydream about it, but when it comes right down to achieving it, they constantly back off. They just can't quite get the motor started. There's always time for another cup of coffee, one more social obligation, or a telephone call. Anything to take them 180 degrees from the stated goal. It's also called procrastination, excuses. When they don't achieve their goals, they may be publicly disappointed, but privately relieved.

Emotional Facts.   There are two primary emotional facts that put the fear-of-success syndrome into play. The first is what you perceive to be the consequences of your success. Rather than viewing success as empowering, it feels (or potentially feels) like a loss. Pressure is an example. When you succeed under pressure, you're not sure you want to do it again. You worry about never again being able to indulge in the pleasure of goofing off. No more being carefree. All eyes will be upon you because you now have to become stodgy, superresponsible, and a role model for others.

A second emotional fear is your sense of belonging. This is a new feeling to you, it's virgin territory. You feel uncomfortable and perhaps that you are operating outside or above your abilities. It's not you; you've pushed the envelope too far and it feels unnatural and strange. In your own mind, the "others," the ones who you felt were always more successful, are now your peers. You're not supposed to compete at this level; this is not your place. You were okay and had some good qualities, but being this successful was not one of them.

Again, many female entrepreneurs struggle with this issue. Being successful and female haven't always gone together. Women have traditionally been taught to cooperate, not compete. They were encouraged to do well but not to take their accomplishments too seriously. Suddenly they face a new threshold, and they wonder if they dare to cross. The fear is that if they cross this threshold, will it be an emotional loss—either rejection or abandonment from someone who matters? Once you understand the dynamics involved, you are well on the way to resolving a fear-of-success dilemma.

The roots of fear of success come from low self-esteem, and low self-esteem comes from not knowing what you want out of life. When we are children, we look for evidence that we can survive by our own resources. Our natural tendency is not to be constantly protected, restricted, or indulged. We like to learn to deal and cope with different problems and difficult situations because that makes us feel we can tackle life. We need to learn not to run away from problems, but to deal with the things that are most difficult.

Doesn't this sound like a typical entrepreneur? Sure, independent, take charge, get things done, a whirlwind of action. But be sure that behind these positive traits there is not the weight of a fear of success. A person can delve into this by truthfully searching the following points. An Ultrapreneur inquisitor should carefully inquire and consider these also.

Fear-of-Success Triggers

Fear of success/low self-esteem can come from our parents. It's how we think they saw us and how they treated us. We may believe we don't *deserve*. Signs of this are:

Were your parents overprotective?

Did they not give you any responsibility?

If you're in between careers, do you think about going back home?

Were they big on analyzing? Are you?

Did they say, "meet the right people" or "be something"? (This subliminally implies that you aren't something.)

Did they always step in and do things for you? (The message is that you aren't capable yourself.)

Some additional signs are:

When you take on a new role, do you feel guilty about it? A lot has been written for and about women in this area under the topic of *impostoring*. Because they are breaking a lot of new ground in what has been a male-dominated business world, they have fears and concerns about their true levels of business capability. Their self-confidence is lacking primarily because they may not have a female role model.

The fear-of-success syndrome that can cause the demise of new companies is more common with the "lone ranger" type of entrepreneur of the past. It can be circumvented in Ultrapreneurial companies and ventures by insisting that the Ultrapreneur share responsibilities, that they build a team where their decision making does not affect every aspect of the company. This becomes more apparent when we look at some guides to recognizing fear of success.

Guides to Recognizing
Fear of Success

1. Recognize you have a fear of success by getting in touch with what and who you *really are* versus what *you perceive* yourself to be. Many entrepreneurs just haven't spent any time getting in touch with themselves; they're too busy doing things. Consequently, they have an overinflated opinion of how good they are in too many areas.

2. Why do you have such low esteem? You need to feel that you deserve to be happy, not weighted down with fear, guilt, and self-defeating thought patterns. Many entrepreneurs carry immense amounts of guilt for past failures or what they perceive as past failures for not living up to the expectations that parents, teachers, spouses, or others have put on them. "Why didn't you become a doctor?" "You're so smart; why aren't you getting better grades?" "Why can't you earn more money for a bigger house?"

3. Solve problems creatively and assertively from a base of self-trust. Learn to respond to trouble and squarely face challenges. Many entrepreneurs tend to crawl into their shells when confronted by problems that they feel inadequate or ill-prepared to solve. As pointed out in #1 above, their ego is at stake. Instead of really knowing who they are, they tend to think that they and only they are able to solve all problems. They need to be encouraged to reach out for help, to get their team involved in problem solving.

4. It takes time to gain self-discipline and get what you want, as well as being willing to pay the cost of being in charge of your own life. Paying the cost in this case is letting others add significant value to a team effort.

Entrepreneurs are notorious for giving lip service to team concepts; only those who have risen above the fear of success make successful Ultrapreneurial leaders. They have learned to accept themselves for their outstanding talents, to be patient with their development, and to feel they can express opinions without taking replies too personally. Most of all, they have to believe in the team concept and prove this by surrounding themselves with key team leaders as smart as or smarter than themselves. Ultrapreneurs have a low fear of failure and a high need for success, coupled with the spark and desire to make it happen. Bottom line: They delegate responsibility and pass on authority with confidence.

Three Steps to Help You Learn
to Accept Success

Sometimes in Ultrapreneurial situations, we find that we are directly faced with working with a team member who is suffering from a fear of success. Ofttimes, this may be temporary and may have been caused by a setback in their plan to achieve certain goals. You can help. With all this grounding in the dynamics involved, here are three steps you can use for yourself or to help others to bring the fear out into the open and deal with it.

Examine Your Rationale. First, rationally examine what you believe to be the true consequences of your success. What would happen if you were more successful? What impact would it have on you and those around you? Who would be pleased? Who would be envious? What would be expected of you? What would you expect of yourself? The basic idea is to ferret out the downside or loss that you fear losing.

Now face up to what you are concerned about. Is it what *has* happened? Is there any other attitude or posture that could develop? If someone would be upset or envious of you, what can you do about it? What is it about their disapproval that is so powerful for you? How did they become so powerful? (Hint: You gave it to them.)

Redefine Your Situation. Second, redefine where you belong. But first own up to where you belonged in the past. Where was that? How come? Is that where you want to be? What needs in you are served by keeping yourself in the same place?

Now visualize where you would like to be. What shifts in your view of yourself will be necessary to ensure a genuine accommodation to this new place? What will you need to do to accomplish this?

Expand Your Comfort Zone. Third, work on getting comfortable outside your "comfort zone." Those afflicted with the fear of success tend to work inside their own personal comfort zone. First, define what activities constitute your present comfort zone. Now draw up a list of activities that raise anxiety—the things that you avoid doing and prefer not to do. Don't start rationalizing that those things don't work and that's why you won't do them.

Take Action. Finally, slowly but systematically begin to do some of the things on your list. If you are determined and committed in overcoming your fear of success, you will need to tolerate some anxiety as a signal that you are on the right path. It will allow you to become more successful and, most important, free yourself from those fears of success.

As was mentioned in the opening of this section, there is a growing school of thought that the fear of success lies behind some entrepreneurial failures. The concern is such that many venture capital firms today require that the key members of a prospective management team take a formal psychological test to help the venture capitalist discover if this is a problem prior to their making an investment.

We can learn from this by developing an awareness of the subject and then using some of the key points just discussed. Ultrapreneuring doesn't leave room for many mistakes. Make sure fear of success isn't one of them.

What Ultrapreneurs Should Not Do

It's very easy, almost a natural tendency, for Ultrapreneurs, especially those on the Ultragrowth path, to be or become workaholics. In fact, it's expected. Simply put, workaholics work excessively. Our society encourages this and rewards achievement. It teaches us that we are good if we are productive. We sacrifice a full night of sleep, regular eating habits, and close relationships. By putting in excruciatingly long hours and facing one stressful situation after another, we inflict serious health consequences on ourselves as well as those who work with and for us. This creates anxiety attacks, work-related headaches, coronary heart disease, cardiovascular complications, and tends to adversely affect family lives, not to mention the ultimate effect all these side complications have on the Ultrapreneurial project itself.

Does it have to be that way? For most Ultrapreneurial endeavors, the answer is probably *yes*. Ultrapreneurs not only envision that the rewards are worth it, but deeply feel and believe that, not if, but when they achieve their goal, they will have the luxury to suddenly change their habits and lifestyle. Maybe there are some balances, some middle-of-the-road compromises. It's possible to find areas where they can draw the line between being compulsive and simply working too hard. An Ultrapreneuring effort requires extreme focus, devotion, and commitment for an extensive time period. It's important that this effort isn't jeopardized and that every Ultrapreneur has an obligation to keep the workaholic balance in perspective, both personally and in their surrounding team members. Following are some warning signs of workaholic tendencies.

Symptom Spotters

1. Frequently declined social invitations and missed family events. Nothing else is as important as work, especially when you are so intensely involved. What's more, you believe that every aspect of the business requires your involvement and that nonbusiness events are only a way to lure you away from your intended goal.

2. You resist any form of outside hobby or sports. To you, pleasure reading is to catch up on industry publications. Other outside activities are a waste of time and effort. Besides, they don't help further your gaining of your business goal.

3. Business is foremost on your mind and the main, if not only, topic of your conversations. You don't know the sports scores unless it's your clients' team. You have only a nodding acquaintance with what's happening on the national political scene. And the last movie you saw? You slept through most of it.

4. No one ever beats you to work, and you always lock up. In fact, you frequently avoid completing the previous day's work so you have some compelling reason to roar right back into a pressing task the first thing the next early morning.

5. You confirm your belief of indispensability by insisting on handling every last detail yourself. Why delegate? You're a workaholic.

6. At the end of the day, you frequently question what you accomplished that day. All that rushing, all that effort and nothing to show for it. Workaholics spend their time spinning their wheels because they're disorganized. They have high energy levels but are unable to channel it properly.

7. Be sure to take on lots of projects, volunteer for everything no one else wants; in fact, invent some new ones. This feeds the need to work harder, which helps you procrastinate, which means you get even less done, which means you can come in earlier tomorrow and, if you're lucky, you may get to stay even later.

A Balancing Act

How do we get caught up in this all-too-common syndrome? For lot's of folks, it happens without them even being aware. They get pushed into various pursuits or projects by peer or societal pressure rather than their own innate desire to pursue something. All of a sudden, they are stretching for a sense of control, they take pride in their work and in controlling their activity, but they are headed for trouble.

Can a successful Ultrapreneur stop being a workaholic and stay successful? The simple answer is *yes*. But it takes a concerted effort to take control. For many, it means consciously cutting down from the normal 70- to 90-hour weeks. It means weaning themselves down to a mere 60 to 70 hours a week instead. But they'll be better Ultrapreneurs and people for it.

Write into your normal day all the tasks you usually do after hours. Don't promise customers the moon. Be realistic when setting deadlines; most things can be negotiated. Take some time away to totally disassociate from work. Success is not just winning or achieving; it's also having fun and staying healthy.

Building a business often takes three to five years of 60- to 90-hour workweeks. You have to commit from the marrow of your bones and decide up front what you are willing to give to get what you're after. However, it's important to see yourself as two people—a businessperson as an Ultrapreneur—but also a son, wife, father, or friend. This gives you a source of self-esteem unrelated to your business. If the business endeavor falls apart, you still have an identity apart from your business.

The Ultrapreneurial key is to maintain realistic goals, delegate, put effort into a balanced life, and be around to really enjoy the rewards.

Success Qualities

We have spent several sections in this chapter looking at some of the negatives that can affect accelerated entrepreneurial ventures. This is helpful both from a personal standpoint and as some guidepoints if you're considering teaming up with an Ultrapreneur. But how about the success points? What good qualities should you be on the lookout for or, as an Ultrapreneur, be trying to cultivate? Here are some answers:

Hard Work

It's never easy getting to the top and it's even tougher staying there. Very few people who have it made on a long-term basis did it without working extremely hard. They worked at least 60-hour weeks with a lot of Saturdays and many long nights. You need a highly cultivated work ethic; you'll never make it on eight-hour days. Eight hours are for survival, and anything over eight hours is an investment in success.

Enthusiasm

For you, your business has got to be the greatest thing that you can do. Enthusiasm sells, but because once in a while business is tough, your enthusiasm is inclined to wane. This becomes apparent to your coworkers and customers. Maybe you need to take a little time to yourself or to spend "unbusiness involved." Pull back to pull yourself up to regain your belief and enthusiasm in what you have chosen to do.

Creativity

In today's Ultrapreneurial business world, you have to be creative in all areas. The things you did three or four years ago won't work today, at least not the same way. You've got to look for and develop new ways, new ideas. Use your imagination to solve problems and generate solutions. Cookie cutter and one-size-fits-all approaches don't work. Customize and innovate.

Flexibility

Adapt to change. It's a key characteristic because business is evolving and changing so rapidly. The market is always doing different things and there are new twists to learn. Look forward to change, welcome it with open arms. Sometimes it's hard to accept, but today, flexibility is a way of life and an Ultrapreneurial must.

Empathy

It is important that you show empathy to your coworkers, employees, suppliers, and most important, your customers. Everyone wants someone to understand and acknowledge their problems, maybe even display some empathy. They want someone to care about them, to be kind to them, to show some interest, build a relationship, or offer a solution. Empathy and kindness never go out of style; in today's cold, sometimes hard business world, it's an Ultrapreneurial key to success.

Knowledge

Knowledge in Ultrapreneurland is not power, but potential power. You must have the knowledge base, coupled with conviction and enthusiasm, to sell your dream. You've got to spend time and effort, on a continuing basis, obtaining more knowledge to be able to offer viable solutions to problems. Knowledge helps solve problems and problem solving is another key to Ultrapreneurial success.

Differentiating Factors

Along these same lines, what might be some of the factors that differentiate between entrepreneurs and successful Ultrapreneurs? These would include:

Entrepreneur	Ultrapreneur
First time start-up	Prior start-up experience
Not sure where to go for advice	Knows where to seek advice
Doesn't know what advice is needed	Knows what specific advice is needed
Feels competent in all areas	Feels weak in certain areas
Seeks professional help in response to problems	Seeks professional help in anticipation of problems
Lacks key skills in industry	Has acquired key skills
Operations-oriented	Total business-oriented
Fairly well educated	Slightly better educated

These are the success qualities and some interesting factors for Ultrapreneurs. Study, absorb, learn, and above all, put them into practice.

An Age-old Debate

Morris Massey is the creator of a videocassette entitled, "What You Are Is Who You Were When." In some ways, it addresses an age-old debate as to who makes better Ultrapreneurs: the young with youthful drive and determination, or the older with experience, organizational and managerial skills?

Risk Is Back

Massey feels that what was right for entrepreneurs 20 years ago may not be right today, "A lot of entrepreneurs are not risk-oriented or aggressive in terms of research and development." He's right; risk-free orientation won't work in the '90s, because opportunities change too quickly and the markets are characterized by world mushrooming competition. The Ultrapreneurial '90s risk is team-oriented.

He also maintains that it's not age that determines people's belief systems or values, but "when we grew up." He contends that what was reality then remains reality now.

There Are Four Generations of Risk-takers

Massey suggests there are four different generations in the entrepreneurial field today: the synthesizers, nuagers, in-betweeners, and olagers.

The olagers, early fifties plus, tend to be conservative and traditional. They identify with their jobs, and their underlying belief system says, "He who dies with the most toys wins." As children of the depression, the olagers consider overtime work an opportunity.

The in-betweeners, early forties to early fifties, believe you can have your cake and eat it too. They may be former hippies (thus challengers) with a foot still in the traditionalists' camp. They are the flip-flop group. They have been in midlife crisis since puberty and still can't make choices. They want choices, but can't make decisions.

Next are the baby boomers, the new-agers, late twenties to early forties. If you didn't like the above descriptions, wait till you read this. New-agers are like the cast of the TV series *thirtysomething*. They talk, talk, talk, but never do anything. They grew up challenging the olagers establishment; however, they are not particularly responsible. They want "balance." Massey says, "They want to make it, but they don't want to sacrifice in order to get it." They consider overtime work as an infringement, not an opportunity.

Last, and surprisingly not the least desirable entrepreneurial candidates are the synthesizers. They're what's left, the group in their early twenties.

They grew up in the decade of the '80s when the most current entrepreneurial boom got its start. Massey feels this group is comprised of "responsibility-focused individuals." Assuming he means both female and male, he feels they have a "deep belief in themselves and a purpose in life." Recognize they grew up with the computer as a toy and consequently can synthesize many variables at once—an acknowledged Ultrapreneurial trait. Also remember they grew up in a time of major upheaval in the employment markets when a lot of traditional industries started to restructure.

Could their marching tune be titled, "We want success and the best way to get it is by becoming Ultrapreneurs"? They grew up knowing, reading, hearing, seeing, and using—first-hand—the Ultrapreneurial success tools of the '80s; Apple computers and Microsoft computer software. Those two companies' founders have become very rich, famous, and powerful heros for the synthesizers.

I doubt the age-old debate can be answered yet. But there's a lot of persuasive evidence beginning to surface that the olagers theme song of "experience is what counts" is going flat. Experience doesn't count as much today because knowledge is easily accessible and the world changes so fast.

Ultrapreneurs Build a Mixed Team

While Ultrapreneurs have to have energy—a fire in their belly—a little gray on the sides indicates there's some season there. I'm tempted to wonder if the "risk-it-all attitude" is still valid. Then again, youth is being cocky and feeling that success always goes on. Where in truth, Ultrapreneurs realize that business success comes in periods, no one does well all the time, and a big key is being prepared and then capitalizing on the opportunity, whether by chance or choice.

Actually, I suspect that the successful Ultrapreneurial team, perhaps led by a synthesizer, managed by an in-betweener, marketed by a nuager, and guided by a olager, is probably the winning team for this decade.

Female Entrepreneurs and Entrepreneuring

In this enlightened age of nondiscrimination it has become impossible to attempt to discuss or write about entrepreneurs and Ultrapreneurs without reference to women and their increasing impact on entrepreneurship. In the mid-seventies, about 5 percent of all businesses were owned by women. By the year 2000, it's projected to be between 45 percent and 50 percent. According to 1992 statistics released by the National Foundation for

Women Business Owners, sometime during 1992, the 5.4 million women-owned businesses will employ more people than the Fortune 500 companies. Twenty-eight percent of U.S. businesses are women-owned and -managed. Nine percent have annual sales of more than $1 million, compared with 14 percent of all businesses; 40 percent have been in business longer than 12 years; and contrary to many stereotypes, women are active in all economic sectors.

The following chart shows the percentages of women-owned firms compared to all firms.

Category	Women	All
Agriculture, mining/construction	6.2%	7.1%
Business services	18.7%	10.2%
Finance, insurance, real estate	5.6%	9.3%
Manufacturing	11.8%	25.2%
Professional services	20.4%	17.3%
Retail	28.0%	18.8%
Transportation, utilities	4.0%	7.1%
Wholesale	5.4%	5.0%

The Female Touch Is Growing

It's obvious when reviewing the statistics on women-owned businesses that the majority are service-oriented. This is natural because service firms tend to require less capital to open and operate. As female entrepreneurs continue to build their numbers, as the business world learns to accept them and appreciate the valuable contributions they continue to make, we'll see more and more female owners in nonservice businesses. However, one can be sure that a reward for this will be that the nonservice businesses will have a larger emphasis on service. This is a female touch that is continuing to permeate our business society.

Female Ultrapreneurs who have an interest in learning more about the organized activities of women business owners are urged to contact the National Association of Women Business Owners (NAWBO); national offices are located at 600 Federal St., #400, Chicago IL 60605, (312) 922-0465. NAWBO has many local chapters across the United States who support female entrepreneurship under the banner: NAWBO is an organization of growth- and profit-oriented women business owners, representing the interests of more than 6 million women entrepreneurs in the United States. NAWBO provides its members access to contacts, opportunities, and power—locally, nationally, and globally.

Cultivating an Ultrapreneurial Corporate Conscience

Various cliches, such as corporate conscience, company responsibility, and caring capitalism, are getting kicked around. In essence, it's the positive trend of the '90s that indicates that the company cares for its employees, community, customers, and all the various environments in which it operates. This is one of the subtle but significant changes from the gunslinger '80s entrepreneur. It's a change that must be incorporated into the thinking and beliefs of the Ultrapreneur.

At first blush, this is almost dichotomous thinking, a complete switch from high-growth companies that are thought of as irresponsible and exploitative to Ultragrowth companies that are kinder and gentler. How can a company innovate a new product or service, drive it into an unforgiving marketplace, capture a dominate position, and not be thought of as ruthless? This is the Ultrapreneur's challenge.

The '90s mean that "green"—not "greed"—is good. Everyone is getting on the socially responsible bandwagon. Universities have added ethics courses to their business curricula. Organizations have implemented awards for corporate conscientiousness. McDonald's has received large amounts of publicity for their dramatic improvements in packaging. Walt Disney Co. is getting praised for appointing a vice president of environmental policy. Wal-Mart, contrary to prior practice, is making a big push to work closely with the leaders in the communities in which it has locations. It's a reshaping of American business.

Just as the lone wolf is out and strategic alliances are in, corporate irresponsibility is out and Ultrapreneurial conscience is in. And guess what—it works! Howard Rothman and Mary Scott, co-authors of the book, *Companies With A Conscience: Intimate Portraits Of Twelve Firms That Make A Difference* (Birch Lane Press, 1992), spent several years interviewing founders, managers, and employees of various companies that were identified as having a high level of corporate conscience. They determined that there are six key points that distinguish socially responsible companies. These points make a good guideline for companies led by Ultrapreneurs.

People Are Always the Backbone

From the president and CEO to the shipping-room people, the company is staffed with employees who are unusually committed to both their communities' and the companies' bottom line. The Ultrapreneur sets the tone and example. Salaries are generally above industry averages and perks and benefits are extraordinary. Working conditions are uniformly superb.

Everyone Is Encouraged to Participate

Everyone is given the opportunity to own a piece of the action, to gain equity in the company. They are given the opportunity to participate in company-sponsored seminars relating to the companies' finance and operations as well as personal and other business matters. They are kept abreast of the companies' efforts to participate in philanthropic activities and encouraged to develop their own. This leads to decreased turnover and increased productivity.

A Humanistic Orientation Is Apparent at Every Level

Executive parking places are out and company cafeterias are in, attended by the president and hourly wage-earners alike, often at the same table. Everyone is on a first-name basis, and employees, their spouses, and children are sincerely considered part of the extended family. Management goes to great lengths to ensure that the workforce is satisfied at work and at home.

There Is Life after Work

Top Ultrapreneurs have to commit to long, irregular hours, but that doesn't mean they don't know what else is going on in the world. They nurture a wide variety of interests, global to local. Companies sponsor speakers to address their employees on topical subjects in private, onsite gatherings, and regularly send them to offsite meetings and seminars. Bottom line: The Ultrapreneur is concerned with issues besides the bottom line.

Community Involvement Is Commonplace

Employees at all levels actively work for the betterment of their neighborhoods and cities. They always have the support of management, as personal involvement in local affairs is considered critical. Employees learn the seriousness of this by observing top management's behavior.

The Past Is Heeded but the Future Is Never Ignored

Forward-thinking management is always cognizant of the lessons of history and the management theories that have proven successful in the past. But in Ultrapreneurial organizations, this is intertwined with progressive leadership thinking and philosophies. Flexibility, and a willingness to refocus, are thus always possible and encouraged. Some efforts come easily, others are long fought. Examples are encouraging recycling, onsite daycare, community outreach programs, and minority education classes.

Caring capitalism is growing. Ultrapreneurs can show that they care and still make money. People are watching with a high level of interest as the socially responsible business movement rolls on.

Passion

In this chapter, we've noted that the characteristics of an Ultrapreneur evolve as our business climate evolves. We've seen that the Ultrapreneur does differ from the entrepreneur in many ways. The main way would be the departure of the long-standing perception of the lone individual who through grit, much personal sacrifice, and dogged determination finally break through the norm of their particular business and rockets to the top of an industry. Tomorrow's Ultrapreneurs, although they endure trials and tribulations, do so with a defined goal, an organizational plan, and a distinctive team who designate and share responsibility, moving ever forward to a predetermined harvest.

The Ultrapreneur has one final characteristic that sets him or her apart from ordinary mortals. It's *passion*. And it's a passion of *love*. Ultrapreneurs won't succeed at anything that they don't love. Sure, they have a lot of help making a decision. But in the final analysis, they make the decision, they live with the problems, they make it work. Mainly because they have the key ingredients—the passionate desire and motivation—to face the situation and see it through.

In short, few start-ups or Ultrapreneurial ventures succeed without this passion. Yes it's true, many passionate entrepreneurs fail, and even some would-be Ultrapreneurs. But that's not the point. Almost none succeed without passion. Ultrapreneurs follow their hearts toward things they care about. How else can you expect to succeed if it's an area that doesn't move you? Simply, if you're an Ultrapreneur, you'll do what turns you on. That's how you capture Ultrapreneurial passion.

4

Building the Inside Ultrapreneurial Team

Ultrapreneurs build world-class products that fill worldwide needs, and their companies need world-class teams to fulfill the promise. Many times it is very difficult to attract these team members the first time out, at the startup stage. Like eagles, first-class executives don't flock. The Ultrapreneur has to seek out the team members individually while pursuing the business goals. This chapter helps define the challenges and provides suggestions and solutions for Ultrapreneurial team building.

The Primary Goal

The biggest point—which becomes the largest difference between Ultrapreneurial and common business teams—is that all key players *must* agree on the basic Ultrapreneurial approach. There has to be agreement among the team members that they are working toward a defined harvest. *This may even include selling themselves out of a job.*

One or More Ultrapreneurs?

In Chapters 2 and 3, we explored the characteristics of entrepreneurs and Ultrapreneurial growth. We uncovered the traits that contribute to Ultrapreneurial success and what drives the individuals themselves. Our concentration in this chapter is to determine if a whole Ultrapreneurial company needs to be comprised of Ultrapreneurial types, or just part of it, or if only one is needed. Basic instinct tells us that it's probably just one or, at most, a

83

couple of individuals with specialized management talents, like inventors or marketing types. The lead Ultrapreneur and the quality of the team is *the* most important factor to success.

This basic instinct is correct: Only one is needed. However, for Ultrapreneurial companies, that one person must be supplemented with a team that is entrepreneurially oriented. They can't just be run-of-the-mill, ordinary managers. They have to be superior in their chosen management discipline, confident of their talent and ability to get the job accomplished—on time, within budget, and with spectacular results.

The team—often made up of the Ultrapreneur, a techie, and a management type—are responsible for creating a carefully crafted Ultragrowth mentality in their company. This mentality is a sort of "us against the rest of the world, we can beat 'em" mindset. It has to be carefully established so that it doesn't turn into a negative "me versus you" internally. This can result in everyone pointing the finger at the other person when something goes wrong. The Ultragrowth management team needs to be sure that when problems arise, they get addressed and solved. The positive us-versus-them mentality seeks out the problems, identifies the causes, works together to solve them and goes on, ever-mindful of the ultimate goals.

Staff

When lead team members have been selected, which is addressed in more detail in the next section, they then become responsible for selecting staff personnel, organizing their tasks, and putting systems into place.

Ultragrowth companies tend to create an invigorating work environment where a lot of the key people as well as staff employees acquire a will to succeed that can border on missionary zeal. This can result in absolutely spectacular results. It builds on itself and is part of the excitement of being associated with an Ultrapreneurial project. But how do make sure you are hiring people who have this unseen quality?

Hire the Well-Qualified

Although there is no sure way of enhancing your chances, one way is to hire overqualified personnel. This is a tough assignment when operating within a limited budget, but it can make a big difference in the final outcome. One way to lessen the hiring mistakes (and there will be some) is to attempt to develop well-defined job descriptions. Management's challenge is to be sure the new employees understand their jobs, are able to perform them, and are supplied with a super support structure. If this is not done properly, it results in mass confusion and lack of work productivity, not to mention rehires.

Rehires in all personnel are extremely time- and dollar-consuming, but even tougher in staff positions. It takes a minimum of three months for new staff employees to learn their jobs. Many times, in reality, this is more like six months before you can count on them as building blocks for new responsibilities. This ability to hire, organize, and manage is an important quality to look for when putting together the top team members. One caution: When hiring overqualified people, there is a tendency for them to instigate too many controls when the company is still small. This overregulation can destroy the missionary zeal that Ultragrowth companies thrive on.

Ultrapreneurial Management Types

It's commonly acknowledged that Ultrapreneurs see opportunity where no one else knows it exists. This ability to retrieve something meaningful from a lot of unrelated places is usually backed with high energy levels and a good deal of creative drive. For true success, they need someone to back up their innovation, someone to keep the pieces glued together. They need managers—managers to find them money, to account for it once it's found, to prepare legal documents for their endless stream of deals, to prepare the brochures and coordinate the sales trips, to be sure the products are getting produced, shipped, and that they work when they arrive at their destination.

This ever-roaring Ultrapreneur, who is always creating work, needs other bodies to sort out the pieces, solidify disorganized plans, and implement the whole. According to A. David Silver,[1] these bodies need managers who are thorough and don't get distracted from the task at hand. These persons are frequently older, more likely to be in a stable, long-term marriage relationship, live in the suburbs, drive a luxury American car, and vote Republican, whereas the ultrapreneur is likely to be single or divorced, live in the city, drive foreign cars, and vote Independent. Ultrapreneurs live for the great achievements which lie ahead; managers, while optimistic about the future, are pleased with their accomplishments to date.

While not risk-averse, managers typically don't have a high level of risk tolerance. They're seeking a balance between challenge, risk, and reward. They want, need, and deserve equity, a piece of the action. They make the team stronger by creating better business plans with more concrete market and product research along with systematized launch strategies.

There must be depth, maturity, and experience in the industry in which the company operates. It's best if the Ultrapreneur has had prior profit cen-

[1] *The Entrepreneurial Life,* John Wiley & Sons, 1986, p. 69.

ter responsibility; if the Ultrapreneur doesn't, there better be plenty of it in other team members. There also needs to be an intimate knowledge of the market and a well-thought-out strategy for penetrating the market. The management team is the most important consideration in the investment decision, and the Ultrapreneur needs to assemble the eagles for a world-class team.

Getting Intimate with the Management Team Requirements

Since Ultrapreneurs come in lots of sizes, shapes, and with varying talents, the blend and unique fit among the founders is what is most important. The object is to take the talents of the Ultrapreneur and combine them with the capabilities of equally talented and committed partners. Mix in the wishes that they can work well together and that the critical mass can seize and execute the opportunity, and the chances for success are dramatically improved.

The functions of a management team differ for different companies, depending on the nature of the company. For instance, a high-tech-product company may need a large research and development department, whereas a service firm may not. In another example, a company that sub-contracts all of its manufacturing most likely won't need a production manager; however, they may need a quality control expert. Specific management abilities function in specific designated areas. The following is a general list of guidelines, qualifications, and fundamentals outlining abilities by various members of a management team for a variety of Ultra-preneuring companies.

Administration and General Management

Communication. Ability to communicate clearly and effectively to all parties and the public in both written and oral form.

Making Decisions. Ability to take input from the team and implement changes.

Negotiating. Ability to solicit differences from all sides, balance opinions, and arbitrate fairly for mutual benefit.

Planning. Ability to identify obstacles, establish attainable goals, develop and implement action plans.

Problem Solving. Ability to gather and analyze facts, anticipate trouble and know what to avoid, how to implement solutions effectively, and follow up thoroughly.

Project and Task Management. Ability to properly define and set goals, organize participants, and monitor a project to completion.

Operations Management

Inventory and Quality Control. Ability to establish suitable inspection standards, maintain accuracy, and set realistic dollar benchmarks for raw, in-process, and finished goods.

Manufacturing. Demonstrated experience in the process, openness to continuing improvement techniques, people power, machinery, time costs, and quality needs of the customer.

Purchasing. Ability to seek out the most appropriate sources and suppliers, considering cost, delivery time, and quality; and to effectively negotiate contracts and manage flow, balancing current need and dollar resources.

Financial Management

Capital Raising. Ability to determine the best approach, form, structure debt/equity, short- versus long-term, and familiarity with sources.

Money Controls. Ability to design, implement, and monitor all money management and to set up systems for overall and individual projects.

Ratios Applications. Ability to produce detailed pro formas for profit and loss (P&L), cash flow, and balance sheets; and to analyze and monitor all financial areas.

Marketing Management

Evaluation and Research. Ability to conduct thorough studies using proper demographics, and to interpret and analyze the results in structuring viable territories and sales potential.

Planning. Ability to provide promotion, advertising, and sales programs that are effective with and for sales representatives and distributors.

Product Continuation. Ability to determine service and spare parts requirements, track customer complaints, supervise the setup and management of the service organization.

Product Distribution. Ability to manage and supervise product flow from manufacturing through the channels of distribution to the end user, with attention to costs, scheduling, and planning techniques.

Support. Ability to obtain market share by organizing, supervising, and most important, motivating a sales force.

Engineering and R&D Management

Development. Ability to guide product development so that a product is introduced on time, within budget, and meets the customers' basic needs.

Engineering. Ability to supervise the final design through engineering, testing, and manufacturing.

Research. Ability to distinguish between basic and applied research, keeping a bottom-line balance.

Personnel Management

Conflict. Ability to confront differences openly and determine resolution with teamwork.

Criticism. Ability to receive feedback without becoming defensive; and to provide constructive criticism.

Culture. Ability to create an atmosphere and attitude conducive to high performance, rewarding work well done, either verbally or monetarily.

Development. Ability to select and coach subordinates and pass this ability on to peers.

Help. Ability to determine situations where help is needed.

Listening. Ability to listen without prejudging, really hear the message, and make effective decisions.

Legal Management

Contracts. Experienced in and knowledgeable about the broad procedures and structure for government regulation and commercial law, including warranty, default, and incentives.

Corporate. Experienced in and knowledgeable about the intricacies of incorporation, leases, distribution, and patents.

This list covers the basic qualifications, abilities, and characteristics the Ultrapreneur should take into account when assembling a management team. Common to all the above management disciplines are five basic man-agement functions.

Five Basic Management Functions

It's the Ultrapreneurs' responsibility to ascertain if their prospective team leaders are proficient in the following basic management functions:

1. *Set objectives,* in clear, concise terms.
2. *Organize*—entails analysis and classification of work, and grouping these into an organizational structure.
3. *Communication* with, and the motivation of, people. This is essential because it is the people who in the final analysis get the job done. How well they do it depends on the quality of the communication and degree of motivation.
4. *Follow-up,* measuring of performance and results.
5. *Development* of good people, in present jobs as well as in anticipation of future advancement.

With the qualifications and functions defined, the Ultrapreneur can turn to the tasks of identifying, interviewing, and putting together a team.

Ultrapreneurial Hiring

"Should I use a headhunter?" Whether to employ the services of a head-hunter is a common question for Ultrapreneurs when searching for execu-tive team members. It's not unusual for two or three key people to be pre-identified; however, it's also not uncommon for there to be two or three big holes in the team lineup. This may also apply to some key middle-management people, who may be critical right from the start, who have not been identified or retained. Professional executive search firms can be a blessing to help find these people. This section gives some helpful hiring tips to use, with or without executive search firms.

Executive Search Steps

Jon Fitzgerald, President of Health Industry Consultants Inc. in Denver, Colorado, heads one of the country's top executive search firms in the health industry. His firm has a guide for the nine steps involved in a com-prehensive executive search. It provides a good outline for an Ultrapreneurial company to use as a guideline when it must go outside its inner circle to find and qualify potential top-management candidates. In an abbreviated form, the following describes the executive search process from a management recruiter's standpoint in nine steps.

Step One—Client Review.   If at all possible, the head of the executive search team does a presearch interview in the client's facilities. This includes gathering information regarding products/services, market share, and competitive information; also, assessing and getting a feel for such items as working environment, management style, organizational structure, reporting relationships, compensation packages, and the candidate's qualifications. Additionally, interviews are conducted with key people. These initial familiarity sessions help the senior search team to assess the existing and potential chemistry needs between the Ultrapreneur and the management candidates.

The Ultrapreneur should also consider these factors prior to initiating a search. They should prepare a "brief" that addresses the companies intended positioning in its industry, the "style" of the company, and the "feel" of the management. With these points in mind, the fit with a prospective employee can be better balanced.

Step Two—Planning.   Assignments are made in the search office or by the research staff. Strategy meetings are held, and a forecast of completion dates for each step in the search project is drawn up.

Ultrapreneurs do this thinking naturally, backed by the timing schedules dictated in their business plan. (See Chapter 5, "Assembling The Outside Ultrapreneurial Team.")

Step Three—Research.   Research is undertaken to gather data on competitive sources, previous internal search records, university affiliates, and other sources. For Ultrapreneurs, this step takes some extra effort. They have to force themselves to look outside their normal circle of business contacts and uncover and explore new sources.

Step Four—Candidate Research.   The research at this step is expanded to include many other sources that may reveal potential candidates. This can include management directories, "Who's Who" directories, industry directories, and others. A potential list, often over 100 names, is usually prepared.

Step Five—Recruitment and Evaluation.   Prospective candidate contact is now initiated, making preliminary interest inquiry and soliciting resumes.

Extensive telephone interviews are conducted and some initial personal interviews may be conducted.

Again, for Ultrapreneurs, this takes an extra effort. It requires the commitment of blocks of time to concentrate on soliciting candidates and the preliminary interview process. There's a hidden benefit in this step. It is that the Ultrapreneur makes new personal contacts and many times gets some scoops on the latest happenings in their industry.

Step Six—Documentation of Results.   An initial report is prepared that summarizes each candidate contact, and then a review is completed to reduce the list. Relocation sensitivity is determined and additional promotion of the employment opportunity is presented to the candidates.

Step Seven—Interview Cycle.   This step requires interaction between the candidates, the search executive, and the client. Personal interviews, as well as additional phone discussions, are conducted. Information is exchanged all around and client-preferred types of interviews or testing are conducted including psychological interviews when required. In-depth reference audits are also performed.

This step is the most difficult for Ultrapreneurs. Parts of it require an unemotional attitude, and ofttimes Ultrapreneurs have a hard time backing off their natural sales enthusiasm and just presenting the facts about the company and the position.

Step Eight—The Hire.   This is the final elimination. Salary negotiations are conducted, an offer is extended, and further consulting by the search team is provided, as needed to result in an offer being accepted. Many times, the Ultrapreneur is the lead in this step.

Step Nine—Termination of Search.   Backup candidates are notified and follow-up discussions are held ninety days after employment with both the client and the new employee.

The executive search by a headhunter can take from two to six months with costs varying from hourly fees to set annual retainers, all plus expenses. Most venture capital firms have established contacts with favorite executive search firms as well as a large collection of industry contacts.

Ultrapreneurs are encouraged to retain professionals for team member searches when they don't have all the players identified. The Ultrapreneur is naturally handicapped in this area because an Ultrapreneur's life is built around selling. Consequently, the tendency is to sell themselves and their project, as opposed to making rational, logical, and unemotional personnel hiring decisions. As the Ultrapreneurs or their team members get involved with interviewing prospects, there are some specific techniques to observe.

Ultrapreneurial Interviewing Techniques

You are about to make a decision you may have to live with for years. Don't do it lightly. Hiring decisions are supercritical for Ultrapreneurs, whether for top team members, middle management, or line employees. You can't afford the loss in time by making a bad hiring decision. Each employee is part of the value-added process; when you consider that every person takes three to six months to get up to speed before they can make continued meaningful contributions, you realize that attention to detail applies in hiring just as it does in all Ultrapreneuring steps.

It's important that you spend some time prior to an interview to square yourself away and get into the proper frame of mind:

Keep in mind the position to be filled.

Read the resume immediately prior to the interview.

Know in advance what questions you wish to ask.

Give the candidate your undivided attention.

Choose a quiet, private, comfortable location.

Your Attitude

Be impartial. First impressions can be prejudicial.

Use the candidate's name frequently.

Think of candidates as interesting; learn something.

Smile; be friendly.

Treat the candidate as you would wish to be treated.

Meeting the Candidate

Introduce yourself by using your name and title.

Mention that you're going to take confidential notes.

Ask questions in clear, concise, conversational tones.

Don't ask "yes" or "no" questions.

Ask open-ended questions: who, what, when, where, how.

Attempt to determine the candidate's goals.

Avoid snap judgements; draw the candidate out.

Don't sell; interview.

Give the Facts

Review the facts about the position, good and bad, including job requirements, hours, working conditions, job security, opportunities for advancement, benefits, pay.

Make no promises you can't keep; don't exaggerate; remember, this is a high-stress situation for the candidate; speak slowly.

Asking Questions

Keep them clear and concise.

Ask one at a time.

Start with easy ones.

Ask what they have done, what they want to do, what they can do, what they are willing to do.

Pay attention to their answers.

Pay attention to their questions.

What You Want to Learn

Are interviewees:

Industrious or lazy?

Alert, observant?

Open-minded or opinionated?

Self-starter, enthusiastic?

Willing to learn new things?

Thorough, have common sense?

Honest, take pride in job?

Interview Guide

Some further techniques are presented in the following guide. The "ask yourself–ask them" (prospective employees) question format is very effective. The Ultrapreneurial team members should spend some time prior to an interview with the candidate's resume in hand to formulate some specific questions. This is a critical step that will assist you in getting below the surface of the individual to determine if they really fit your company's needs.

Ask yourself	Ask them
1. Attitude	
Can compete without irritation?	Ever lose competition, feelings?
Can bounce back easily?	Uncertain about making a living?
Balanced interests?	How can American business improve?
What is important?	Are you successful to date?
Loyal?	Describe best boss?
Take pride?	Favorite duties/least favorite?
Team player?	Feel about coworkers?
2. Motivation	
Settled in work of choice?	What ambitions do others hold for
Work from choice/necessity?	them?
Make day-to-day plans?	What done to improve job skills?
Make long-range plans?	Mortgages, debts pressing?
Leisure for self-improvement?	Will job help get what's wanted?
3. Initiative	
Self-starter?	How got into line of work?
Completes tasks?	Work better alone or with others?
Follows through?	What likes/dislikes in job?
Works independently?	Do supervisors let them work alone?
4. Stability	
Excitable/even-tempered?	What disturbs you most?
Impatient/understanding?	Get along with people they dislike?
Show likes/dislikes freely?	What childish actions irritate?
Use words showing strong feelings?	Describe unpleasant work?
Poised/controlled?	Describe pleasant work?
Impulsive/erratic?	What most admire about spouse?
Perform under pressure?	What most admire about others?
Enthusiastic about job?	What irritates about others?
5. Planning	
Ability to plan/follow up?	What part work like best/least?
Ability to coordinate others?	What part most difficult?

Ability to fit into company?	How spend typical day?
Think of new improvements?	Where will be in 5 years?
See whole or details?	If manager, how run job?

6. Insight

Realistic in self-appraising?	Tell me strengths/weaknesses?
Desire for self-improvement?	Weaknesses important to do some-thing about?
Problems of others interest?	
Reaction from others?	Size up last employer?
Will take constructive action?	Most useful criticism received?

7. Social Skills

Leader or follower?	Do with spare time?
Learn new ways to deal with people?	Start any groups?
	Prefer new or old friends?
Make friends easily?	How go about making friends?

Rate a candidate in each category. Keep in mind: "What is this person telling me about themselves? What kind of person is he/she?" Other parts of the interview should cover education, previous experience, and other matters related to specific qualifications.

You're in a search posture when interviewing. Your charge is to gather facts, establish feelings, and confirm information which will lead to a critical decision. Ultrapreneurs are always seeking ways to add value to their enterprise. Putting together a team of eagles by effective interviewing is one of the most effective value-added tasks.

Your Board of Directors: Who, Why, and How

In the early seventies, there was a popular television commercial which depicted a dress-shirted and loosely tied executive walking the well-tended grounds of his executive headquarters in quiet contemplation. The voiceover stated that this executive's decisions were now much easier since he had access to a powerful new mainframe computer to help him. If the public thinks it's tough making decisions with the help of a mainframe computer, one should try the Ultrapreneurial style with just the help of a hand-held calculator.

Of course, today we have PCs that are just as powerful as the seventies mainframe, so that part is equal. But there is an even more important executive tool available to both yesterday's and today's Ultrapreneur. It's a well-qualified and supportive board of directors.

The Difference between Good Boards and Bad Boards

A good board of directors is composed mainly of outsiders. A startling statement? For many entrepreneurs, yes. Those who have a little experience understand that selecting outsiders for the board often goes against the grain for the CEO. It's true that there could be outside members who don't have a stake in the company. It's understandable if one dislikes involving outsiders in important policy decisions. Thus CEOs tend to enlist people who are involved in the day-to-day operations of the company, such as the key management team members. This is a *bad* board of directors.

Most entrepreneurs will deny this, but employees and managers tend to rubber-stamp the CEO's decisions and inhibit rather than encourage frank comment—not to mention that they may be too close to the situation. It's called self-preservation. It's hard to be objective when one's own job may be at stake. Therefore, it's in the Ultrapreneurial CEO's best interest to choose board members who will give independent, unbiased feedback, and who will not be afraid to disagree or say "no."

Another good reason to limit insiders on the board is to preserve the CEO's own infallibility. No one has all the answers, but when the CEOs can't come up with answers it can weaken their leadership position in the eyes of management. It's not a good idea for subordinates to know when CEOs are frustrated and unable to come up with the solution to a problem or to discover they are not the great leaders they seem. All of us, at one time or another, face a decision we just don't know how to make. Strong boards of directors can serve as psychological support teams to help Ultrapreneurs make the important decisions.

Determine the Outsider's Role

Outside board members serve a very important function in an Ultrapreneurial company. They are outsiders only in that they do not actively work in the company as employees or in management. A board member could be a major shareholder (most valuable), a business associate (valuable), a retired chief executive (valuable), an investment banker (good). Also acceptable, but lower on the ladder, are lawyers, accountants, and suppliers with a financial stake in the company. The common feeling is that they should be reviewed very carefully, since they may have personal interests at odds with the company's best interests. Other excellent candidates for the board are persons engaged in businesses different from the company's, who can appreciate and understand the risk of running an Ultrapreneurial company.

A good board member plays many roles—from assisting in formulating long-term policy and plans, to critiquing existing financial, production, or marketing practices. But the board's most powerful role is that of confidante, mentor, and peer to the Ultrapreneur. With a good board, rather than the president making decisions alone, the directors become involved in setting company policies and strategies and reviewing operating results.

Overall, the board of directors should demonstrate respect for the Ultrapreneur. They should like the Ultrapreneurs and want them to succeed. They should have unquestioned integrity, good judgment, relevant experience, problem-solving skills, and a capacity for action- and risk-taking. That's why a good board is hard to find.

An Informed Board
Is a Helpful Board

One of the prime responsibilities the Ultrapreneur has to the board of directors is to keep it informed. Directors must be given information on a timely and continuing basis. They must have meeting agendas and pertinent background information sufficiently in advance of scheduled meetings to allow them time to prepare for the meeting. They must be furnished with monthly financial statements, including comparisons to budgets. At all meetings, they must be given detailed reports on the company's progress.

Although most directors may know what is expected of them, it would be a good idea for the company, usually through its legal counsel, to furnish each board member with a copy of the *Corporate Director's Guidebook,* published by the American Bar Association. This book provides a general overview of the functions and responsibilities of the corporate director and will help the directors to perform their directorial functions responsibly, as well as to adhere to the company's bylaws and any governmental regulations. Consider it a *must read.*

What to Expect
from a Board of Directors

The Board of Directors Does Not Run the Company. The board of directors does not run the company; management runs the company. The board sees to it that the company is well-managed.

The Board of Directors Does Not Develop Company Strategy. The Ultrapreneur and management develop company strategy. Board input can be indispensable, however, in coming up with ways to test and evaluate management strategy.

The Board of Directors Enhances Company Performance. The attention of the board of directors can be turned to immediate needs, such as controlling costs, or it can apply its expertise to planning ahead to future needs, such as defining and penetrating a new market. The board must be flexible enough to deal with all matters in the best interests of the company.

Directors Should Be Experts in Their Fields. It's up to the Ultrapreneur to assess the management team's strengths and weaknesses and the company's direction, and then select the best candidates for board positions. The intent is to fill or supplement voids in the management structure and thereby help improve the company's performance. The Ultrapreneur will probably be pleasantly surprised to find the high caliber of outside people who are not only flattered, but would gladly serve on an Ultrapreneurial board of directors. The ideal board is composed of top-notch people who are experts in the industry, such as a scientist with an interest in business dealings who would benefit from the experience.

Directors Must Attend Meetings. At the very minimum, board meetings should be held quarterly. The frequency of meetings depends on the needs of the company. According to national surveys conducted annually since 1971 by Korn/Ferry International, one of the world's largest executive search firms, the boards meet an average of eight times a year. Ultrapreneurial companies may find it necessary to schedule meetings 10 to 12 times annually. The Korn/Ferry survey also determined that the average outside director devoted more than 150 hours annually to company business.

By contrast, a survey by *Venture* magazine found that 38 percent of private companies held board meetings only when needed, 29 percent held monthly meetings, 25 percent held quarterly meetings, and only 8 percent met semiannually.

Directors Get Paid. As far as compensation goes for directors, no two companies do it the same. Compensation can take many forms, including annual retainer fees and hourly or per-meeting fees, plus expenses. In a recent Korn/Ferry survey of 31,000 companies, meeting fees for outside directors ranged from $100 to $1000, with an average of $534. In addition, many firms have established annual retainers of $5000 to $10,000. For Ultrapreneurial companies there may be no fees at all, although $100 per meeting seems to be a common practice.

Another form of compensation, especially for cash-short companies, is the issuance of stock in lieu of money. This practice can prove to be a disadvantage over time, as it makes outside directors insiders. If a director is also a shareholder and the company is faced with a decision that may adversely affect the value of the shares, that board member may not be totally objective.

Directors Can Get Sued. By way of explanation, in 1977 the Foreign Corrupt Practices Act (FCPA) was passed by Congress as a part of our securities regulations. This act stated that officers and board members should create an environment whereby middle and lower levels of management, as well as employees, understand the nature of corporate accountability. It urged board members to be cognizant of their responsibility to monitor the totality of corporate performance. This well-intended legislation was probably the forerunner of many lawsuits, especially against public companies.

Most of these lawsuits are nuisance suits, but they are very expensive to fight. There were hundreds of such suits filed up to the mid-1980s against both private and public companies. This resulted in skyrocketing premiums by liability insurance companies. Many insurance companies just plain stopped writing officer and director policies, and many fine outside director prospects turned down offers to serve on boards of directors.

In response to a major outpouring of protest from the business community, many states passed legislation that limited officer and director liability. The SEC compliance became stricter; tighter financial accounting rules to promote more control were instituted. The increased adverse publicity resulted in companies policing themselves more carefully, and court awards were reduced. These cases were no longer plums for the lawyers seeking to make big, quick bucks, because plaintiffs had to prove that the company, its management, and more particularly, individual directors, were purposely negligent in performing duties, or committed willful acts of omission, especially fraud. The result has been that these types of suits have really subsided and, in fact, liability insurance is now again becoming affordable.

Makeup of the Board

There is no standard operating procedure regarding the number of members that must constitute a board of directors or the mix of outside directors versus management members. It depends on the scope of the company, egos, and personal preferences of the Ultrapreneur.

Five directors on the board is a good number for several reasons. It's an odd number, which avoids tie votes, the rigged taking of sides, and bitter personality battles. Three members may not allow for sufficient diversity of opinion or fill weak areas in management. Two outside directors seems to satisfy the vague FCPA rules and the court's feelings about the need for outside objective input. Using two inside managing directors and rounding a board out with one outside major shareholder may be ideal. For an Ultrapreneurial company, five directors is ordinarily sufficient and, as the company grows, it can easily expand to seven. Thus a company can add expertise from either inside or outside to fit expanding needs without the board becoming cumbersome and overly expensive.

Committees of the Board

Because of the proliferation of liability suits against companies, management, and boards during the last decade, as mentioned earlier, companies
were compelled to become more accountable. Committees were established to validate accountability. Many Ultrapreneurial companies today
maintain committees composed of board members, management, and outside experts. These include:

Audit Committees—Comprised entirely of outside directors, the audit
committee reviews the company's internal accounting procedures and
controls. They also choose and interrelate with the outside audit
accountants.

Nominating Committees—This committee reviews the performance of
the directors and recommends nominees for directorships.

Conflict of Interest Committees—Composed at least of two-thirds outside
members, their function is to oversee significant transactions between
the company, its subsidiaries, and members of management.

Compensation Committees—Reviews management compensation including salaries, bonuses, perks, and stock incentives.

Executive Committees—A mini-board that may act on behalf of the full
board to see that policy is implemented.

The Board of Advisors

The board of advisors is not set up as a committee of the board, although in
some corporate structures it is considered to be one. One or two board
members may head the advisory committee and act as a buffer between the
advisors on the outside and the board itself.

As a rule, the formal setup of the board of advisors is accomplished
through an amendment of the bylaws. The advisors are appointed by the
board of directors, but they are distinct from the board. In most companies,
advisors may not be officers, directors, or employees of the company. They
are experts in various fields whose function is to consult with directors and
company management on technical, management, and economic factors
that affect the company. Well-chosen advisors add prestige and credibility
to an Ultrapreneurial company, especially when it comes to fundraising.

It should be noted, too, that members of the board of advisors serve at
the pleasure of the board of directors and receive compensation as determined by the board, often only in the form of consulting fees. They are also
provided with indemnification by the company.

There are no requirements for formal group meetings by the board of
advisors and, in fact, it's not unusual that they never meet as a group. Indi-

vidual members of the board of advisors are consulted as necessary in their areas of expertise.

After considering the insiders, the Ultrapreneur as a person, the management team, and the board of directors, we focus our attention on some other key team members. Team building is not restricted to full-time employees of the company. Ultrapreneurial companies cannot afford to have all the needed management disciplines in-house. Consequently, the next chapter addresses some other important *outside* team members.

5
Assembling the Outside Ultrapreneurial Team

Unlike many entrepreneurial efforts, Ultrapreneurs recognize that their inside team members don't necessarily complete the picture. They know they need and depend on some outside players also. There's even a greater difference. Ultrapreneurs know that these outside members are not just ordinary professionals, but people that must be integrated into and support the Ultrapreneurial concept. These outside team members are always highly qualified, very knowledgeable in their areas of specialization, and motivated to assure that the Ultrapreneurial effort succeeds.

Consultants and Advisors

The old adage that too many cooks spoil the broth doesn't apply when it comes to hiring consultants and advisors for Ultrapreneurial companies. No matter how professional a management team may be, and no matter how well staffed the company, there are usually areas of the business where it can use outside expertise. That's why consultants were born.

A *consultant* is a person with specialized expertise. Consultants are often retained on a one-time basis for a specific problem. *Advisors,* also discussed in this section, may also serve as consultants, but are expected to have a broader knowledge of the business. Advisors are usually retained to advise the company's management team on a longer term. They can be especially useful when working through the Ultrapreneurial approach.

What Consultants Are Really For

Bringing in a consultant is not the same as hiring another person on the staff of the company. Consultants should be retained only for the period of time required to assist the management team in identifying, isolating, and solving problems or deficiencies. The consultant's function is to bring a particular problem into focus and zero in on the solution.

If there is a marketing problem, the marketing consultant may advise the company when to put the product on the market, whom the product should be directed to, and where the product is likely to receive a good reception. Or a consultant can provide expertise on product packaging improvement or production techniques. There are countless situations where management could be served by help from an outside professional.

A consultant or consulting firm is *not* someone management turns to in desperation; rather, they should be used as a source for helpful guidance. Many consultants, where an Ultrapreneurial company is concerned, like to get involved during the conception phases of the company. If they really know their craft, they can be very helpful in starting a company off on the fast track.

Consultants Can Come from Anywhere.   Anyone can call themselves a consultant. Some people who call themselves consultants are simply self-promoters. Some work on a temporary basis. They are often people with good management skills who are between jobs, or they can be former CEOs who offer expertise in their particular fields.

There are tens of thousands of private consultants in the United States today. Most work on their own, but there are also consulting firms that employ as many as several hundred people. These range from national to international in scope. Their clients are usually major companies. They prefer long-term projects and their fees are commensurately high. Many major companies operate on this premise: the higher the fee, the better the consultation. The question is whether the consultant's expertise and experience fits your company's needs. Look for proven professionals in their field who have successfully helped others with similar problems to those facing your company.

Hire When Ready!   When enlisting the aid of a consultant or consulting firm, the company should first be convinced of the need. Management consultants are generally hired for the wrong reason; once hired, they are generally poorly employed and loosely supervised.

Therefore, it is important that the company do its homework before hiring a consultant. Most consultants have an area of expertise and specialty. Some may claim broad expertise, but their experience may actually lie in a special industrial or technical area. The company should find out this information in advance. The fact that a consultant has an excellent background in one field does not make him or her an expert in another field. The company should also determine in advance the precise problem needing a solution, thus eliminating some consultants from the running.

Consultants Are Not Always Necessary. Properly utilized, a consultant can appreciably help a company's operations, but too often management may already have the answer to a problem and only need to convince key people. The consultant can serve that purpose, but at a price. Consultants also are often asked to explore areas the company has no intention of pursuing. Yet another misuse of company money is to hire consultants to research information that is readily available.

A sharp management group can solve many consulting chores without paying unnecessary consulting fees. For instance, suppliers can usually advise a company whether it is more advantageous to buy or lease certain assets, or how to go about computerizing a business with the right kind of hardware or software. Insurance company agents are trained to determine the most efficient insurance and employee benefit plans. Advertising agencies and marketing firms interested in working with the company will usually provide sound, useful information for free. All it takes is a little talking to the people a company does business with or plans to do business with. Remember, a consultant is not the only one who can supply answers.

Consultant is not a magic word. Consultants should not be left to their own devices. Management has an obligation to stay on top of consultants' activities as well as to make certain they get the necessary support from the company's staff. Consultants should be encouraged to bring solutions within a reasonable period of time. It's your time and money.

How Much Should You Pay? Consulting fees can take many forms. They are often open to negotiation, but some consultants are firm in their charges. Much depends on the complexities involved. Fees can be based on hourly time or a weekly amount. Some consultants ask for a fixed fee or retainer. Some companies prefer to have consultants work in-house, but some consultants will only work offsite.

The ideal way for the company to approach the consultant situation would be to contact several possible consultants. Brief them on the problem. Secure proof of their expertise and information on several similar projects they have worked on. Besides asking for their credentials and resume, request specific proposals on how your project could be handled.

Before the final decision is reached, management should feel confident working with the consultant and satisfied that the four items listed in Figure 5-1 will be received.

The effort and time involved in securing the services of the right consultant for a particular need will pay off handsomely. The chemistry must be there, for with it comes the confidence and security the job will be done right.

Specific Things You Should Expect from a Consultant

1. A realistic and reasonable charge for services
2. A determined attempt to produce results
3. A cooperative attitude toward the people involved
4. Maintenance of a continuing relationship

Figure 5-1.

There are many sources for locating consultants. They can be found through the Small Business Administration, colleges and universities, and professional placement services. Bankers, attorneys, and accountants are very good resources. Some of the best sources may be recommendations from other companies; if you put the word out in your daily networking, you should get solid results.

Some Advice on Advisors

As mentioned earlier, advisors differ from consultants in that they are usually connected with your project for longer time periods. The best advisors—the most dependable ones—are those persons or consulting firms that have been through the Ultrapreneurial battle from beginning to end more than once. You may have to search, because there are not many out there. What's more, even though the advisors may have been through the process, they'll find it different every time. Markets change, financing methods change, and the exit strategies change.

Advisors are best used if they are integrated into the Ultrapreneurial process as early as possible. It really helps if they can have a handle on the progress as it ramps up and carries on. They should be able to temper the eagerness of the Ultrapreneur and the management team, ignore minor pitfalls, offer encouragement, act as sounding boards, and help get on with the show. Advisors are best used in strategic planning, in helping to form policy, and in identifying other professional outside team members.

Accountants

Although it's not a strict requirement, and there is no law that states so, it is very advisable that an Ultrapreneurial company has an audit-capable certified public accounting (CPA) firm involved with it from its opening stages. For the small company, hiring an auditing accountant to verify the comptroller's figures may seem like paying to have the same job done twice.

Generally, startup and early stage companies do not have a need for a detailed or complex accounting system. In all probability, a part-time bookkeeper or comptroller could easily handle the accounting. The situation is different for an Ultrapreneurial company.

Since the premise is to employ all resources to the max, to gain the greatest financial return, and to do this in maximized time, a qualified CPA is an important part of the outside team.

It easiest to look at the accounting functions of an early stage Ultrapreneurial company as being three distinct parts: a bookkeeper/comptroller, a Chief Financial Officer (CFO), and an audit accountant.

The comptroller is the onsite, most likely full-time, person who is a full-charge bookkeeper. They set up the books and keep them going, hopefully in a very accurate way.

The Chief Financial Officer (CFO) may be full-time, but most likely a part-time consultant or advisor. As the company grows, it may be the intention to bring this person in on a full-time basis. Regardless, this individual will most likely have an accounting degree and often is also a registered CPA.

The audit accountant is optional, but for very reasonable cost should at minimum be used as a consultant at the startup stage. They will assist or be sure that the initial accounting systems are properly set up to assure that the company's books will be in order for an eventual audit.

Compilations, Reviews, Audits

The following are brief descriptions of the three types of reports that CPA firms issue. They can be confusing, but an Ultrapreneur needs to have a good understanding of the differences.

Compilations. A *compilation* is the simplest of the CPA reports, generally performed for internal use only. The purpose is to give the accountant a general understanding of the nature of the company's business, the accounting records, and company policies. The CPA reads the company's prepared financial statements and makes sure that they are in appropriate form, free from clerical errors. The figures are supplied by management, and the CPA does not express any opinion about them.

Reviews. A *review* is a report that goes beyond the compilation. It provides some assurance about the reliability of the financial statements. The CPA reviews the accounting principles and practices of the company and its industry, and analyzes and compares expected trends, past results, industry data, and internal projections. The review may also contain some of the specific procedures that would ordinarily be performed in an audit. The CPA firm will state that they have reviewed the financial statements *but* will not express an opinion about their validity.

Audits.   An *audit* is a confirmation of the creditability and reliability of the financial statements of a company. An audited financial statement is prepared by an outside audit accountant (who is a CPA) to guard against company manipulations in the report. The accounting firm reviews and evaluates the effectiveness of all accounting procedures and internal financial controls. The accountant must attest (issue an opinion) to the legitimacy of the company's financial statements and to the company's financial position for the period covered. This is the toughest type of accounting report.

Be Prepared

Companies in the early stages of doing business should start making preparations for their planned exit. They should start this process right from the beginning of corporate formation. If a qualified Chief Financial Officer (CFO) is not part of the startup team, a qualified advisor should be in place.

   At minimum, a bookkeeper or comptroller should be on the job, but need not be a full-fledged accountant. The position includes responsibility for day-to-day routine bookkeeping functions and coordination with the outside accounting persons. As the company grows, there will probably be an increasing need to bring in a full-fledged accountant.

Ultrapreneurial Consideration with Regard to Audit Accountants

Audit accounting is a subject warranting a closer look. Audit accountants must be completely independent of the Ultrapreneurial company. They must not have any financial or ownership interests in the company, and they cannot take stock for fees. They work in teams, and their job is to look for trouble in the books, so they tend to be suspicious. They seem to trust no one, especially in the company. They can be expected to cross-check every item because that's what they're paid to do.

Qualifying the Audit Accountant.   There are many ways to qualify an auditing firm. One of the best is to get recommendations from a trusted business friend that is familiar with audit accounting. Seek information from your advisors and attorneys. A word of caution to Ultrapreneurial companies contemplating going public as a harvest strategy. Any CPA firm can work the numbers game, but not all CPA firms can play the public company Security and Exchange Commission (SEC) numbers game to the benefit of the client. If your harvest strategy includes going public, or being acquired by a public company (both of which require audited financial statements), you should carefully consider using an SEC-qualified CPA firm

---

Specific Questions to Ask Prospective Accountants

What are the firm's areas of expertise?

Do you have useful investment contacts?

Who will work with your company day-to-day?

What are the billing methods? Hourly? By job?

What is the billing cycle?

When can someone begin?

How long will it take?

Will they give you an estimated total cost in a written proposal?

Figure 5-2.

from the beginning. Although heavy SEC experience is not critical for the accounting firm, since set SEC guidelines are followed by all firms, it is nonetheless essential that the firm have some experience in SEC accounting. Obviously, the more the better, and the more recent, even better yet.

Another way to qualify an auditing firm is by interview. In fact, this should be done even with highly recommended firms. Select promising candidates and request proposals for final evaluation. Ask such questions as those listed in Figure 5-2.

Familiarity Is a Must.   Every effort should be made to hire audit accountants familiar with the company's type of business and industry. Familiarity helps because audit requirements differ vastly from industry to industry. For example, an oil pipe supply company's inventory occupies many acres of outdoor storage whereas the inventory of a fast food franchise is turned over by being eaten every day, and a manufacturer of high-tech small parts may fit three months' inventory in a few fireproof file drawers. Bookkeeping, payable, and receivable methods and standards vary from industry to industry. This results in special rules being applied to different types of companies and to their various stages of development. The audit accountant must have the skill and knowledge to work through these differences. That is why familiarity is a must.

GAAP Must Be Observed.   *GAAP* is an industry term. It stands for *Generally Accepted Accounting Principles*. GAAP dictates the principles for presenting audit information. As an example, accounting methods of private companies are generally aimed toward decreasing taxable income and depreciation. Inventory booking and write-downs are adjusted accordingly. Private companies frequently switch back and forth from cash to accrual accounting methods to assist tax adjustment. These practices are not allowed for companies which function under GAAP. All accounting for public companies must be done on an accrual basis.

Although the process of auditing an existing company that has not been previously audited can be costly and time-consuming, it can be done, providing the company has maintained fairly complete financial records. However, getting into the area of inventory may be a different matter.

Inventory verification within GAAP can be very complicated. For most auditing, there are pieces of paper that provide an "audit trail"—something that shows what happened when, for what number, and for what amounts between what parties. The audit accountant can verify these facts. Sometimes it involves writing to a supplier or customer to request verification that on such-and-such a date, they sold or were owed X number of items at X costs or X number of dollars. It almost always includes that the company's bank verify the amount of money in various accounts or in loans on certain dates. But until we perfect a time machine, it is very difficult, if not impossible, for the audit accountant to verify that on such-and-such a date, there were X number of some part sitting on some backroom shelf that was included in an inventory count. How do they know for sure that there were 28, not 29, pieces? This is why, at minimum, having an audit accountant monitor an inventory check becomes so important. That way they can certify that they did indeed physically observe all inventory. The audit trail is complete.

Time Costs Money.   An Ultrapreneur with the goal of exiting their company should seriously consider enlisting the services of an audit accountant to monitor and audit inventory procedures from the very start of the company. The costs will be considerably less than a fully audited financial statement. It won't eliminate the necessity of a full audit if a buyer insists, or if the company intends to exit via going public, but it will save time and dollars, not to mention making the company much more creditable for acquisition, sale, or merger.

Any audit for a small existing company can take from a few weeks to possibly six months. It depends on the problems the auditing process may uncover. Previously unaudited companies—if they haven't conducted their accounting according to auditing standards—are typically beset with such deficiencies as poor accounts payable systems, uncollected accounts receivable that haven't been written off or down, unreconciled bank accounts, notes payable with double assets pledged as underlying collateral, and incorrectly recorded depreciation expenses.

Accounting ethics require strict adherence to due diligence procedures. For instance, if the company purchased a major piece of equipment, the accountants will have to see copies of purchase orders, invoices, receipts, and canceled checks.

Areas that can present very complicated problems for previously unaudited existing companies include personal financial dealings by officers and directors that were placed through the corporation. Even advances and loans made to officers by the company, which aren't by nature wrong, may require special schedules to be filled out.

All of these issues take time to resolve, and the costs vary according to the time expended. An acquiring company may require an audit before it hands over the check. Wouldn't it be nice to say, "No problem, we're audited," instead of waiting for weeks or months to seal the deal while getting an audit performed? It makes sense, both time-wise and dollar-wise, to consider setting up the Ultrapreneurial company's books for audit right from the start.

Attorneys

The Difference between Large and Small

Like shoes, legal firms come in different sizes and styles. Many of them specialize in various types of legal services. It's up to company management to choose the firm that best fits the company's requirements as to size, compatibility, competency, and potential worthwhile business contacts, including investment contacts.

A large legal firm is not the answer for all companies. True, a large firm may have several hundred lawyers with many areas of expertise. On the surface, that may seem advantageous. Many large companies prefer such firms, as they can call upon the services of different specialists in one office. That arrangement may serve the purpose of a diversified, multinational company with many divisions and different companies under its corporate umbrella. An Ultrapreneurial company, lacking that corporate makeup, wouldn't need a firm with all those attorneys, and faces the possibility of getting lost in the shuffle.

Large legal firms with many partners and associates traditionally also have many young, inexperienced junior associate attorneys. These are usually assigned to work with small companies on a day-to-day basis. Since the associates must often clear their advice with a partner, dealings can become frustrating for the Ultrapreneurial management as well as time-consuming and costly. These new, bright young lawyers, although capable and intelligent, lack experience, and they can make a lot of mistakes. It's a learning process for them, but it's usually the Ultrapreneurial client who pays for their mistakes.

Depending on the benefits and prestige derived from engaging large law firms as opposed to small ones, it may be preferable for the Ultrapreneurial company to work with a smaller legal firm. For one thing, the company will get closer attention. Junior associates or paralegals become involved usually only to help out on routine matters. Many small firms can be fully competent to handle all the corporate information, including a good surface knowledge of SEC rules and regulations for the Ultrapreneurial companies contemplating going public as an exit.

Getting Along

Too often the attorney's image is that of a necessary evil. Attorneys have been typecast as arrogant, nonresponsive, and overpriced. In fact, some of them are very nice, but rarely do they come cheap. However, in the eyes of reasonable entrepreneurs, the price is right if it helps get their Ultrapreneurial company results.

There must be no secrets kept from counsel. The more an attorney understands the company's industry, its management team, and its aspirations, the more helpful they can be, and the less frustrating for all. Forthrightness will also save time, which translates directly into dollars when dealing with legal counsel.

Questions to Ask

When interviewing for counsel, it's advisable for management to prepare a list of questions for a potential law firm or attorney to answer to assist the CEO in the selection process. The questions shown in Figure 5-3 can prove helpful in making the decision.

When the interviewing and cross-checking of references is complete, the most important selection criterion comes into play. It's called "comfortability." Are you comfortable with the personal rapport between you and counsel? Do you sense a good level of mutual respect? Will you feel comfortable working with this person on tough problems under possibly stressful conditions? If your answers are affirmative, trust your gut and go for it.

What Lawyers Are Selling, and How They Charge

Attorneys typically bill by time; they count not just hours, but minutes, including phone minutes. Their rationalization is that they do not sell products or services, but knowledge and past experience which can be invaluable to the client.

> #### Specific Questions to Ask Prospective Attorneys
>
> Do you have particular areas of specialty, and are they compatible with our company's industry?
>
> Who will be our day-to-day contact?
>
> What is your billing procedure?
>
> Can you give us your best estimated total costs, including expenses and fees, for a particular project?
>
> Do you have any useful investment contacts? Underwriters, brokers, private investors?

Figure 5-3.

Although hourly rates vary considerably from less than a hundred dollars to several hundred, a good round figure for the primary senior contact member of a law firm would be about $150 per hour. Junior associates could bill in the area of $75 to $100, and administrative functions (typing and copying) could range from $35 to $50 per hour. These are give-and-take figures, but every minute counts.

Ethical law firms usually provide an estimate of the total costs on a project basis. It's safe to assume that the final amount will seldom be less than the estimate. Although some firms are willing to put a cap on a project cost, they usually leave an out for themselves for unanticipated exigencies. The entrepreneur can make book there will be something.

It's also unrealistic to assume that legal counsel will work on a contingency basis for normal Ultrapreneurial legal needs. It's best to plan on a deposit or advance of at least the first month's work or first stage of work. Rarely will any substantial work be performed by a law firm prior to an initial payment, usually made at the time of the signing of an engagement letter.

Other Forms of Payment

Generally speaking, the legal profession is not adverse to taking a limited flyer with the company. Many attorneys like Ultrapreneurial companies, not only because they generate handsome fees and are fun to work with, but because they like taking a portion of their fees in stock. The structure of the legal business in itself does not generate capital appreciation or equity buildup. Consequently, accepting stock as part payment allows lawyers to become more intimately involved with the company and gives them an opportunity to invest without actually putting out any hard cash.

Paying stock in lieu of money can create problems. For one thing, it can dilute ownership among shareholders in the company. It can cause disagreement among the partners of the law firm, too. Especially in larger firms, it often happens that partners who are not directly involved with the project may not feel as positive about the company's potential. They would prefer cash to restricted stock that has no guarantees.

The strongest argument against stock as payment is the potential conflict of interest. Some company managers may question whether the advice they receive is in their interest or their advisor's interest. Attorneys in the law firm may question a conflict of interest regarding outside parties involvement. The ability to remain objective when negotiating non-arm's-length transactions may also be questioned. These may seem extreme concerns, but should not be ignored in a decision whether to offer stock for the services of legal counsel.

Double-Check the Cost

As mentioned earlier, the cost of doing business with a law firm is high under the best of circumstances. Therefore, it's just good common sense to make a practice of regularly reviewing counsel's billings. To err is forgivable. To not check the error is expensive. Time and again, good relationships between management and legal counsel have dissolved because it seemed counsel was taking advantage regarding billings. This assumption, more often than not, turns out to be unfounded. That is why professional legal counsel is always ready to discuss, substantiate, and if necessary, adjust billings. It's up to the company to keep the lines of communication open and frank. Establishing a good working relationship and then maintaining it is of benefit to both company and counsel.

The Multiple Counsel Approach

It's common practice to have more than one type of legal counsel working for a company. It frequently happens with Ultrapreneurial companies that they may have used a general practitioner type of attorney for years to advise them on a variety of needs. Then when they get involved with an Ultrapreneurial company, this old legal counsel friend may not be able to fill the bill. Don't fear, the comfortable long-time relationship doesn't have to be abandoned. Attorneys are used to working together, and the good ones recognize their legal expertise limitations. So if you need more sophisticated corporate advice—say, acquisition or merger, to explore a contemplated public offering, or for patents, trademarks, real estate, or other specialties—don't hesitate to obtain it, and use your long-time trusted counsel to coordinate. The two lawyers can complement each other and probably at a cost savings to you and the company.

Conclusion

The entrepreneurial scene in the nineties has changed. You still need eagles, but today's multifaceted Ultrapreneurial international business world requires sharing the nest and understanding team responsibilities. This applies for both inside and outside team members.

Empowerment—Is Your Company Headed for Divorce?

The relationship between employers and employees, between clients and outside contractors, can be like a marriage. It's hard to find a really good one, and when they go bad, both sides get hurt and blame each other.

The use of empowerment is a way to prevent company divorce. Empowerment is to give power, to authorize, to enable. For Ultrapreneurs, it is not a set of techniques—it is a path of self-management. It is giving employees more and more freedom. It's granting them personal responsibility for their own selves, to encourage them to survive and prosper. The Ultrapreneur encourages them to express value in their work, their achievements, and their contributions to life. In turn, they see themselves as forces for positive change and improvement by having control over their business destiny, discovering what's possible, and creating a place to believe in.

Ultrapreneurial empowerment is achieved by open lines of communication, delegation in decision making, and reward sharing. It is the single most important job benefit for employees. People will stay because of the right empowering atmosphere. By treating both your employees and outside team members as customers, you will save hundreds of thousands of dollars. You can do this just by listening, really listening, to their feedback. As part of this communication empowering process, educate them and let them know how they fit and contribute to the big picture.

The primary point is that by empowering Ultrapreneurial team members, they agree to the company's basic approach. They have some common ground on which to build. Most importantly, they become supportive of the fact that if they are successful, they may be selling themselves out of a job. Just the kind of company divorce that Ultrapreneurs seek.

After the team is selected, the initial project is to firmly establish the goals. With goals defined, the challenge is to assemble a business plan that will serve as a guide to achieving the goals. Compiling the business plan is the subject of the next chapter.

6
Planning the Ultrapreneurial Venture

Business plans boil down to operating the company on paper. The aim is to validate an idea and challenge every aspect of the business. A business plan is a written presentation that carefully explains the business, its management team, its product or services, and its goals, together with strategies for reaching the goals. The entrepreneur or team members who write the plan will find it a painstaking process. But keep in mind, this is *the* selling tool, and it requires careful consideration of all the multiple facets of a start-up or business expansion. It cannot be written as an afterthought, and it should not be taken lightly. Check with any professional investor anywhere in the country, and you'll hear horror stories about ill-conceived, poorly written, or sloppily put together business plans. As great as the company's potential may be, it is essentially doomed to rejection, before it can even get a foot in the door, if it has a poorly conceived business plan.

This is even more important for Ultrapreneurial businesses. The planning margin for error is less, the timing is up-paced, and the benchmarks have to be results-oriented. Several more points differentiate the Ultrapreneurial plan from what you would normally expect to see. These include a more clearly defined exit strategy which requires a closer look at company structure and the Ultrapreneurial business plan valuation approach. Prior to looking at some of the Ultrapreneurial details, let's review some basics.

Your Primary Business Plan Purposes

There are two primary purposes to a business plan. The first has an outside objective—to obtain funding. There's no business without the bucks. The second serves an inside premise—to provide a plan for early corporate development: to guide an organization toward meeting its objectives, to keep the Ultrapreneurial business itself and all its decision makers headed in a predetermined direction, to explain in an engaging way with interesting information on how the company will be run for the next three to five years. The Ultrapreneur must put all the "hows" and "needs" together in one neat package. The human and physical resources must effectively interrelate with the marketing, operational, and financial strategies of the company. Unless an Ultrapreneur has magical powers of persuasion, this is not the time to try to fake it.

The business plan is considered a vital sales tool for approaching and capturing financial sources, be they investors or lenders. They will want to know that the plan has been carefully thought out by the Ultrapreneurial team. They want to be convinced that the team has the skills and expertise needed to actively manage the company and that it is prepared to seize opportunities and solve the problems that arise. That's why the business plan must be well prepared, professional in tone, and persuasive in conveying the company's potential.

It cannot be stressed too strongly that *a good business plan is the cornerstone of successful financing*. If you want investors' money, you've got to give them good reasons to buy in. The business plan is where you lay out the reasons. It doesn't have to be unduly lengthy or complicated, but it must be informative and relevant. It needs to maintain logic and order, and show the company as effectively positioned as a good investment.

More important, the business plan should be specifically directed to the funding source and satisfy its particular concerns. For example, you would orient and write the plan differently for presentation to a banker than you would for a venture capitalist, an underwriter, or a private investor. The venture capitalist would want to know what risks are involved, whereas the banker wants more information about how good the security is. These concerns must be individually addressed. There are no hard and fast rules for preparing a business plan—no established, formal format. The key word is *ingenuity*. Strive for inventiveness, strive to be interesting and captivating.

Incorporate the Nine Guiding Principles into Your Plan

Here are some general guidelines covering the basic elements of a business plan. These should be helpful in writing any business plan, no matter whom it is directed to.

Make It Easy to Read

There is so much competition for investment dollars today—that is, if you want to get the jump on the next person, your plan will have to be well formatted and easily understood. Your introductory statement summarizing your operation is one of the most important sections; it must capture the readers' attention and motivate them to read the balance of your plan. Caution: If they need a dictionary at their side in order to read, they'll stop. Construct a glossary if you have to use a lot of technical words.

Your Approach Should Be Market-driven

Not product-driven. If you want those magic doors to money to open, you must understand that investors are primarily interested in how the product or service will react and be received in the market. They want to see your research demonstrating and substantiating how the customer will benefit and be motivated to purchase, before they buy into your plan.

Qualify the Competition

Start by qualifying your product according to cost or time savings and revenue generation. Also show your projections for sales growth, how your product or service is superior to others, and how you intend to exploit the competitive advantage.

Present Your Distribution Plan

Be specific as to how the company will sell and distribute its product or service. Clearly describe the methods and what it will cost to get the product or service into the ultimate customer's hands.

Exploit Your Company's Uniqueness

Explain what will give your company a competitive edge in the marketplace—special attributes like a patent, trade secrets, or copyrights.

Emphasize Management Strength

Show proof that the company is comprised of highly qualified people who can cover all the bases. Indicate the incentives that will keep them together, and how they, the directors, and the advisors possess the necessary credibility.

Present Attractive Projections

Paint a realistic picture—substantiated by assumptions—of where your company is going with funding. Be detailed and keep it credible. Good validated projections and forecasts are impressive.

Zero In on Possible
Funding Sources

As mentioned earlier, it's different strokes for different folks. Design versions of the plan to fit the idiosyncrasies of each source you plan to approach. A banker's interest lies in stability, security, cashflow coverage, and sound returns, whereas a venture capitalist is more interested in high leverage resulting in outrageous returns. Both want to know how the proceeds are going to be spent.

Close with a Bang

Drive home the point that you're offering a good deal. Be definite about how the investor will get their money back and when. Specify the return rates; state how the risk investor will receive a 30 percent or 50 percent compound annual return, or whatever you're offering. For lenders, show that their funds are adequately secured and that your cashflow more than covers their interest and principal payments.

The Next Step:
Obtain Critical Reviews

You're not finished yet. One of the big differences between ordinary plans and Ultrapreneurial plans is that they have been critiqued to work. After you have drafted your business plan, solicit feedback on it. Ask a cross-section of people whose judgment you respect, to review it. Don't fall in love with your wordsmithing. Make any revisions that are necessary, and then prepare a good oral presentation. In fact, you should have both a 2-minute and a 5-minute oral attention grabber. Follow up with a detailed 15- to 30-minute presentation, all of which are modeled on your written business plan.

A word of caution: When preparing your financial projections, avoid the shortcut of relying on packaged computerized information—those preset formats in which you plug in figures and percentages. Individualize your financial projections. Think them out carefully. No two businesses are alike. Show when you bring on additional personnel, and remember that each new hire adds other costs over their pay—items like benefits, desks, and supplies. Maybe another computer or additional travel expenses. These items need to be tracked for each expense period. Don't just show advertising costs as a percent of sales. Most advertising expenditures are made some months before sales result. A lot of them have to be prepaid before they are run. It's just not justifiable to show "plugged" computer figures for most expense items. Individualize them. And keep in mind that a new startup company will not fit the standard industry norms, especially one that is on an Ultragrowth track.

Your projections should include the financial obligations of bringing your product or service to the marketplace: enlisting new management people as well as workers; taking on more physical space or manufacturing capacity; purchasing support materials and services; and buildups in inventory and accounts receivable.

Outline for a Business Plan

There are many specifics that should be included in a successful business plan. The following outline, although general in nature, contains many suggestions which may seem obvious, but one could easily forget to include the basics. Again, this outline should be used as a preliminary planning guide. It's up to the reader to add lots of detail, meticulously gathered and presented in succinct Ultrapreneurial form.

Cover Sheet

Indicate full formal name of company
ABC Company/ABC Corporation/ABC Inc.
(If you have a logo, use it.)

Indicate ownership status
A sole proprietorship/A New York corporation

List full street address
555 West Fifth, Suite 55, Anytown, State, ZIP USA

List mail address if different
Mail address = P.O. Box 55, Anytown, State, ZIP USA

List phone and FAX/telecopier number

List principal contact name and title
Mr. E. E. Ultrapreneur, President
Home phone number optional

Date the plan
Month and year

Table of Contents

Categorize the contents. Use section names and page numbers. You have a choice of only main category headings (History, Management, Product, etc.) or detailed categories (History—date founded, founding members, place founded, etc.). Make note of any charts, tables, or graphs.

Executive Summary

A very important part, this summary briefly sets forth the contents, taking key sentences from each section of the plan to overview the project for the reader. Devote two or three pages; more is too many. Consider using your mission statement or a brief visionary type of paragraph. It should be concise and to the point. This section is the first thing read by an investor and they may not read further if you haven't captured their interest.

History

The first several paragraphs should briefly describe the product/service, to whom it is sold, the current status of your industry, and where your new company fits in. This is your second chance to give the reader an overview to establish a basis of a detailed understanding. After this brief introduction, include a description of how, when, and by whom the company was started, its achievements, acceptance setbacks, and bringing these experiences to current-day status.

Product or Service

To succeed with an Ultrapreneuring company, you must know your product or service; to succeed in obtaining capital, you have to be able to clearly describe your product/service. After a simple, straightforward description, then proceed to describe the need for the product or service in today's marketplace, how it will make a difference, the benefits derived from using it or what will make the customer buy it, as well as its advantages. Explain any special training needed to sell or use it. Include all relevant regulations that may affect its sale or use. Expound on any exclusivity or technological uniqueness. Unless your plan is going only to those persons who are specialists in your industry area, assume you are writing for the layperson. Forget industry jargon and replace it with words that the nonspecialist can understand. If you tend to write technical descriptions, then engage a professional writer.

Market Description and Analysis

This section profiles three key areas: customers, industry, and competition.

Prepare a Customer Profile. Describe what persons form your market, where they can be found, why they purchase your product or service rather than another, and whether it appeals to a single individual or to groups. Document quality, warranty, service, and price significance; pinpoint the buyer and user. Point out political influences, if any. Describe market coverage, whether local, regional, national, or international.

Prepare an Industry Profile.   Discuss pertinent trends, past, present, and future. Offer available statistical data on sales and units. Use charts, graphs, and tables if they can make the presentation clearer and more impressive. Refer to trade associations if helpful.

Prepare a Competitive Profile.   Stress advantages of price, quality, warranties, service, and distribution. Include the operational strengths and weaknesses. Project potential market share trends in sales and profitability.

Don't guess in this section. Check all your facts and note all your sources. You can be sure that these will be checked with a fine-tooth comb during an investor's due diligence process. If you're citing voluminous reports or statistical information, note that you have them available for further review.

Marketing Strategy

This is a critical section that should clearly specify the company's goals, how they are to be achieved, and who will have the responsibility for achieving them. Qualify all distribution methods (representatives, dealers, and so forth) and describe any planned advertising or public relations activities. Include references to sales aids, foreign licensing, and training plans as appropriate. Simply, detail how you are going to sell the product or service.

Operations Plan

This section is primarily oriented toward facilities, manufacturing capability, and equipment. Disclose all present capabilities as to equipment and facilities, as well as further projections for offices, branches, manufacturing, and distribution. It often helps if you include current floor plans as well as expected future space plans for production or manufacturing companies. For all Ultragrowth companies, task/time charts can be especially useful in this section. They help impress on the reader that the Ultrapreneur has a real handle on the operational challenge.

Research and Development

The length of this section depends on whether you're a product or service company—further, if a product company, how technical your product is. The object is to explain all past research and development efforts and accomplishments as well as future expectations. Here is your opportunity to justify past time and dollar expenditures. Substantiate the patentability of inventions, proprietary processes, or other advantages the company will have over competition and the resultant, anticipated market impact.

Schedule

Describe the timing and sequential steps that will be taken to bring the company up to full speed. Graphs or charts help indicate the timing and interrelationships of the major events in the company. Take it month by month for the first year. Thereafter, indicate the progress expected quarterly. Areas that may be important include completion of prototypes, starts of beta tests, early significant sales, when key people are to be hired, physical expansions or moves, opening of branches, trade show or convention dates, major equipment purchases, etc.

Management

In the eyes of the investors, the quality of the management team often determines the potential success of the company. Consequently, this section should cover career highlights, accomplishments, positions held, and emphasis on good performance records. Describe how the team has worked together in the past. List all directors, consultants, advisors, and other key professionals who will be involved in company operations and point out how they add value. Detailed resumes of key management should be appended with bios of others as appropriate.

Risks and Problems

These could be a red flag. There are diverse opinions about the inclusion of this category. Some investors object to the obvious and prefer to discover their own negatives. Others prefer that the company openly acknowledges risks and potential problems. It's a toss-up; however, high-profile, success-threatening risks should be brought out.

Use of Proceeds

Judiciously present a timetable indicating how much money will be needed, when it will be needed, and how it will be used. Most Ultra-growth companies require multiple stages of financing, including both debt and equity. Show the proposed capital structure as to who is going to own what part or percentage of the company at what stage. Startup plans need to detail startup use of proceeds and then generalize on the additional stages.

Finances

Present the company's current equity capital structure as well as future plans. Itemize the equity payments made with dates paid. List all outstanding stock options. Include both historical and current profit-and-loss statements and balance sheets. Present current and proposed salary structure for those already on board and those who will come on board at a later date. Show projections including balance sheets, profit-and-loss statements and cashflow studies. These should be month by month for the first year, quarterly for the second and third years, and yearly thereafter. It is mandatory that detailed assumptions accompany all projections. It is also very helpful if the very first part of this section summarizes the details. In fact, in many cases, details can be appended or supplied separately.

Appendix

Include a glossary (if pertinent) and all essential pieces of evidence, such as resumes, product brochures, customer listings, testimonials, and news articles.

Your Plan Is a Lot of Work

It's suggested that you seek out available books on writing a business plan. They can be found in many bookstores and all libraries. Read two or three to give you the essence of a good background for specifically outlining your plan. Each company is different and your plan must be tailor-made to fit your particular situation. The ideal business plan just doesn't exist, and generic plans just don't cut the mustard for Ultrapreneurial companies. Expect to spend a minimum of two or three months and 200 to 300 hours writing your plan. It's not unheard of that an Ultrapreneur spend up to a year putting together a detailed plan. Additionally, you'll have to spend some time in preparing and rehearsing your oral pitch. Remember, your words and story not only have to paint a pretty picture, they must be persuasive as well.

It's of little use to approach the writing of a business plan as a necessary evil. Rather, look at it as a helpful tool that can be used to exploit the advantages of your product or service.

The Plan's the Thing

Some companies may question the necessity of a business plan, citing successful firms that never had one. Times are changing. When the goal is to raise money, it's not only the entrepreneur's money that is at stake. Advisors, team members, directors, investors, and bankers need to be thoroughly convinced. They want to know that they won't be wasting their time and money. They want to know that the Ultrapreneurial management team has a clear sense of direction and is prepared to move toward its established goals.

A good business plan is the answer. What's more, much of the same information would have to be gathered anyway to be made available to any potential shareholders before they place their money in the company.

The Ultrapreneurial Difference

As was mentioned earlier, the Ultrapreneurial plan has some peculiarities of its own. These are concentrated in the fact that execution of the plan must be as precise as possible, that timing is tight, and that all resources must be stretched to the max.

The primary difference is in the fact that because the whole operation is on an Ultragrowth track, constant change is inevitable. These changes, some caused by leaps forward, others caused by setbacks, require that the business plan be almost constantly updated and that flexibility be acknowledged. Quarterly reviews may not be enough. Updates may have to be done every six weeks. Ultrapreneurs are always making progress or subtle changes of direction in their companies. It may be a new contract, it may be approval for a new product, it may be a successful beta test. It could easily be a new member of the management team. Regardless, one will fast discover that a business plan often goes stale as the first copies go out the door. Don't hesitate to do simple update sheets as supplements to a plan. Further, it's not the least bit unusual that continuing revised versions are made in the plan itself. That's why it's so important that the key members of the Ultrapreneurial team be intimately involved in business plan writing and revisions. This ongoing revision process brings home the strategic value that both the management team and the plan play in assuring that everyone is singing from the same songbook.

When an Ultrapreneurial team is established, many problems are confronted on an ongoing basis. The solving of these problems—some small and faced on a daily basis, others that may only be faced once in the lifetime of the company—are all important in their time. Many of these problems can be identified in the process of constructing, implementing, or revising business plans. It's an Ultrapreneurial difference: seeking out potential difficult areas, addressing them upfront, and determining solutions before they become problems.

Ultrapreneurial Structuring and Valuations

Another important Ultrapreneurial difference regards the initial company structure, ratios, and valuation strategies. While these are points to be considered in any business, they are very important to the Ultrapreneur. They have to be tested right upfront. You have to be sure that the end goals are feasible, that enough monetary gain can be had, and that the risks and work effort to be made can be justified. While these topics are books unto themselves, we'll briefly address each point sufficiently to make the Ultrapreneur aware of what points come into play and the primary fact that both legal and accounting counsel should be sought pertaining to these key areas.

Choosing the Right Structure: Legal and Tax Advantages

By structure, we're referring primarily to the legal entity of the company, i.e., sole proprietorship, partnership, corporation, or otherwise. Commonly, a corporate entity is the vehicle that is chosen. It offers the best liability protection for the principals and is the easiest to financially structure and comprehend.

Sole proprietorships, where one individual owns the company lock, stock, and barrel aren't conducive to Ultragrowth where multiple members of a management team must receive equity consideration. The same with partnerships, with the exception of the very early stages prior to the injection of any significant amounts of financing. Incorporation is the way to go and even here there are several choices to consider. This is why the Ultrapreneur should involve corporate legal counsel from the beginning. Many start-ups are formed as Sub-Chapter S corporations which allow the initial shareholders to treat the expected early losses with favorable personal tax considerations. As the company's capital needs grow, the corporate legal structure can be changed to what is termed a straight *C Corp*. As the most common corporate vehicle, it's preferred by most professional investors because it is treated as a legal entity distinct from individuals or other legal entities. C Corps offer the maximum liability protection of any legal business structure.

Several Points of Caution. It is imperative that experienced legal counsel be retained to input these decisions. There are many pitfalls that can cause unneeded problems downstream that can be addressed early on. For instance, a corporation should adopt a Section 1244 Stock Plan under Internal Revenue Code right upon incorporation. This allows the initial investors an identified way to write off their equity investments up to one million dollars should the company fail. Another caution is to be sure that legal counsel understands the Ultrapreneurial goal of harvesting the company in a relatively short time period. The company may just as well be formed with the thought of taking it public right from the start. This requires some subtle differences in the construction of the initial articles of incorporation and initial bylaws, neither of which add much cost at the start, but which can require extensive costs and time loss, not to mention management flexibility, after the fact. Again, discuss these points with both legal and accounting counsel prior to adopting a formal structure.

Looking Forward to Limited Liability Companies. A final structure point: As this book goes to press, a new type of corporate structure is being explored. It was initially conceived in the state of Wyoming and is now being accepted by numerous other states across the country. It is called a *Limited Liability Company* (LLC). While some attorneys are counseling their clients to adopt the LLC as their business entity of choice, others are continuing to show caution pending clarification of a few sticky issues, primarily oriented to taxation.

An LLC provides the opportunity to have your cake and eat it too. It is intended to provide the same opportunity for tax saving and flexible tax planning as sole proprietorships, partnerships in various forms, and the S corporation, but also the shelter from personal liability afforded by the traditional corporation for all owners. All this without the restrictions on the number and nature of shareholders and other matters imposed by the S corporation legislation.

So what's the problem? The problem is that the IRS has not yet issued a revenue ruling confirming that it will treat the LLC as a "partnership" for federal income tax purposes. Although such a ruling has been granted in connection with the Wyoming statutes, and is being requested by many others states, the Ultrapreneur should ask their legal counsel about the status in their particular state.

The legal structure of the Ultrapreneurial company can play an important role in successful Ultrapreneuring. The key is to obtain top-notch accounting and legal counsel at an early stage and to then maintain a close watch that anticipates Ultragrowth.

Previewing Valuations

Valuation, for our purposes, is the total dollar value of the company at any point in time. Obviously, at the beginning, this value is nothing, zero. Hopefully, when the company is harvested, it's multimillions. The challenge then, with the small exception of making it all happen, is how we determine these dollar values at various stages in the company's evolution. How do we know how much the company is worth so that when we are seeking new capital infusions, we don't under- or overprice the percentages of the company we're selling? How do we project these values, especially in the early stages, and how do we keep these valuations consistent throughout the Ultragrowth process?

Tough questions with no easy answers. In truth, valuations are not simple science. They are a subtle combination of art combined with some science. Given this nature of the animal, one can readily see that there could be lots of room for continued disagreement; in fact, that is the one reality of valuation.

The Ultrapreneur's bottom-line challenge is to justify the valuations with a substantial, substantive, and convincing story—a story backed with realistic marketplace facts and sound comparative data. To accomplish this, the first thing needed is a basic understanding of the fundamentals of valuations. What are the commonly accepted guidelines? Part of these guidelines are contained in what are called *ratios*.

Previewing Ratios

All financial planning relies on *ratio analysis*. This applies to both existing operations and future projections. Ratios become the science when projecting valuations or the anticipated worth of a company in the future. The Ultrapreneurial company's interest in these ratios is to use them, along with their internally prepared projections, to assist in determining valuations and to self-qualify for financing sources. For example, a venture capital firm may have an internal policy that states that due to their past experience, they are not interested in investing in projects that carry less than a 20 percent return on sales. In another example, a conservative bank may feel that loaning to companies with less than a 1.8/1 current ratio is too risky.

These ratios, which relate to two or more categories of financial data, are used to forecast future needs as well as judge present and past performance. Past ratios are very useful because they can be compared across time periods, against former projections and to industry averages. They can be used to identify and track problems as well as to maintain management consistency. There are six basic financial ratios that are commonly computed from balance sheets and income statements, whether they are historical or projections.

Expense Ratios

These show the company's various expense categories all in relation to its revenues. They are used to compare the company's recent performance with past time periods, project future results, and to compare to industry norms. These expense ratios are calculated for all major expense categories such as cost of goods sold, various material costs, selling expenses, general and administrative expenses, and just about everything one wants to track.

$$\text{Expense ratio} = \frac{\text{expense category}}{\text{annual sales}}$$

Profitability Ratios

These show a company's profitability in relation to either sales or investment. They are used to indicate the *operational efficiency* of the company. The most common are return on sales, return on assets, and return on equity.

$$\text{Return on sales} = \frac{\text{profits after tax}}{\text{total sales}}$$

$$\text{Return on assets} = \frac{\text{profits after tax}}{\text{total assets}}$$

$$\text{Return on equity} = \frac{\text{profits after tax}}{\text{total equity (assets - debt)}}$$

Utilization Ratios

These indicate a company's ability to manage short-term assets. They are used to show the *financial efficiency* of the company. The most commonly used utilization ratios are receivables in days, inventory in days, and payables in days.

$$\text{Receivables in days} = \frac{\text{accounts receivable}}{\text{annual sales divided by 360 days}}$$

$$\text{Inventory in days} = \frac{\text{total inventory}}{\text{annual cost of goods sold divided by 360}}$$

$$\text{Payables in days} = \frac{\text{accounts payable}}{\text{annual purchases divided by 360 days}}$$

Liquidity Ratios

These show the company's ability to meet short-term debts. They are used to indicate *credit strength* or financial risk. The common liquidity ratios are the current ratio and the acid-test ratio.

$$\text{Current ratio} = \frac{\text{current assets}}{\text{current liabilities}}$$

$$\text{Acid-test ratio} = \frac{\text{current assets} - \text{inventory}}{\text{current liabilities}}$$

Debt Ratios

These indicate the proportion of debt in the company's capital structure. The ratios are used to indicate the credit strength or financial risk of the company. The common ratios are debt-to-equity and the long-term debt percentage.

$$\text{Debt to equity} = \frac{\text{total debt (current liabilities} + \text{long-term debt)}}{\text{total equity (assets} - \text{debt)}}$$

$$\text{Long-term debt} = \frac{\text{long-term debt}}{\text{total capitalization (assets} - \text{current liabilities)}}$$

Coverage Ratios

These indicate the company's ability to meet fixed financial charges of long-term debt in the capital structure. They are also used to show the credit strength and financial risk of the company. The common coverage ratios are number of times debt interest is earned, and the number of times debt payments (both interest and principal) are earned.

$$\text{Debt interest} = \frac{\text{company profits before interest and taxes}}{\text{annual debt interest payments}}$$

$$\text{Debt payments earned} = \frac{\text{company profits before interest and taxes}}{\text{annual debt (interest and principal) payments}}$$

Assuming the Ultrapreneur knows these financial qualifiers, they can test their internal projections against them and, at minimum, have a sense if they can make a first-round cut when seeking financing. This can save a lot of time, not to mention frustration, which for the Ultrapreneur is very valuable when contemplating or executing an Ultragrowth plan.

Investor Equity Valuation

The Ultrapreneurial question here is: "How much of my company do I have to give away for the financing I'm seeking?" As with all valuation questions, there's no simple answer. Generally, the later the stage of development or the further advanced the company, the smaller the percentage of ownership the Ultrapreneur has to give up. Most Ultrapreneurial start-ups need to secure some amount of outside investment to support their Ultragrowth. Consequently, the challenge is to give up the smallest amount of equity and still assure that the ultimate goals can be achieved. Although there are some guidelines, some ranges, the final figures are the result of negotiations or a persuasive story.

If the Ultrapreneurial company is pure startup, no prototype, or much less sales, the investors are taking the vast majority of the financial risk. At this stage, it's not unusual that the investor will request 50 to 80 percent of the deal, maybe even more. However, if the Ultrapreneur or the team is investing at the same time, their money should buy equity stock on the same terms as the investor(s). Even for high-quality projects that are the dreams and prey of venture capital firms, the venture capitalist likes to see the Ultrapreneur retain a 20–25 percent stake. They feel that anything less reduces the incentive and commitment to make the deal work.

So if this could be considered the normal range for startup investing, how can the Ultrapreneur increase their stake? Many factors affect this, including:

A complete management team with proven, above-average prior startup experience, indepth knowledge of the product/service, substantial experience in marketing

A proven beta test or market test that indicates viability of the product/service

A strong patent or proprietary position

A generally acknowledged real need for the product/service

Strange as it may sound, if the company has a need for substantial second- or later-round financing, most sophisticated investors don't want the original team to get so diluted in the initial rounds that they lose their incentive commitment. If this seems to be a potential problem, one solution can be to structure it so that the Ultrapreneurial team has some performance incentives which allow them to regain equity percentages or exercise options that make their Ultrapreneuring efforts very worthwhile.

In more advanced stage deals, the valuations are also always negotiable. However, reality plays a part; good common sense, tied into the realities of the financial marketplace, set the guidelines.

A Valuation Example

Here are some valuation reality checks.

1. If you are seeking a $1 million investment for 50 percent of your company, what you're saying is that the value of your company before the investment is $1 million. Can you justify that figure? Can you show cause that your concept or idea, what you have put into the company so far, is worth a million dollars? A lot of entrepreneurs cannot.

2. Here's a more complex, but very real-life, example of a venture capital valuation scenario. Assume your projections show $150,000 in after-tax profits in year three. Also assume that the prospective investors feel comfortable with your projections and won't impose a discount factor. And finally, the assumption is that similar companies in your industry are being valued at four to five times after-tax earnings. Based on these three assumptions, you can figure the value of your company as follows:

$$\$150,000 \times 4 \text{ to } 5 = \$600,000 \text{ to } \$750,000$$

Now we can carry this to the next step: It takes two more assumptions. First, that you're seeking $200,000 from investors, and second, that most investors would feel that a 30 percent annual growth (return) on their money would justify the risk of their investment in your deal. Thus, the $200,000 investment, if it grows at 30 percent a year, would be worth approximately $440,000 at the end of three years. If your company value is $600,000 to $750,000 at the end of year three, and the investors' value must be worth $440,000 to meet their return objective, the $200,000 today must buy from

$$\frac{\$440,000}{\$750,000} \text{ to } \frac{\$440,000}{\$600,000}$$

of your company which would be from 59 percent to 73 percent.

Remember, this is a starting point for negotiations. You're confident that you will exceed your projections by leaps and bounds and the investor is very skeptical that you're capable of meeting the third-year projections until the fifth year. This type of valuation is very subjective. The more you can do to substantiate your case, to convince the investor that you not only have a good product/service but also a superb Ultrapreneurial team that can execute the plan flawlessly, the better your chances of receiving better valuations and less dilution.

The above formula is commonly known as the *present value* formula, where PV = present value, FV = future value, i = investment rate of return, and n = the number of years that the investment is held. It is expressed as follows:

$$PV = \frac{FV}{(I+i)n}$$

Thus, $$\$200,000 = \frac{FV}{(1 - 0.30)3} = FV$$

There are additional valuation methods which are used by investors; in fact, although some of the science methods are basic or common to most investors, almost all investors have their individual approach to the art. The Ultrapreneur's challenge is to build a convincing Ultrapreneurial plan that can withstand investor scrutiny and then be prepared to negotiate aggressively.

Creating a Special Executive Summary

Another Ultrapreneurial business plan difference is the putting together of a *Special Executive Summary*. This summary is not the same summary that is part of the business plan; it does, however, take advantage of the high points in the plan. It serves as an entering wedge to semi-interested persons as well as potential investors.

The business plan executive summary, discussed under the Business Plan Outline section, usually summarizes the business plan in two or three pages. The Special Executive Summary expounds on the most enticing parts of the business plan for about six to eight pages. In essence, it's a condensed business plan that shows a company to best advantage. It's an entree, when initially seeking help, to locate and identify potential financial sources. It can also be used as an overview for persons who do not need to know all that much about the company (like staff personnel or suppliers), or for those from whom management wants to keep proprietary information. It can be changed and adapted to any particular audience. It's kind of the bait before the hook, a plan used to capture one's initial interest and motivate one to request more information. Above all, a Special Executive Summary should not be taken lightly. It is indispensable, and should be kept updated. This is easier to do than revising a whole business plan if the Ultrapreneurial team simply wants to test some new plan ideas or gain some quick feedback. It may very well be the key to reaching the right source.

Making the Transition from Business Plan to Operating Plan

A final Ultrapreneurial business plan point: Business plans should be converted to *Operating Plans*. Once the company is up and running, management should convert the business plan to an Operating Plan. This process is simply retitling the plan to an Operating Plan and then religiously keeping it updated, using it as an operational guide on a continuing basis. It helps keep both management and staff focused on the tasks at hand. The parts that are pertinent to various departments can be pulled from the master plan and passed on to the appropriate individuals responsible from a staff position. This should be given continuing top priority for all Ultrapreneurial companies. The basic plan should be reviewed quarterly, at minimum semiannually. Remember, for investors, the business plan is what they buy into. It becomes the benchmark for accountability. They intend to hold management responsible for achieving the goals and objectives that are set out in the plan. It is inevitable that things will change as the company achieves full operation. In some cases, these changes will have only a small effect on operations. In others, they could result in a drastic move in total company focus. Keeping the ultimate Ultrapreneurial goals in mind, it's apparent that a continuing update of business plan strategy in the form of an Operating Plan helps keep everyone singing from the same songbook.

Ultrapreneurial Plans Take Your Best Effort

All companies should have a business plan. However, if a company's objective is to be Ultragrowth, it *must* have a business plan, and that plan must be detailed and flexible. Preparing it may take months, but you won't get to first base without it. The outlines presented in this chapter may not fit every company's particular requirements, but should contain enough general information and suggestions to provide a solid base for preparing your plan. More detailed materials and information on writing business plans can be found in many bookstores and libraries.

For Ultrapreneurs, there are some very important points that need to be given extra attention to set their plan apart from ordinary business plans. These include continually updating their plans, paying special attention to the corporate structure and valuation portions of the plan, creating a Special Executive Summary, and finally, converting the Ultrapreneurial plan to an Ultrapreneurial Operating Plan.

A company should give its plan its very best efforts. You will discover that a well-prepared Ultrapreneurial plan will prove a solid sales tool when approaching any financing source, investor, or lender, as well as provide management with a written game plan for guiding operations and maintaining a check on expectations.

A final note: *Failing to plan is planning to fail.*

7
Securing Ultrapreneurial Debt Financing

Ultragrowth companies are constantly on the search for new capital, either through debt or equity, and it is seldom easy to come by. The Ultrapreneur understands that raising money is a way of life.

During the decade of the eighties, many capital-raising incentives disappeared. Tax shelters in the form of limited partnerships were discontinued. Tax breaks for capital gains, both short-term and long-term, were dropped. The Small Business Administration stopped making direct loans. The Securities and Exchange Commission tightened the rules for trading smaller capitalized stocks. This left the entrepreneur with fewer choices for raising capital, and imposed tighter regulations on the process of financing itself. For many, this became a major stumbling block on their road to success.

In short, many of the '80s financing methods are gone. The '90s decade will see an evolution, not revolutions, in financing. Strategic partnering, joint ventures, and subtle forms of private equity sharing will become the bywords.

Sure, there will still be "quick flash" methods of financing. That's the American free enterprise way. The Ultragrowth generation of capitalists' challenge will be to determine how to adapt their company's approach to the kinder, gentler marketplace that continues to evolve, yet still create financing that supports the Ultragrowth approach.

Only experienced entrepreneurs realize that the financing of companies is done in stages and that they have to be flexible in identifying the latest trends in financing. Many first-timers erroneously believe that they can successfully generate sufficient cashflow on a near-term basis, then bootstrap their way to financial success. *This doesn't work,* especially in many of today's medium- and high-tech areas or Ultragrowth companies. This chapter discusses this fact and other potential problems, and offers many solutions to financing.

There Are Several Types of Financing: Debt and Equity

Contrary to the dreams of many startup entrepreneurs, initial financing can be the hardest part of launching their new business. There are many popular misconceptions that an idea, a startup team, and a preliminary business plan will get them in the venture capitalist door. They expect to exit, happily, with the check in hand. They don't realize that traditional venture capital—venture capital funds that are supported by institutional investors—only finance a fraction of a percent of the new companies started each year. They are not cognizant of the fact that 90 percent plus of startup money comes from private sources.

The first thing to do is to put together a business plan to use as a fundraising tool (see Chapter 6). Second is the actual raising of the financing, or *financial marketing.* Each alternative to raising money requires a different approach to the business plan. Financing never happens quickly; it is never simple. In fact, it is usually quite painful and exasperating. Ultrapreneurs frequently find themselves chasing down blind alleys.

There are a number of sources of financing and a variety of forms of capital. Some are used to finance seed or startup companies while others are used for expansion or Ultragrowth. Start-ups are usually limited to the type of financing they can get, like personal savings used as equity or personally secured subordinated debt. On the other hand, companies with a proven track record have a much larger choice of financing alternatives—such as banks, venture capital firms, or public offerings. What all Ultrapreneurs soon discover is that there are several factors that they must constantly reckon with, in pursuit of the elusive dollar. These are the dilution of equity ownership, potential restrictions on daily operating flexibility, and debt-imposed constraints on future growth. These factors will be touched on time and time again throughout this chapter.

Your Two Basic Choices for Financing

For all intents and purposes, the Ultrapreneur has two basis choices when considering financing: debt or equity, pledging a part of one's soul or giving away a piece of it. Commonly, one does both.

In simple terms, debt is borrowed money secured in some fashion with some type of asset for collateral. Equity, on the other hand, is contributed capital, usually hard dollars. Debt may be secured by a personal signature only, and equity can also be in the form of a contributed asset. But most often new businesses require long-term debt or permanent equity capital to support major expansion and anticipated rapid growth. The advantage of borrowing is that it is a relatively simple process to arrange. It does not take a great deal of time and does not dilute equity ownership. The disadvantages are that it is a high-risk strategy as far as company growth is concerned, in that incurring debt subjects the company to a firm obligation, usually including the principals as cosigners. A downturn in business or an increase in interest rates could result in the inability to service debt payments.

Your Two Basic Sources of Financing

Likewise, there are two basic sources of financing: self-funding and external funding. Self-funding, although the most preferable, is seldom the most practical.

Advantages of Self-Funding

Self-funding involves Ultrapreneurs investing their personal money. It has the following advantages:

1. Allows the Ultrapreneurial team to take their time on their business plan and initial product development.
2. Means the only financing source they have to answer to is themselves.
3. Saves them the time otherwise devoted to finding a financial partner(s).
4. Establishes a strong internal discipline regarding the spending of funds.
5. Frequently shortens the time needed to get the product to development stage.
6. Usually lessens overhead costs.

The biggest point in favor of self-funding is the fact that this is the best way to build additional value, and hence equity, into the company. A company with a prototype product or service that has been self-financed is worth much more than several individuals with just an idea.

External Funding Is More Complicated

External funding, while not as preferable in concept or seed stage, comes from a lot of different sources of both debt and equity. They can be divided into two groups: informal and formal investors. The informal are the traditional family and friends. The formal include venture capital firms and the more formal type of investment groups—usually brought together in a private placement. With all these possibilities, it makes external funding more complex.

There are pros and cons to all of these areas, debt, equity, self-funding and external funding. We'll address all of them as we proceed through these chapters on Ultrapreneurial financing.

Ultrapreneurs Use Combinations

Unlike oil and water, debt, equity, self-funding, and external funding do mix well. In fact, it's an Ultrapreneurial secret. Ultragrowth companies *must* mix their financing sources and choices.

Which to use, and when, becomes a matter of individual option although there are some pretty well established precedents. Founders' personal investments, including both personal assets and family and friends' equity and loans, are usually what finances concept or seed stage companies.

Development stage companies commonly seek funding from private placements, early-stage venture capital firms, and various grants from both foundations and government sources.

Early-stage production companies may receive financing from bank loans, leasing companies, and research and development partnerships (for incremental product development). Strategic partnerships are often entered into at this stage with potential customers, suppliers, and manufacturers.

Companies at the next stage of ramping up, which is full-scale production and expanded marketing, often receive additional dollar injections. These come from second and larger rounds of traditional venture capital, larger companies that are looking for product distribution opportunities, institutional investors, more venture leasing companies (for manufacturing equipment), and additional strategic partners (often seeking secondary manufacturing and distribution rights both domestically and for foreign countries).

After this stage, the Ultrapreneuring company has some heavy choices to consider. Here is where the harvest point is a natural. They still need more money (what's new), but their choices are a lot broader: more venture capital, bridge or mezzanine financing while going public, being acquired (perhaps by one of the earlier-stage strategic partners), or selling out to a cash-rich company.

So Debt or Equity?

If we're saying that Ultrapreneurs use combinations, how do we distinguish which and when? The use of debt almost always requires that some equity has come in first. A rough rule of thumb is that a dollar of early stage equity can support a dollar of debt, *if* there is some additional security to further back the debt. Lenders feel that a start-up has little ability to generate sales or profits. Consequently, the lender wants to have their debt secured, and even then, they feel that the asset value will be decreasing with time and there's always the possibility that management may not be up to the company-building challenge at hand.

This debt will most likely be short-term debt (one year or less) to be paid back from sales. Short-term debt is traditionally used for working capital and small equipment purchases. Long-term borrowing (one year or maybe up to five) can be used for some working capital needs, but usually is assigned to finance property or equipment that serves as collateral for the debt.

While commercial banks are the most common source of short-term debt, there are more choices for long-term financing. Equipment manufacturers provide some, as does the Small Business Administration (SBA), various state agencies, and leasing companies. These are discussed in more detail in the following sections.

It's true, Ultrapreneurs can finance start-ups with more debt than equity, but there are some distinct disadvantages. If they negotiate extended credit terms with several suppliers, this restricts their flexibility to negotiate prices. Heavily leveraged (i.e., debt-financed) companies are constantly undercapitalized and will experience continuing cashflow problems as they grow. Paying close attention to strained cashflow requires a lot of management time be diverted from company growth. It also affects the balance sheet, making it difficult to obtain additional equity or debt.

On the other hand, there is one big positive in using debt. Debt doesn't decrease or dilute the Ultrapreneur's equity position and it provides nice returns on invested capital. However, if credit costs go up, or sales don't meet projections, cashflows really get pinched and bankruptcy can become reality.

Ultrapreneurial companies use varying combinations of debt and equity. They determine which is the most advantageous for the particular stage of growth they're financing. Their aim is to create increasingly higher valuations to result in highly profitable harvests.

Understanding the Stages of Ultrapreneurial Development

Prior to delving into the details of Ultrapreneurial debt, it's helpful to establish an understanding of the traditional stages of development for Ultrapreneurial companies. These are: seed or concept, startup, first, second, third, and harvest. They are briefly described as follows:

Seed or Concept

This is the wild-eyed, perhaps incurable, inventor stage. There is an idea, a concept, no management team, no prototype, and patentability has not been determined. No business plan, timetable, or market research has been assembled. Founder(s) may be technicians.

Tasks.   To begin development of a prototype, assemble some key management, develop a business plan, assess market potential, structure the company, and assess patentability or proprietary standing.

Traditional venture capital firms have little interest in funding a company at this stage. The risk level is just too high, and the time for achieving a payout or harvest is not determinable. Personal savings or friend and family money funds this stage. It ends with the completion of a seed stage business plan and the formation of the company.

Start-up

At least one principal person of the company is pursuing the project on a full-time basis. The prototype is being developed, the business plan is being refined, a management team is being identified, market analysis is being undertaking, and beta tests are being set up or initial customers are identified. More formal funding is being accomplished.

Tasks.   Complete and test the prototype and obtain evidence of commercial interest. Assemble and identify an initial management team, finish the business and marketing plans, establish manufacturing and initiate sales.

Traditional venture capital firms may show an interest at this stage, assuming that a top-rated management team is assembled, patentability or proprietorship is proven, and marketability is demonstrated. Fundraising is a major effort at this stage and it may take from several months to a year or more.

First Stage

The company is now a going concern. The product has proven manufacturable and is selling. If it's a service company, some customers have tried the service. The management team is in place, the company has experienced some setbacks, customers can confirm product usage, marketing is being refined, adjustments are being made in the business plan and the moneyraising efforts continue.

Tasks.   To achieve market penetration and initial sales goals, reach close to breakeven, increase productivity, reduce unit costs, build the sales organization and distribution system.

At this stage, traditional venture capital firms are interested in investment—in fact, it's their most preferable stage. Financing is needed to get the production bugs worked out and to support initial marketing efforts.

Second Stage

Significant sales are developing as are assets and liabilities. The company is sporadically achieving breakeven, and cashflow management becomes critical. Second-level management is being identified and hired. Export marketing is being explored and more sophisticated management systems are being put into place.

Tasks. To obtain consistent profitability, add significant sales and back orders, expand sales from regional to national, identify international marketing plans, and obtain working capital to expand marketing, accounts receivable, and inventory.

More sophisticated and second-round venture capital financing comes into play at this stage. The founders and investors are forming plans for the harvest.

Third Stage (also Mezzanine Stage)

All systems are really go and the potential for a major success is beginning to be apparent. Snags are being worked out in all areas from design and development of second-generation products; to marketing and distribution; to management and all its applied systems.

Tasks. To increase market reliability, begin export marketing, put second-level management in place, begin to "dress up" company for harvest.

At this stage, the company may need to obtain "bridge" or "mezzanine" financing to carry increased accounts receivable and inventory prior to harvest. There is a great amount of pressure to prove second- and third-generation products, increase profitability records, improve the balance sheet, and firmly establish market share and penetration.

Harvest

The end is near for Ultrapreneurial companies. The company is sifting and sorting out its options including going public, being acquired, selling out, or merging. What started out as a dream probably at least three years prior, has become an Ultrapreneurial reality. The next challenge is to start all over again, but this time with a pocketful of dollars and a lot deeper insight as to the extent and rewards of the challenge.

With an understanding of the stages of development of Ultrapreneurial companies, we can delve into the various types of debt used in Ultrapreneurial financing.

Identifying Debt Financing: Forms and Sources

Pure debt (loan/borrowing) financing can take several forms. It is available from various sources such as banks, finance companies, factors, or leasing companies, not to mention individuals. Another important, but often overlooked source is trade payables. This is considered increased risk for the company since borrowed funds require repayment. However, loans do increase the borrower's return on equity (leverage). Costs to be considered in using debt financing are not only interest, which can be high, but also indirect costs that can be associated with some forms of debt, such as *compensating checking account balances,* where the borrower is required by the lender (bank) to maintain a stated minimum balance in a non-interest-bearing checking account.

This means if the borrower received a $100,000 loan from a bank, the bank could insist that the borrower keep a minimum $10,000 in the checking account, with a stipulation that the account cannot go below the $10,000 (or the full amount of the loan would be automatically callable for repayment). The borrower is required to pay interest on that $10,000, even though it can't be touched. Additionally, the lender may impose strict loan covenants in the form of company performance ratios that must be maintained. These could be items such as:

- The company's net worth versus assets cannot fall below a certain level.
- The company's inventory must be maintained at a certain level.
- The receivables cannot go over a specific level.
- The payables cannot exceed a predetermined ratio.

If any of these situations occur while the loan is in effect, the total loan or portions of it can be called due and payable.

Understanding the Forms of Debt Financing

Prior to getting into a detailed listing of debt sources, it is helpful to have an understanding of the principal forms of debt financing provided by the various sources.

Accounts Receivable Financing. For this form of short-term debt financing, the company pledges its receivables as collateral for a loan. Commercial banks are the most common provider of accounts receivable financing; however, it is also done by commercial finance companies and factors (see Factoring, page 149)—banks seldom factor.

The bank will discount the face value of a company's invoice (commonly 10–25 percent), and immediately remit the balance to the company. Accounts receivable loan lines can be increased as receivables increase, remembering that they are discounted as to the value of the receivables pledged. Receivables usually will not be accepted if they are over 90 days old, and the bank will reject invoices for companies that they do not feel meet their credit standards. The invoice may be payable directly to the bank (a notification receivable, where the company notifies the customer that the receivable has been sold to the bank) or a non-notification where the invoice is paid directly to the company and the company then remits the monies to the bank. A non-notification is preferable, as some customers deem that a company using receivable financing may be in financial difficulty.

Conditional Sales Contracts. When a company knows that by purchasing a new piece of machinery or equipment it can increase its productivity and profitability, it should consider making that purchase under a conditional sales contract. Under this contract, the company agrees to the equipment purchase with a nominal downpayment and then paying installments over a one- to five-year period. The bank holds the title to the equipment and usually has full recourse against the original equipment supplier for the balance on the loan should the company default. When the contract is completed, the bank turns over the title to the company since the "conditional sale" has been satisfied.

Equipment Loans. Equipment loans, also called *chattel mortgages,* are made to secure loans on machinery, equipment, and business property that collateralize the loan just the same as a mortgage on real estate. They are commonly executed through the security agreement forms of the Uniform Commercial Code (UCC). The title (chattel) remains with the company unless there is a default, in which case it reverts back to the bank. These are used mainly for new equipment and for periods of one to five years.

Lines of Credit. A bank will make a line of credit agreement with a company on either a formal or informal basis. They will agree to extend a maximum loan balance for a one-year period. Often, the bank charges an extra ½–1 percent line of credit fee for making this commitment. The loan funds are commonly used for seasonal financing to build inventory or carry receivables. They are generally paid back as the inventory or receivables are liquidated.

Banks usually collateralize these by pledges of inventory, receivables, equipment, or any other assets they can get their hands on. If unsecured, the bank will require that all debt to the company's principals or shareholders be subordinated. Often, line of credit loans are accomplished by renewable 90-day notes. The bank will insist that once a year the complete line is paid off and remains at a zero balance for 1–2 months (called "resting the line"). A compensating balance is also common with the company keeping a checking account at the bank that maintains 10–20 percent of the outstanding line of credit. Some banks may "discount" the loan by deducting the interest in advance. One can see that line of credit loans can be very costly considering that extra fee charges, discounting the loan, compensating balances, and resting the line all add up to a higher effective interest rate.

Plant or Property Improvement Loans. This type of loan is not seen too often with Ultrapreneurial companies since they seldom own their plants or property. They are simply expanding too fast to take on long-term (10- to 20-year) mortgage commitments. However, should they make significant plant or property improvements, the loans will be mid- to long-term and are secured by first mortgages on the improvements and second mortgages on the underlying plant or property.

Time-Sales Finance. Another name for time-sales financing can be *floor planning*. It is used when the company offers to arrange the financing of its products to its dealers and then on to the ultimate customer. The most common suppliers of this type of financing are commercial finance companies, although some commercial banks also offer this service. The company sells its products to a dealer via an installment or conditional sales contract and then sells the contract to a finance company. Some larger companies have subsidiary divisions which do nothing but finance the company's product sales. Many times this same type of contract is then used to sell and finance the product to the ultimate user.

From the company's point of view, this is another way to obtain long-term financing using short-term methods. The bank, who frequently discounts the contract, obtains double or even triple security. The bank takes the contract on a full-recourse basis, first from the company for the dealers obligation, and secondly from the dealer for the ultimate customers' installment obligation. Collection of the installments may be made directly by the bank or indirectly through the dealer or manufacture. Time-sales financing can be an Ultrapreneurial key to Ultragrowth. The company is making sales by helping its dealers make sales by helping their customers buy financing and the product.

Unsecured Term Loans. The key words here are *unsecured* and *term*. Unsecured is pretty simple. A loan is made that doesn't have any underlying collateral which can be pledged to liquidate the loan in the event of default by the borrower (company). Term, on the other hand, has three key features:

1. They are made by banks for periods of up to five years.
2. Periodic repayment is required.
3. The loan agreements are tailored to fit the special needs of the borrower; as an example, small interest-covering payments may be made with a balloon (large) payment at the end of the term. Banks watch term loans with a special cautionary eye. This is because the loans are for longer periods and a lot of changes can take place in a company over three to five years. They frequently place covenants which prohibit additional borrowing, merger or sale of the company, or payment of dividends, as well as other special restrictive clauses.

You May Have to Sweeten the Deal. The last several decades have seen wide fluctuations in the costs of borrowing money. Interest costs have been as high as 25 percent. What's more, long-term loans often carried *equity kickers* in the form of stock warrants or rights to purchase stock. (This is common practice with venture leasing companies and many sources that provide side or off-balance sheet financing.) An equity kicker is a deal made by the lenders with the company. The gist of it is that because the company is new and considered high-risk, the lenders are betting that the company will become successful. To offset that high risk for the lenders and to entice them to make loans, the company issues them a warrant that allows them to buy x number of shares of the company's stock at today's prices at sometime in the future.

It may not sound fair, but savvy Ultrapreneurs know that these are often the costs of borrowing money for early-stage companies.

Subordinated Debt: An Alternative

An alternative to bank borrowing is the placement of subordinated and sometimes convertible debt debentures with private lenders, venture capital firms, or organizations such as Small Business Investment Companies (SBICs, discussed later in this chapter). Most subordinated debt is unsecured, semisecured, or secured by a specific type of collateral, but is always junior (secondary) to senior or common bank loans. For example, the company has a bank loan for $500,000 that is secured by inventory, receivables, and equipment. The company wants to buy some new equipment to open a new production line. The equipment, with a small downpayment, will be enough to secure the new loan. However, if the company should go bankrupt, the bank has first claim against its assets. and the new equipment lender would have to take a secondary position against the assets after the bank. That's what makes the new lender subordinated.

But let's assume that the new loan helped the company reach its goals, the loan agreement may contain a convertibility clause that allows the new lender to convert their subordinated debt (or debentures) to common stock at an agreed-upon date at prices most likely determined at the time of the loan. In essence, the loan is a *subordinated convertible debenture,* that is, debt that can be convertible to equity as stock.

Putting together subordinated and/or convertible debt placements takes experienced legal and accounting advice. Additionally, careful consideration must be given to the long-term effect of equity dilution, as it could be possible that the subordinated convertible debenture holders could team up with other minority shareholders and, by their conversion rights, gain effective control of the company.

Understanding the Sources of Debt Financing

After looking at the forms of debt financing, let's look at some sources for getting debt financing. The following section describes a number of them. Descriptions include some key narrative as well as costs for the debt, the lengths of maturities that are common, how the use of proceeds can be spent, and advantages and disadvantages in using the particular debt source.

Commercial Banks

Banks are traditional lenders for secured short- or medium-term loans. They are "no-risk" lenders in that they insist on some form of collateral and are likely to require the personal guarantees of the company's officers. These loans are usually revolving lines of credit to finance inventory or receivable built-up and are quite often seasonal or loaned against a particular contract. Term loans require systematic payments over the life of the loan. Banks will also make mortgage loans on a longer-term basis against buildings, real property, and equipment. They do not ordinarily provide loans that are unsecured, or lend to startup companies. The overall banking crises of the late 1980s and early 1990s have made traditional bank financing at minimum difficult, and in many areas of the country almost impossible to obtain.

Costs	Floating rates to 5 points above prime
Maturity	30–90-day notes; credit lines to 3 years; long-term mortgages to 7 years
Proceeds	Working capital; inventory; receivables; machinery
Collateral	Unsecured; secured against specific assets' personal guarantees
Advantages	Usually lower costs than other lending organizations; many branches
Disadvantages	Prefer established businesses; require personal guarantees and/or collateral; restrictive covenants

Commercial Finance Companies

Commercial finance companies provide asset-based lending, most commonly against receivables and occasionally against inventory. Their rates are usually higher than those of banks, and they usually require regular monthly reconciliation of their collateral (receivables or inventory). They are more aggressive lenders than banks, but seek highly liquid collateral which they are apt to discount highly. If they make equipment loans, which must be backed by appraisals, the maximum period is five years and they insist on stiff prepayment penalties. They most likely will insist on receiving monthly financial reports on the company.

Cost	Floating rates to 7 points above prime
Maturity	Depends on loan size, usually 1 to 8 years
Proceeds	Working capital; acquisitions; machinery; equipment; real estate
Collateral	First liens on assets; personal guarantees
Advantages	Fairly quick processing
Disadvantages	Higher costs, monthly tracking

Factors

Firms whose primary business is *factoring* are called factors. Simply, factoring is accounts receivable financing. In other words, the company sells its accounts receivables, at deep discounts, to a factoring company. A standard practice is for the factor to buy the company's receivables outright, without recourse, immediately upon proof of shipment of the goods. This applies only to preapproved customers of the company, and the company is still responsible for returns or defective merchandise. Factoring is common in such industries as clothing and furniture manufacturing, plastics, shoes, textiles, and toys. In recent years, some factors have entered into some high-tech areas. However, their terms are stiff because of the high rate of technology changes. Factoring is high-cost financing, but saves some clerical costs (credit checking, cost of bad debt collection and writeoffs) and turns receivables into cash quickly.

Costs	Floating rates 5 to 10 points above prime
Maturity	90-day to one-year agreements
Proceeds	Unrestricted
Collateral	Often personal signatures
Advantages	Quick cash
Disadvantages	Requires top credited customers; high costs

Leasing Companies

Leasing companies (which include some banks and most commercial finance companies) tend to offer the entrepreneur more flexibility than commercial banks. The company may lease an asset (equipment, office equipment, trucks, autos), or buy it, sell it to the leasing company, and then lease it back (lease-back). Leases can often be made for longer time periods and set up with varying payment plans.

Payments can be scheduled monthly, quarterly, semiannually, and in some cases annually. Depending on tax advantages, the lease contract may also contain balloon payments. Most equipment lessors encourage and offer easy upgrade plans for fast-growing companies that continually need to move up to faster or next-generation equipment without major penalties. In recent years, a new type of leasing company has made major inroads in the leasing area. Spawned by venture capital types of financing, these new lessors are know as *venture leasing companies* because one of their primary requirements is that the company has received considerable venture capital financing. This adds a higher level of creditability to the new company; however, it's not uncommon that the company may have to issue warrants or options for its stock to obtain the most favorable leasing terms. Sometimes, lease-backs can also be arranged with private individuals.

Costs	Prime plus 6–8 points
Maturity	Negotiable; operating leases as short as 6 months; financing leases for useful life of asset
Proceeds	Machinery; equipment; real estate; acquisitions
Advantages	Easy deals; 100 percent financing; lessor carries risk
Disadvantages	High costs; no ownership benefits

Savings and Loan Associations

S&Ls in general have been experiencing major upheavals, changes of ownership, and a lot of financial setbacks. But many are still operating. The entrepreneur should not overlook the fact that with all their problems, S&Ls are still viable financing sources. The distinction between S&Ls and banks continues to lessen, except that S&Ls are still more inclined to finance against real property.

Cost	Competitive with banks; fixed or variable rates tied to the prime rate
Maturity	Long-term to 15 years; occasionally lines of credit
Proceeds	Real estate; some working capital; equipment
Collateral	Always secured; personal guarantees
Advantages	Attractive rates; experienced real estate lenders
Disadvantages	High minimum loan amounts; restrictive covenants

Small Business Administration

The SBA has always been considered a lender of last resort. In the past, a company had to be turned down by two other traditional lenders to qualify for an SBA loan. However, in recent years, the SBA has instigated a variety of new programs that are in place with varying degrees across the country. One major improvement is what is termed an SBA bank. These banks' primary business is originating, placing, and servicing SBA loans. You can find information about the SBA banks in your area by contacting your local/regional SBA office. Basically, SBA has a number of different loan programs with various qualifiers. Their rates are reasonable, but subject to government funding availability guarantees. All SBA loans have a lot of restrictive covenants and require a lot of paper processing. The entrepreneur who is successful in obtaining SBA assistance is one who acknowledges and adapts to the paperwork system.

Cost	Floating and fixed rates tied to prime
Maturity	5 to 25 years
Proceeds	Working capital; machinery; equipment; real estate
Collateral	Secured by liens; personal guarantees
Advantages	Low-cost considering risk; do not finance some types of assets
Disadvantages	Liens; personal guarantees; paperwork

Small Business Investment Companies

The SBA licenses and provides leveraged financing to SBICs, which in turn provide various forms of venture capital to entrepreneurial enterprises, usually in the form of convertible/subordinated debt.

Amount available	$100,000 to $1 million
Structure	Convertible debt; debt with warrants
Cost	Reasonable interest; dividends; equity
Proceeds	Working capital; acquisitions; leveraged buyouts
Advantages	Subordinated capital; 5-year debt; fixed interest
Disadvantages	Equity dilution; must prove fast growth

Minority Enterprise Small Business Investment Companies. MES-BICs are identical to SBICs except for the fact that they are designed for, and only available to, minority-owned businesses.

Industrial Revenue Bonds

Industrial revenue bonds are not for startup or early stage companies, with the exception of those companies that have substantial equity financing. They are mostly issued to finance companies with large real estate needs or companies with large equipment needs. Also, in most cases, the issuing agency holds title to the property and leases it back to the company.

Costs	Floating or fixed rates at 70 to 85 percent of prime at tax-exempt status
Maturity	Usually 5 to 15 years or more
Collateral	Secured by fixed assets
Advantages	Low rates; good maturities
Disadvantages	Depends on market availability; strict government rules; high closing costs, especially legal

Life Insurance Companies and Pension Funds

This type of debt financing is specifically for established companies with substantial equity financing. Additionally, it is obtainable for large investment projects that frequently run into the millions.

Costs	Fixed rates tied to long-term markets
Maturity	5 to 25 or 30 years
Proceeds	Real estate; machinery; equipment
Advantages	Reasonable interest rates, long-term maturity
Disadvantages	High minimum amounts; restrictive loan agreements

Government Sources

SBA, SBICs, and MESBICs are just some of the better-known government sources for debt financing. However, since both federal and state governments seem to have frequent policy changes, it makes it difficult to include any type of comprehensive listing. It is suggested that the Ultrapreneur leave no rock unturned when exploring debt financing. Both federal, state, and local government programs can be uncovered that apply to specific types of industries or financing applications.

The best starting place is to inquire with your state's economic development commission. However, don't take no for an answer when you ask them about new business development programs. Keep inquiring—ask friends, business associates, chambers of commerce, and larger city economic development commissions (they take on all kinds of bureaucratic names and titles). Some very innovative financing deals have been put together by Ultrapreneurs who dug deeper and used a lot of creative thinking to combine several different government assistance programs that saved the companies lots of tough-to-find financing dollars.

Small Business Innovation Research Grants

Several grant programs are funded and administered by various federal agencies. The grants (first stage up to $50,000, second stage to $500,000) are primarily available for new product research and development. The products that result, if successfully developed, belong to the company. But the stipulations are that the government has an option to purchase or use the technology. These grants are offered to both individuals as well as companies.

Amount available	First stage to $50,000; second stage to $500,000
Structure	Grant by federal agency
Cost	Documented proposal must be submitted
Proceeds	Seed capital for R&D of a product
Advantages	Low cost; no equity giveaway; no debt
Disadvantages	Limited capital commitment

Other Grants

Numerous grants are available from the federal government, state governments, foundations, and private sources, and not exclusively for research and development. It is estimated that the total grants from all sources amount to $100 billion *annually*. A directory listing most of the grants available in the United States is published by the Office of Management and Budget.

Leveraged Buyouts

Leveraged buyouts (LBOs) is a form of financing that has been around for decades, but became glamorized in the eighties. It simply amounts to borrowing against the assets of a company and then using the cashflow realized from the operations of the company to service the debt. Buyers, after purchasing a company, frequently sell off some of the assets to reduce the debt load and, as part of their operating procedure, drastically cut operating costs to increase cashflow. Obviously, LBOs are not applicable for pure start-ups because there are no assets. However, if the Ultrapreneur is buying out an existing company to then exploit a particular technology, or purchasing a group of companies for the basis of expansion, LBOs may apply. Sources of financing for LBOs are commercial banks, asset-based lenders, industrial bonds, venture capital firms, and private investment pools. LBOs usually get their funding assembled from and through investment bankers.

Credit Enhancement

This is a debt financing technique that is not used too often because it's difficult to set up. However, it is worth some Ultrapreneurial think time to determine if you have the right connections or potential to pull it off. Often a company cannot borrow from a lending source unless it is able to provide liquid or semiliquid assets as collateral. The challenge is to find a third party who has an interest and a belief in the company and who is willing to provide the needed liquid collateral to secure the debt. The collateral is usually in the form of marketable securities, certificates of deposit, or letters of credit. In exchange for "enhancing" the company's credit, the third party usually receives a fee, payable at the time the loan is provided, along with warrants to buy stock in the company at some future date.

Trade Credit

One of the best is saved till last. In small, fast-growing companies, trade credit—in the form of accounts payable to suppliers—can make up large percentages of a company's total balance sheet. If you can buy goods and services and be given 60 to 120 days to pay for them, it's the same as having a *no-interest* loan for 2 to 4 months. Suppliers offer such terms to induce new companies to buy from them. It takes careful attention on the part of management not to abuse these generous terms.

The Ultrapreneur wants to be sure they keep their word with these suppliers, lest they need additional help to fill a quick order and suddenly find themselves in the position of being put on a COD basis.

A couple of other trade credit forms are: seasonal or special dating terms, where a supplier ships in advance knowing that payment will not be made until after some predetermined time; and consignment terms, where the supplier will ship and does not require payment until the item is sold. Again, be sure you honor these type of terms with prompt payment when the time period finally arrives.

There can be a big side benefit to warming up to suppliers for trade credit. Suppliers can also be used for inexpensive research and development, also for market research. They frequently have internal design departments to help customers and potential customers work up engineering. Don't hesitate to ask them to help you work up a design, patterns, drawings, or for technical expertise. They may have a CAD system available that's just what the doctor ordered. They frequently are a vast depository of marketing data and information. Don't hesitate to ask; you just might get what your looking for.

As mentioned earlier, debt financing is one of the primary choices in putting together the total financing package for Ultrapreneurs. In the next chapter, we'll take a look at the other primary choice, equity.

8

Securing Ultrapreneurial Equity Financing

Seed Stage Financing

Obtaining money for an Ultrapreneurial company is really pretty simple—it's just another sale. Your customer has something you want—their money. You have something they want—equity or a piece of the action of your high growth potential. The key, as in all sales, is to determine the right price and close the sale. To do that, you have to develop a *financial marketing* mindset. Just as you would prepare a marketing program, you need to prepare a financial marketing program. That means you prepare a plan and a pitch, develop a marketing scheme, present the package, and close the sale. It takes intimate knowledge, unbounded enthusiasm, and a scuff-resistant ego.

Your business plan is going to show you how much money you will need, if it should be debt or equity, and at what stage or time period it's needed to accomplish what tasks. By consulting with your peers, legal counsel, and accountants, you will have determined the most proper legal structure for your company as well as the proposed valuations. From this, you can then develop your financial marketing program which in turn will help you narrow in on the type of investor you will be seeking.

For seed and concept companies. this invariably means the Ultrapreneur starts with family and friends' money, and then proceeds on to obtaining informal investor financing prior to attracting the interest of the more formal investors such as venture capital firms.

You're Looking for Angels

Part of the contingent of private financing sources, or informal investors, are persons affectionately referred to as *angels*. Along with family and friends, they are the largest providers of early-stage financing, both from a dollar standpoint as well as their sheer numbers. They are a homogeneous group that is very difficult to identify and capture. They may be your next-door neighbor or a relative of your friends. They may be *affiliated* in that they have some contact with you or your business, or they could be *nonaffiliated* in that they currently have no idea you even exist. Obviously, it's easier to start with someone who is already familiar with you and has a vested interest in the relationship. Recognizing that there is no typical angel, just like there are no typical Ultrapreneurs, it's still helpful to establish a characteristic profile of angels.

What's an Angel Look Like?

Various surveys and research reports have yielded some interesting characteristics for identifying angels. Although the exceptions probably overrule the norm, the profiles lend some interesting food for thought:

90-plus percent are male

Typical ages are 40 to 60 years old

Hold master or multiple advanced degrees

Have prior startup experience

Personal income between $100,000 and $250,000 per year

Invest minimally once a year; average is 2½ times

Invest $25,000 to $50,000 per deal, totaling $130,000 year

Seldom take more than 10 percent of a deal

Seek a minimum 20 percent compound per annum return

Expect liquidation in 5 to 7 years

Strong preference for manufacturing deals

Like technology they're familiar with

Prefer start-ups, early-stage companies

Dislike moderate growth

Like consulting role, board of directors/advisors

Like to invest with other sophisticated investors

Invest close to home (50 to 300 miles)

Primary investment motivation is a high rate of return

Secondary motivation is capital appreciation

Learn of investment opportunities from associates and friends

Less than 30 percent of referrals come from attorneys or accountants

Would like to see more opportunities than they currently see

Refer investments they make to their investment network

Contrary to venture capitalist, angels don't rank comprehensive business plans on the top of their criteria list. However, they rank management ability the highest, and seek a clear, demonstrated market need, plus a large market potential for the product or service.

How to Find Your Angel

The financial marketing mindset with angels is a little different than that of dealing with venture capitalists. Venture capitalists know what they want and how to go about getting it. Their primary focus is financial; they're investing other people's money and are getting paid to obtain outrageous returns. Angels, on the other hand, react to your proposal by determining in their mind if you're being fair. While they are also looking for a financial return, they frequently are seeking a psychic or intangible reward like helping minorities, creating jobs, revitalizing urban areas, or simply contributing back to society for their success.

Your First Task Is to Locate Them. It's a tough task. They don't advertise, they network quietly. Start with your calling card file; it may contain some hidden angels but most likely will lead you to more angels. Spread the word that you're seeking financing, that you have prepared a business plan, that you're prepared to talk with anybody, any time, any place, and that you're prepared to pay finders' fees. That's right—many times you will have to pay a fee to someone who puts you in touch with someone who writes the check. It's a financial marketing reality.

Professional service providers are always a good place to start. Attorneys and accountants are very good networkers with a potential vested interest. Suppliers or vendors can be helpful. Sometimes they invest, many times they may furnish leads, but frequently it's a good way to break into the subject of extended credit terms. Try customers and even employees (they may have some home equity to borrow against). Competitors, especially in other parts of the country, may reveal some strategic alliances as well as information that may lead to an angel. Dialing for dollars, also called telemarketing, works when you can obtain a list of wealthy individuals. Don't forget any already successful entrepreneurs, ex-entrepreneurs, or dentists and doctors. Not only can they bring in their money, but they can help attract other angels.

Bottom Line—It's Networking. Attend local venture capital groups; there are 80 to 100 of these located in almost every larger city in the country. Check the business events listing in local newspapers or regional business magazines. These groups meet specifically to network and exchange business opportunities. Many of them have a forum for presenting prospective business projects and a lot of angels attend or are plugged into the networks surrounding these groups. They are prime hunting grounds for Ultrapreneurs.

A final source is boutique investment banking firms and some business brokers. They focus on financing start-ups and matching angels. As intermediaries, they charge fees which can vary considerably. It's suggested that you qualify them and their principals by soliciting advice from your accountant and attorney.

The Best Ways to Approach Angels

Once angels are identified, the common approach is to furnish them with a copy of your business plan; after they have reviewed it, you'll hope to get together with them face to face. I suggest you handle this a little bit differently. If you can't arrange to meet them in person, furnish your Special Executive Summary first. Better yet, if you have your company up and operating, invite them to come in for a first-hand look. Assuming your Special Executive Summary captures their interest, then arrange for an in-person meeting. This is your opportunity to sell them on what your company has to offer—that is, management and a product/service with a lot of potential. It's just like any other sales job—display the wares and convince them you have something they need.

Initial contact via phone or nonpersonal referrals don't cut it. They're just not enough. The angel has to understand your company and gain a feeling for the enthusiasm that backs it. Your challenge is to get them personally involved, to buy into your determined dedication. If all they have is your business plan, it's too easy for them to refuse. You want to get them emotionally involved.

Keep in mind that you know more about your business than they do. Be cautious about how you present your projections, remembering that you will be expected to achieve them. Be sure they're realistic and achievable. Although angels are a lot more flexible than venture capitalists (and consequently you can close the deal in half the time), you still need to be sure your relationship is established with a strong bond of good faith and that you earnestly attempt to keep all your commitments.

Preparing the Scene

Once you have passed the seed stage, your company is beginning to be attractive to a more sophisticated level of investors. These would typically be venture capital firms. Although some venture capitalists may not be interested in investing at the startup stage, preferring to stand by until you've proven yourself some more at the first stage, it's still a good time to make an initial contact. Remember, you're forming a financial marketing plan and, just like in advertising, "repetition brings it home." By instigating a first-level contact with venture capital firms at seed or startup stage, you can come back at the next round of financing (while keeping them posted on your interim progress) and the familiarity with both you and your project will be in place. You will have had the chance to prove that you can do what you told them you were going to accomplish.

Understanding Traditional Professional Venture Capital

Professional venture capital firms have traditionally thought of their job as the early-stage financing of relatively small, rapidly growing companies. Over the past ten to fifteen years, their internal job descriptions and responsibilities have vastly increased. Sure, their primary objective is to still make a sizeable return on their investment, and they would like to do this from a passive basis. However, they have learned that they also have to take an active role alongside management. They have realized that venture capital investing requires a long-term investment discipline.

A Brief History

The industry of formally managed professional venture capital was started shortly after World War II when several wealthy families, including the Rockefellers, the Whitneys, and the Phippses, started to invest in the new technologies that came out of the war. They went on to seed-finance many now well-known companies: Itek, General Signal, Memorex, and Minute Maid, to name just a few. In 1946, the first formal investment partnership was put together in Boston under the name of American Research and Development (ARD). ARD made many early-stage investments, but its most successful was Digital Equipment Corp. (DEC).

The most successful single individual in early professional venture capital was Alex Rock. His seed investments are legendary, including Fairchild Semi-conductors, Teledyne, Scientific Data Systems, Intel, and Apple Computer.

Traditional venture capital received a big boost in 1958 when Congress passed the Small Business Investment Act which created the Small Business Investment Companies (SBICs) program. Government came to the rescue again (so to speak) when in 1978 it reduced the capital gains tax for long-term investment and clarified the 1974 Employee Retirement Income Security Act (ERISA) that then allowed pension funds to invest in professionally managed venture capital. Billions of dollars poured into these funds as the institutional investors (pension funds, insurance companies, major corporations, individuals and families, endowments and foundations, union and multi-employer plans, and foreign investors) sought the 20 to 30 percent per annum returns that the venture funds had traditionally made.

Today's professionally managed venture capital firms have proven their ability to evolve with the financial times. They have endured the big-time losses from their early-stage investments in computer hardware companies (over 500 initially, down to a handful today) and have entered the biotech era with lots more trepidation. They have adjusted, readjusted, and continue to readjust some more their investment philosophies as they seek to improve the knowledge of the art and science of venture capital investment.

Although the entire industry could be broken into many diverse categories, we will deal with some further explanation in two broad types: traditional and corporate professionally managed venture capital funds.

Venture Capital in General

The formal organized venture capital community can generally be divided into two main groups: traditional private institutionally funded partnerships and corporate venture capital funds. Although they have different objectives for investing—private funds for a money return and corporate for gaining technology—they have some similar operating policies and modus operandi.

They can be very difficult to get an audience with.

They are very select in the deals they get involved in.

They are seeking large investment dollar projects.

They only invest in deals with significant upside potential.

They aren't too attracted to start-ups.

They seek very high growth rates.

They have very stringent investment criteria.

They may be very limited as to their industry focus.

They place a high premium on the quality of management.

They have a concern for bringing more than money to the deal.

Another item in common for both private and corporate funds is the minimum and maximum amounts they're willing to invest. On the minimum side, it's usually in the area of $100,000 to $500,000. While some may go as low as $50,000 for seed projects, others may not go below $500,000. Their line of reasoning regarding minimums is that it costs them just as much time and money for due diligence in making a $50,000 investment as it does for $500,000.

Regarding the maximum amounts, there really isn't any ceiling. Most funds are individually limited to x percent of their total funds. However, all funds are capable of putting together syndicates with other funds to provide almost unlimited financing for the right Ultrapreneurial projects.

Traditional Venture Capital

The traditional venture capital firms manage funds that range in size from ten million to over several hundred million dollars. Funds that manage over one hundred million are called *megafunds*. Besides coming in many different sizes, they also have a lot of different orientations. Some funds specialize in seed-stage investments, while others only do advanced or bridge financings. Others concentrate their efforts on leveraged buyouts, and some only invest in specialized areas. These investment specialty areas may be only medical, or retail; others may prefer manufacturing or just computer software. Some large funds run what is termed a *balanced fund* which invests over a broad spectrum of industries and company development stages.

For all funds, their prime criteria are solid, experienced management teams who have identified a creditable market niche with a large growth potential and the possibility of developing a hundred-million-dollar-plus annual revenue company.

Very frequently, the partners in the fund will have prior experience and current knowledge in the areas in which the fund invests. This results in them being better equipped to take an active part in guiding the company in such areas as planning, marketing, developing supplier connections, finding new personnel, and bringing in additional financing sources.

Here Is Some More Insight.   A little more insight into the formation and operations of all venture capital funds helps in understanding their investment motivation. Each fund typically has several general partners as well as analysts, research and clerical personnel. The general partners have the responsibility to put the fund together and to solicit and obtain the actual limited partner institutional investors. These limited partner investors typically commit to a gross total dollar investment. The actual dollars will be invested in stages, commonly one-third of the money when the fund is started, one-third after the first year, and the balance during the second year. They are expecting that their investment will not be fully returned until the seventh through tenth year. They also expect to earn an annualized 30 percent compound interest on their money.

The general partners, on the other hand, receive an annual management fee to oversee the investment. They make all investment decisions without routine input or approval of the limited partners or passive investors. Additionally, although there are many different types of agreements, the general partners are entitled to receive a percentage of the profits after the initial investments are repaid, typically 20 percent. One can easily see that fund managers are under a large amount of pressure to perform, and those that do are justifiably rewarded.

Although most traditional venture capital funds orient their investments toward products, there are some that seek service-type companies; Computer software and medical services are examples. When seeking product investments, and to some extent in the service areas, there are three categories to consider: revolutionary, evolutionary, and substitute.

There Are Three Categories to Consider

Revolutionary. Examples of revolutionary products would be cameras, televisions, or computers. Venture capitalists tend to shy away from the revolutionary deals. They take too much cash and they take too long to develop.

Evolutionary. Examples would be instant and auto-focus cameras, color or portable television, and personal or laptop computers. These are the ideals for venture capital, the next generation or cheaper versions. To really merit consideration, the next generation should be 30 percent cheaper, 30 percent faster, or have a 30 percent improvement in quality. Better yet, all three.

Substitute. These are products that can develop niche or substitute markets, like fast-food chicken or hamburger, or regional spinoffs on automobile fast or quick lubes. Venture capital firms have differing opinions about substitutes. Some really like them if the niche is well defined, has an easy market entry, and what seems to be a broad appeal. Others beg off on substitutes, feeling they need too much marketing and advertising, both of which are hard to quantify when tracking the expense outlays.

Regardless of the categories, the uppermost consideration for traditional venture capital partnerships is the potential monetary return. This may not be the top criterion for corporate venture capital funds.

Corporate Venture Capital

Many corporations form venture capital subsidiaries for a variety of reasons, one of which is not to make a large return on their initial investment. This doesn't mean that they don't want to make money or that the Ultrapreneur should avoid exploring corporate venture capital as a source of financing. In fact, in many cases, corporate venture capital can be a better deal for the Ultrapreneur than the traditional firms. The corporate firms tend to over-fund their portfolio companies in an attempt to drive the realization of the project to a faster conclusion; because large corporations typically don't have an entrepreneurial mindset, they tend to overstaff and overequip all areas of operations. Consequently, where the Ultrapreneur is striving hard to produce results over a shortened time period, corporate venture capital makes a great fit.

What Corporate Venture Capital Seeks.   If corporations aren't seeking large returns, what are they after? A good start is strategic alliances in one form or another. It could be from a basic or applied research basis, one where they can support a patent or invention. It could also be a marketing alliance where they can obtain exclusive marketing rights. Or it could be a manufacturing agreement where the Ultrapreneuring company manufac-tures private-label products for the corporation. Ofttimes they are trying to find new talent or teach practical entrepreneuring to existing personnel. At other times they may be doing some public relations posturing or support-ing a philanthropic desire.

They look for start-ups where there will be a need for large capital con-tributions. As the company grows and expands, they are prepared to invest sums in excess of $5,000,000, on up to tens of millions. They seek projects that can utilize multiple locations or plant sites, including foreign locations. With this size of investments, it's obvious that they are looking for projects that have very large market potential where their long-term vision means that the company will have revenues in excess of half a billion dollars in 10 years or so, which also means that one-product companies won't do. They need to have multiple product spinoffs that allow for secondary products and licenses for international exploitation.

Why They Need Big Projects.   The reasons they need such big projects is that they are hunting for alliances to incubate future acquisitions that they can grow and support to become whole new corporate divisions. They are seeking to provide work for any plants that they may have which will have unused manufacturing capacity. They need projects in which they can invest excess cashflow and teach entrepreneurial thinking to their middle-management layers. They realize that many new technologies come from smaller companies. Consequently, if they can establish strategic partnerships during the early stages of a company's development, they can gain an insight into the windows of these new technologies and markets.

When one realizes that large companies like IBM or Exxon spend in excess of three billion dollars annually for just research and development—a sum equal to the whole traditional venture capital industry—then one can see that initial returns on their venture capital investments are not the prime motivator. Traditional venture capital firms are seeking to turn or liquefy their investments in three to seven years, whereas the corporate venture firms have longer timeframes of ten to twenty years to grow new ideas into mature industries.

The Negatives of Dealing with Corporate Venture Capital. With all these positive points in favor of corporate venture capital, assuming the Ultrapreneurs project is large enough, what could be negative? The biggest negative is the unstable nature of corporate venture capital. This type of fund has a history of being the *in* thing to do and just as suddenly falling out of favor. Large corporations are ruled by the economic times of Wall Street and its obsession with quarterly profits. This means that when the corporate venture capital firm is plush with excess cashflow, it has a keen interest in making venture type of investments. When things get tight, when pressure is put on budgets, invariably corporate venture capital gets slashed since expenditures of hard cash get sliced first.

Additionally, some corporate venture fund managements are restricted as to the final decisions to invest. They may have to obtain approval from corporate hierarchy to exceed predetermined investment levels or to invest in what may be considered fringe product areas. Since many new Ultrapreneurial ideas cross common product lines, or even combine technologies from different industries, it's not uncommon that corporate venture capital is not appropriate in the earliest stages. Even though venture capital is supposed to be entrepreneurial in style, corporate bureaucracies don't necessarily end at the door of corporate venture funds. It can take an excruciatingly long time to get upper-level approval for the Ultrapreneur who is depending on staying on a fast development track. Be sure you clear this point prior to getting too far downstream with corporate funds. Be sure the fund management has the authority to not only approve your project, but also to write the check.

Watch Out for Management Changes. Another negative is the fact that the upper management of corporate venture funds don't stay around long. The good ones leave for higher personal payouts with the private funds which tend to leave portfolio companies as orphans. These frequent personnel changes add to the confusion for the Ultrapreneur, since one of the many side benefits of making a venture capital connection is that the venture capital management itself has the ability to bring other players into the game. The fund manager that inherits the portfolio orphan may not have the enthusiasm, knowledge, or additional contacts that the original manager had who pushed the Ultrapreneur's deal through to begin with. The result is an orphan company, running low on money and time, without valuable industry contacts, and left without a dedicated lead venture fund.

Finally, corporate venture funds tend to want to establish the maximum values of a deal at the time of original investment. This tends to "cap" the harvest potential for the Ultrapreneurial team. Bad blood can develop if the team loses its high-profit incentive, especially if the project runs into some snags. This is bound to happen when the Ultrapreneurial team is in a bad renegotiation position and they become susceptible to diluting their total package to compensate for the addition of more dollars or time.

The prime motivation of corporate venture capital is an interest in growing their own acquisition candidates. They tend to make initial investments based on an arrangement that enables them to acquire the Ultrapreneur's equity at some future time. They are ideal capital partners for Ultrapreneurial companies that will require large sums of investment, who require longer time periods for development, and who can benefit from teaming up with a large corporate partner in research, development, manufacturing, and market distribution.

How to Find a Venture Capital Firm

Identifying venture capital firms is a fairly simple process. There are numerous directories available, and the bible for the industry is *Pratt's Guide to Venture Capital Sources*. Pratt's, as well as others (including state and regionally sponsored guides) are available in any good city library. These guides furnish name, address, and contact information as well as the size of investments they prefer, and in many cases the particular industries in which the firm prefers to invest.

How to Qualify Them

Qualifying a venture capital firm is a little more difficult than finding one. It requires that the Ultrapreneur use some common sense and recognize some of the ground rules. This includes not approaching a firm that clearly states that it does not invest in biotech if you're a biotech development company. It's surprising the number of companies that spend a lot of dollars sending plans by overnight delivery to venture funds that plainly state in their published information that they refuse investment in a particular industry. Most funds have a list that shows their areas of interest as well as areas in which they do not invest.

While many funds invest in companies located all over the United States, some prefer only projects located within two or three hundred miles or two or three hours from their headquarters. If you identify a firm that likes your industry, but you're located outside their preferred geographical investment area, place a call to them and ask if they know of a firm in your area. Many funds participate in investments with other firms if there is a "lead" investor who will agree to monitor a portfolio company. These lead investors are usually geographically located relatively close to the investment.

When a fund indicates that it has a preference for a particular industry, it usually means that one or more of the general partners has some background in that industry. This can be especially helpful to the Ultrapreneurial team because they don't have to spend a lot of time getting the venture capitalists up to speed on industry knowledge. It's also helpful because the venture capitalist can pick up the phone and get quick answers to due-diligence questions, and after making an investment is usually able to bring a lot of their industry contacts into the deal to help it grow and sometimes even staff the portfolio company.

How to Get in the Door

All venture capital firms will tell you that their best deals come from the companies in which they have already invested. The second best way to get in the door is to have someone who has some preestablished creditability with the fund make an introduction. If you can't find such a person, your legal counsel, accounting firm, or banker can make an initial contact on your behalf. If they are unable or unwilling to do so, don't hesitate to make it yourself. The best approach is to place a phone call to the designated person listed in the guides. When they finally return your call, simply outline your project and ask if you could send them your Special Executive Summary. If after reviewing your summary they have an interest, they will request your complete business plan. It is very difficult, not to mention a waste of valuable time and money, to send numerous plans out blindly to numerous funds.

Every venture capital firm in the country receives two or three plans per day, some thirty or forty. While they may get around to briefly reading them, it may take two or three months. Even then, so many plans are so poorly written that they don't even deserve a reply.

With this many plans coming in the door, you can also see that sending your plan by overnight delivery, or faxing your summary, simply is a waste of dollars. It's suggested you ask, and if they request fast delivery, by all means, do so. Most times, they won't have the time to look at your project for a week or two, so save the bucks.

Again, the best avenue is someone who can front you in the door. When they have made the initial contact, simply send your plan with a brief cover letter and keep your fingers crossed. If you haven't had a reply in two or three weeks, a progress call is appropriate. Calling every few days will only alienate the initial screener of your project and assure that your plan will fall deeper into the bottom of the pile.

However, don't get discouraged after all this discussion about how hard it is to get a receptive ear. Remember, venture capital firms need product, too; it's just the realization of the old axiom that "entrepreneurs run and money walks."

How to Present to Venture Capitalists

Assume a venture capitalist, after what seems an eternity, expresses a further interest in your project. What is likely to happen next? A phone conversation with a request for some more information will most likely occur and include the subject of a face-to-face meeting. There's always the chance that it will be held at your facilities, but again, the most likely scenario is that you will be requested to visit them in their offices.

This initial meeting is a get-acquainted session and the venture capitalist's first "size up the management" opportunity. First impressions count; be prompt, have clean fingernails, suit and tie, be relaxed, smile, and come well-rehearsed. This presentation should be 15 to 30 minutes and modeled after your business plan. The venture capitalists simply want to hear your business story in your own words. They will have read your plan thoroughly, a couple of times, and will have prepared numerous questions. But first off, they want to size you up.

Don't Bring Your Attorney Along. Don't—I repeat, do not—bring your attorney or accountant along. They talk too much about the wrong things. No intermediaries at all is preferable; remember, the venture capitalists want to become intimately familiar with the management team. If there is going to be a wedding, they are going to marry the bride, not the bride's father or mother.

You're seeking to impart your basic philosophy and display the capabilities and skills of your management team. You can do this by making a straightforward presentation that is clear-cut, having the technical aspects simplified. Venture capitalists need to understand the nature of technology and the current and future stages of Ultrapreneurial development. Discuss practical applications and substantiate the size of your markets. You must indicate an in-depth knowledge of your competition by discussing their strengths and weaknesses, followed by why you can replace them and how you are going to do it.

When talking about your management team, describe specific experience that makes each of you uniquely qualified, especially as to what is applicable during the last five years. Note where and how your team has been assembled, how you have worked together in the past, and how you see individual skills complementing each other on your project. If you have a missing management link, discuss it frankly and suggest that you're open for recommendations from them. All venture capital firms have a vast knowledge and network to identify and obtain key management players.

Be Realistic about Your Financials.   Regarding the financial aspects of your project, the keys are truthfulness and reality. If your operations are existing, discuss the good and bad points. Talk about where you made mistakes and blew some time and dollars and where you're really proud of belt-tightening; give some examples of the ingenious methods you used to economize. Be realistic in your projections. Keep in mind that the venture capitalists probably have some practical experience in your industry area. If not, they definitely have seen many more optimistic projections that resulted in bad start-ups than you have. Worst, best, and most likely scenarios aren't bad, but every projection has got to be backed with detailed assumptions. Assumptions can make or break the creditability of any projections. Be sure yours are well grounded.

In summary, the venture capitalist has the following objectives:

1. To meet you and your key team members face to face

2. To obtain more information on the business and how it is going to make money for all parties

3. To determine if they feel they can "cut a deal"

What to Ask a Venture Capitalist

It takes two to tango and the mating dance with a venture capital firm is no exception. If they invest in your company, you're assured of a long-term arrangement. You need their money but you will also want to take advantage of a lot of other aspects of their services. This means you will want to qualify your get-along ability in the early stages of your contact; they understand this. In fact, they respect this approach and are most willing to help create a relationship that is compatible in personalities and style.

Ask them about their investment philosophies. This is very important to the Ultrapreneur who is seeking a predefined harvest. If the venture fund's strategy is to harvest only by public offering, and you feel your most likely early harvest will come from being acquired, you need to reach an acceptable understanding right from the start. Just because they don't agree with you doesn't mean they can't help. There is a good chance they can give you a very good referral to a fund who subscribes to your way of thinking.

Also talk with them about how they feel they can help you. What resources can they bring to the table to complement and enhance your plan? Get a feel for participation on an ongoing basis. Will they be active or passive investors? Do they want a seat on your board of directors and how often will they require what type of reporting?

Inquire about their investors. Are there some who are in the same industrial area as your operations? Are there any strategic partnering possibilities with their investors, portfolio companies, or other deals they are involved with?

Think of it this way. You have a right to a prenuptial agreement just like they have the right to a marriage license. It behooves both parties to gain a deep insight as to the boundaries of the relationship, and the first meeting is the best way to start the process.

What to Expect from the Meeting

Toward the end of the meeting, don't expect immediate decisions or even a lot of indications of where they are at. If you have to know today, their answer is NO.

Typically, they had asked you to bring along some additional documentation to the meeting; if their first impression is favorable, they will ask you to send in some more data as a result of the meeting. The most common response from them to your question "What do you think?" is "We'll be in touch."

What Will Happen Next?

Proceeding on the premise that the venture capitalist is positively disposed toward funding your project, the next step is to conduct preliminary negotiations on the deal. This means that the venture capital firm has completed some additional background-information gathering and is at least comfortable enough to want to be sure that you and they can arrive at some basic agreement as to the valuation and structure of their potential investment.

The venture capitalist is not necessarily cavalier at this point, however; because of their experience, they have a pretty good determination as to what it will take before they agree to invest. A very important point for the Ultrapreneur to understand is that the venture capitalist is not inclined to "beat" the Ultrapreneur into a submissive equity position which the Ultrapreneur does not want or will be uncomfortable with over the lifetime of the project. Venture capitalists attempt to create a win-win deal. They are fully aware that the Ultrapreneur can get back at them while operating the company. They simply have investment parameters and return goals to obtain, and they are keenly interested in exceeding these goals with yours and all investments they make.

Be reasonable in your expectations; listen to their side, their judgments, and then negotiate. Negotiate means give and take. There will be a lot of points to review and a lot of areas for open discussion. The venture capitalist will provide the basic format in the form of a letter of commitment. Follow his or her lead. Discussions don't mean conclusions, and often you'll find ways to enhance your position that turn out far better than you originally thought.

The Commitment Letter: Its Five Sections

Commitment letters come in many forms, from one-pagers to terribly long and complex documents. The subject is too vast to detail in this book and there are just too many variables. Suffice it to say that the Ultrapreneur must have legal counsel involved prior to final signing. It's again suggested that you let the venture capitalist take the lead. They have their preferred format, and your chore is to respond. There are five basic sections to any commitment letter.

Terms. This section will state the terms on which the investment will be made, including loans and equity options. The intent is to state what the venture capital firm intends to do and what it intends to receive for doing it.

Collateral and Security. This section will declare how the investment, loan, and/or equity option will be collateralized. In most cases, this will originally be all assets with some contingencies.

Conditions of the Investment. This section sets forth the conditions which surround the investment. This will include financial and management reporting requirements as well as ratio and default requirements.

Representations. This section includes many different representations that you or the company makes, such as corporate standing, lawsuits, tax positions, investment to date, use of proceeds, criminal convictions, and more. Do not sign any representations that are not truthful or that you cannot fulfill.

Conditions of Commitment. These are conditions that if not met, void the venture capital firm's commitment to fund your project, such as: you may be required to pay them a fee or reimburse certain expenses; all legal documents will be acceptable to them; their due diligence meets with their approval.

This letter of commitment, also referred to as a *Term Sheet,* will be the basis of what is called an *investment memorandum.* The investment memorandum will be the final document that is signed after their completion of additional due diligence. For now, your concern should be to negotiate every item in the commitment letter, but don't get bent out of shape about every detail. The venture capital firm will be reasonable about all the items being discussed.

Due Diligence:
A Complete Checkup

To the uninitiated, few things are more mysterious than the investment or due diligence process. What goes on? What is it comprised of? How long does it take? In fact, what is it?

Due diligence is simply the process of conducting background checks and representations made by the company. It's verifying employment and education, as well as general reputations of the management team. It's studying and reviewing the industry complete with market analysis. It's verifying facts and statements made in the business plan. It's a detailed review of the proposed project, seeking misrepresentations, mistakes, and an independent appraisal of potential.

This is a process that can't be rushed. Every venture capital firm has their own format and schedule. Considering a lot of variables, they will require additional visits with the management team, visit office or plant sites if they exist, ask questions about your management intentions, and ask questions about your proposal.

They Will Check Everything. They will investigate the individuals; check credit records; talk with references, past employers and employees, fellow workers, acquaintances, suppliers, customers, and maybe even neighbors. In some cases they may even request personality or psychological testing. They are seeking to verify experience, leadership qualities, team building abilities, honesty, reliability, guts, and vision.

They will conduct industry studies pertaining to the business by talking with competitors, suppliers, and potential customers. They will query any industry-relevant associations or membership groups. They are looking to verify the uniqueness of the product (is it truly unique or is it old hat in the industry?), trying to determine if your approach is unique or just a variation on an existing theme. They will most likely bring in several consultants, maybe question government sources, attorneys, accountants, bankers, and other venture capital firms.

Recognize that all this sleuthing will have a positive result. Ofttimes, they will uncover information you weren't aware of, and most times their due diligence enables them to better assist and work with you.

How Long Will This Take?   Surprisingly, four to eight weeks is the average. The more you can cooperate, the faster and easier it is for them. If they request information or data sources, reply quickly. They're just as anxious as you are to get this project off dead-center and on the way to providing everyone involved with outrageous rewards.

The Marriage

After the completion of the due diligence process, the next step is the close. As mentioned earlier, this is orchestrated by the investment memorandum. This is a more detailed document than the letter of intent but will cover all the items in the letter of intent. Just more t's and i's. Obviously, you'll need an attorney, preferably one who is experienced in this type of transaction. Be sure you're okay with the terms; you'll have plenty of opportunity to raise questions, make changes, and clear up any misunderstandings during the draft stages and prior to the actual close. A final note: Keep your harvest goals in mind.

The Ongoing Relationship

Trust is the biggie. Make sure you establish it from the start and work hard to maintain it. Keep lines of communication open at all times. This doesn't mean there won't be disagreements, even of the heart-stopping form, but don't let these disintegrate to silence. Use their board of director member as you intend to use all members—working. If you have questions, ask. If you have problems, discuss them. They have lots of experience in assisting companies and appreciate management that will listen to their advice. Their single underlying objective is growth. They want to liquefy their investment worse than you do. Be open, honest, and Ultrapreneuring.

Traditional Venture Capital Funds

These are professionally managed companies who manage high-risk investment portfolios. Their capital is supplied by institutions such as insurance companies, pension funds, and limited partnerships.

Amount available	Usually $500,000 and up; occasionally for start-ups
Structure	Convertible preferred stock
Cost	Generally a minimum 30 percent per annum compounded interest

Proceeds	For very high growth to sales of $50 million
Advantages	Large amount of capital available; easy second- and third-round sources
Disadvantages	Must have high growth potential; require high equity give-up

The Preferred Investment Vehicle

Regardless of the source of your financing—family and friends, angels, or venture capital—you will need some vehicle, forms, or set of papers to make it all nice and legal. On the surface, it would seem that if you're going to sell stock, you could take the investors' check and give them a stock certificate. Or if it was to be a loan, just take the check and sign a note. Unfortunately, it's not quite that simple. And in fact, you don't want it to be.

Today's "sue the buzzards" mentality causes some real problems for Ultrapreneurs when it comes to raising money. The main problem is the Ultrapreneurs themselves. Considering their natural propensity and rightful enthusiasm for their project, they tend to oversell. This is okay if everything works out the way it is planned. But we all know that Murphy will enter the program and that not always what is well ends well. In the worst cases, your company may not survive.

The problem then becomes that the friendly original investor is not the least bit happy about the fact that *you* did not perform up to expectations or lost all their money. Their fee-happy lawyer is more than pleased to take on the case of suing you because you said there wasn't any significant competition, that your engineer was a genius and couldn't miss on inventing the black box, that you had umpteen customers lined up, and the endless list goes on. What it comes down to is your word against theirs, and most likely they have more money (which is why you went to them in the first place) and they can afford the legal upfront fees that will be repaid when they sell your house.

There is a solution to this dilemma, a document that has been blessed by our governmental bodies, that acts like a sort of insurance policy for Ultrapreneurs to protect them against disgruntled investors, be they friend, family, angel, or venture capitalist. It's called Regulation D and is the subject of the next section.

Regulation D

For some entrepreneurs, the best vehicle to accomplish initial equity financing is through the use of Regulation D, which is a limited offer and sale of their company's stock, or securities, without registration under the Federal Securities Act of 1933.

Simply stated, it's against the law to sell stock unless you are licensed to do so or can qualify for an exemption from the Securities and Exchange Commission (SEC) and the various states securities commissions' rules. The very worst that can happen is that you will have to pay penalties or you can be put in jail. For instance, Section 5 of the 1933 Securities Act ('33 Act) clearly states that "it's unlawful for any person, directly or indirectly to sell a security unless a registration statement has been filed, or to sell or deliver a security after the sale unless a registration statement is in *effect* (emphasis added)." The '33 Act does, however, contain some exemptions, but they fall short of really helping many small companies.

Reg D Is the Exception

That concern made clear by small business is the sum and substance of Regulation D, commonly referred to as Reg D, which became effective April 15, 1982. It is not just another exemption. It is *the* exemption for small businesses that want to raise money by selling some of their stock or for incurring some forms of debt. It is also a form of taking a company public without the burden and expense of a full registration with the SEC. Reg D should serve as a welcome alternative for many Ultrapreneurs.

For many years, and justifiable yet today, the principals of many small U.S. businesses have complained about the expense and trouble of complying with government regulation. It goes back 200 years, to Adam Smith's push for a new era in British economic policy. Smith sought to strip away the shackles of government regulations and constraining ideology, and replace them with the freedom of individual initiative and economic enterprise. Well, some things can't be rushed. The same utterance came from former president Ronald Reagan, when he said in 1978, "For several decades, an ever-larger role of the federal government has sapped the economic vitality of the Nation." The result of this early Reaganomics movement was to remove some of the federal restraints on raising capital. In 1980, Congress enacted the Small Business Investment Incentive Act.

One of the agencies affected by the act was the SEC, which promulgated Reg D. This regulation, along with continuing revisions, broadened the exemptions from SEC's regulations, thereby easing restrictions on equity fundraising.

Reg D established a new set of guidelines that replaced older rules that had been adopted under the '33 Act. Those rules required full disclosure on and registration of securities prior to their being sold to the public. The public in this case is defined as anyone not directly associated with the issuing company. It was proposed that the new federal rules be uniformly adopted by all the states, thus following the Reaganomics trend toward deregulation. Reg D returned many responsibilities of government to the states. Many states have been slow to adopt Reg D, and some have chosen to design their own version. Consequently, entrepreneurs who are contemplating this type of action had better check their own state's securities regulations before relying completely on Reg D.

The Regulation

Reg D reduces the registration requirements and costs, and has opened the door to substantial exemptions to the '33 Act. The technical provisions, which were always subject to varying interpretations, have also been eased. The process now is simpler, which is relative, and has, in turn, lessened the chance that the offerer (the company) may be subject to recision (giving back monies raised) to the offeree (investor) if a technical provision happens to be mistakenly violated.

Some risks continue under Reg D, but compliance is significantly easier than before Reg D. A major, major point is that *by complying with Reg D, it provides the company, its officers, and its directors with an insurance policy of sorts regarding disclosure.*

There Are Six Basic Rules

Reg D consists of six basic rules. The first three are concerned with definitions, conditions, and notification. Rule 501 covers the definitions of the various terms used in the rules. Rule 502 sets forth the conditions, limitations, and information requirements for the exemptions in Rules 504, 505, and 506. Rule 503 contains the SEC notification requirements. The last three rules deal with the specifics of raising money under Reg D. Rule 504 generally pertains to securities sales up to $1 million. Rule 505 applies to offerings from $1 million to $5 million. Rule 506 is for securities offerings exceeding $5 million. Here's the details and how they work.

Rule 501

This first rule defines the terms used in the regulations that are applicable to the offering and sales under Reg D. The following are key definitions:

Accredited Investors. The SEC has long had a definition for accredited investors—sophisticated or wealthy enough to be able to assess an offer or stand the risk of the investment without further information about the investment. Prior to Rule 501, it was up to an attorney, accountant, or stockbroker to decide whether a potential investor met the very vague SEC requirements. Now the rule spells it out. Accredited investors include:

- Banks
- Savings and loans
- Credit unions
- Corporations and partnerships with total assets in excess of $5 million
- Brokers/dealers
- Insurance companies
- Registered investment companies
- Nonprofit organizations with over $5 million in assets
- Business Development Companies (as defined under the Investment Companies Act of 1940)
- Small Business Investment Companies (SBICs)
- Minority Enterprise Small Business Investment Companies (MESBICs)

And more applicable for most entrepreneurial efforts to raise money privately:

- Directors and officers of the company
- Individuals whose net worth exceeds $1 million
- Individuals whose income exceeds $200,000 annually (during the last 2 years as well as expected in the current year)
- Individuals whose joint income with a spouse exceeds $300,000 for 2 years

The term *accredited investors* surfaces again in Rules 504, 505, and 506. In conjunction with accredited investors, the term *reasonably believed* is often mentioned. These terms will be used extensively by a company's legal counsel as these persons and the company have a legal obligation to declare (reasonably believe) if an accredited investor meets the requirements of Rule 501. If the company actually believes, and can prove it had reason to believe, it would have no continuing liability as far as accredited investors are concerned. As an extra precaution, however, the company should have the investor attest to the accredited investor facts and qualifications in writing. This accredited investor document should be part of every offering memorandum.

Purchaser Representatives.   A purchaser representative is a person who is not an affiliate, director, or other employee of the company, or an owner of 10 percent or more of the company, or an owner of any class of the equity securities of the company. Furthermore, such persons should possess sufficient knowledge and experience in financing and business matters to make them capable of evaluating, on their own or together with the purchaser, the merits and the risks of the prospective investment. Additionally, they must acknowledge in writing that they are acting as a purchaser representative, and they must make certain written disclosures as to the identification of the ultimate purchaser. This particularly applies to syndicates, multiple syndicates, and partnership holdings.

Number of Purchasers. Rules 505 and 506 limit the number of purchasers, but accredited investors are not included in the total. The rules further state that the company may sell its securities to an unlimited number of accredited investors in addition to a specified number of other purchasers, such as officers and directors. This also applies to *loosely related parties,* which in some cases may be counted as a single purchaser.

Rule 502

This rule establishes the general conditions pertaining to the exemptions. Several areas are notable:

- Qualifying for an exemption under Reg D is not dependent on the size of the company.
- The exemptions are applicable only to the issuer and not its affiliates, such as subsidiaries, or to others, or for resale of the issuer's securities.
- Some offerings of the "same" securities may be considered as a single offering (that is, *integrated*) if they are made within six months of the start or termination of the Reg D offering. This can save legal and registration costs, but there are technicalities involved, so it's best for the entrepreneur to seek knowledgeable legal advice on how best to handle integration.
- To further clarify the somewhat confusing interpretation of Reg D. There can be no general solicitation or quasi-public advertising connected with the offering. However, to add to the confusion, Rule 504 explains how this type of situation can be circumvented.
- Another general condition is that certain procedures must be followed by the issuer to guarantee that the securities are not being purchased for resale. The issuer must make certain that the purchaser is not an underwriter or an agent for an underwriter. Further, the issuer must provide a written disclosure of this resale limitation. And the actual stock certificate itself must contain a legend specifying the resale restriction. This may seem like a no-win situation, but take heart—Rule 504 contains ways of avoiding this problem also.

Rule 503

This is the rule that sets forth the information that must be filed with the SEC. It also specifies the timing and the type of forms that must be used in the filing.

The company (issuer) must file five copies of the notice of sales of its securities with the SEC on the required Form D, one of which must be hand-signed. This filing must be made within 15 days after the first sale, and thereafter every 6 months, with a final filing within 30 days of the last sale. Compliance in filing is extremely critical. Should the issuers not comply, they run the risk of the SEC rescinding the entire offering and requiring that all monies received be returned to the stock purchasers if they so desire.

Also, the SEC has the right to request, in writing, that the issuer provide the SEC with copies of all information provided to the purchasers of the securities. This makes the information public record. However, the SEC rarely takes this action. Even so, don't bet on it.

Rule 504

This rule is considered by many as the perfect answer for the company just starting out that needs to raise less than $1 million but can't afford to go through the whole SEC registration process. Until they grow to a point where they can afford it, Rule 504 offers such companies an out:

- An exemption to raise up to $1 million
- No disclosure criteria
- Few general solicitation and resale restrictions
- No limit as to the number of investors

Actually, Congress's original intent for Rule 504 was to "set aside a clear and workable exemption for small issuers to be regulated by state blue sky requirements, but by the same token, to be subjected to federal anti-fraud provisions and civil liability provisions." Rule 504 exemption is provided for almost any type of organization, including corporations, partnerships, trusts, or other entities. However, it is not applicable to companies already reporting to the SEC (subject to the '34 Act) or investment companies.

You Cannot Exceed $1 Million. The total offering amount under Rule 504 can be up to $1 million in a 12-month period, less the aggregate offering of all securities sold within 12 months before the start of a 504 offering. So, if a company has raised $100,000 in pre-private money in the previous 12 months, it can still raise up to $900,000 without being accused of breaking the rules, or integration. Generally speaking, there are *no* specific disclosure requirements under Rule 504 (disclosing what the company is about, what it intends to do, or who is connected with it). This means that, theoretically, an issuer can have a purchaser sign a subscription agreement and purchase stock without any information about the company being disclosed. However, the rule is dependent on the blue-sky laws of each state in which the securities are offered. This means that if a state's blue-sky rules require disclosure, it must be provided regardless of Rule 504.

Rule 504 also provides that at least $500,000 of securities must be sold pursuant to a registration under a state's securities law. Consequently, an offer must comply with the blue-sky laws of each individual state in which it is offered. In many states, this negates the effective simplicity of Rule 504 and the federal government's intent, because many states' blue-sky laws arc more restrictive than Reg D.

A word of caution to the Ultrapreneur—regardless of the amount of disclosure the issuer is willing to provide, Rule 504 does not dismiss the issuer from the federal requirements, nor is there an exemption from the fraud provisions, including the areas of material omissions or misstatements. The penalties for noncompliance are severe, including monetary fines and mandatory jail sentences.

Commissionable. One interesting aspect of Rule 504 is the provision for payment of commissions. It was reasoned that if broker/dealers got involved with the selling of 504s, they would provide an extra safeguard for investors. Additionally, it was felt that removing the ban on commissions, which can be as high as the market would bear (generally 15 to 20 percent), would bring the expertise and sales organization of the brokerage firms and investment bankers to the aid of the small business persons. Unfortunately, the measure hasn't had the desired effect, except for a few smaller brokerage firms. It seems the medium-size and large Wall Street firms simply could not justify the expense required to merchandise offerings under $1 million.

The one area in which Rule 504 has helped is in allowing the issuer to *generally solicit,* or advertise, for subscribers to an offering. Some states have been quite lenient in allowing it. However, in practice, very few issuers have advertised their offerings in newspapers or through other common media as was expected.

Number of Investors. With its limited disclosure requirements, Rule 504 also allows an issuer to sell securities to an unlimited number of investors. Theoretically, a company could raise $1 million by selling its stock at a penny a share to 100 million different investors. Obviously, the economics are not too attractive, but there's no rule that stops an issuer from selling

$500 blocks of stock to 2000 investors. Rule 504 is the only rule under Reg D that permits an unlimited number of investors.

A final note on Rule 504 is that the exemption provides for sales of securities of either debt or equity. This opens the door for combinations of both via *convertible debentures*. By way of explanation, convertible debentures are a debt issue (debenture) that is convertible to a preferred or, most commonly, common stock at some future date, usually at a predetermined price.

Rule 505

Compared to Rule 504, Rule 505 is comparatively hassle-free.

- It exempts offers and sales of issuers other than investment companies.

- The offering in total cannot exceed $5 million during a 12-month period, less what has been raised by pre-private money, as mentioned in the discussion of Rule 504, plus inclusion of any future offerings contemplated in the 12 months following the last sale under Rule 505.

- The sales cannot be made to more than 35 nonaccredited investors and they must be accompanied by the same kind of disclosure information as is required in Part I of the filing for an S-18 registration, which is the SEC filing document for a company going public.

- Sales can be made to an unlimited number of accredited investors.

- No general solicitation (advertising) is allowed.

- Rule 505 carries the same filing notification requirements as Rule 504.

- Rule 505 carries a disqualification from using the exemption if the issuer, defined as just about anybody connected with the company, including officers, directors, principals, or underwriters, are "bad boys," as defined in Rule 252(c)–(f) of Regulation A. Loosely, a bad boy is a person who has incurred the wrath of the SEC for the potential (without necessarily having been convicted) of having committed a securities violation. However, the SEC can waive the misconduct disqualification. The issuer should seek advice of counsel if anyone connected with the company has had previous problems with the SEC.

- The same fraud, misstatement, and material omissions compliance apply as for Rule 504.

Obviously, the largest drawback to selling stock under Rule 505 is the limited number of nonaccredited investors allowed, which naturally means that the average investment per investor has to be considerably more than under Rule 504.

Rule 506

This is the last rule under Regulation D.

- It exempts offers and sales of issuers, including sales by investment and reporting companies.

- The offering amount must be for offerings over $5 million, with no time restrictions.

- Sales cannot be made to more than 35 nonaccredited investors. The nonaccredited investors must be capable of evaluating the merits and risks of the investment, and it is up to the issuer to verify that the investors are knowledgeable enough to make that evaluation.

- Sales can be made to an unlimited number of accredited investors.

- No general solicitation (advertising) is allowed.

- Rule 506 carries the same notification requirements as Rules 504 and 505, with the primary emphasis on filing every six months.

- Rule 506 does not contain "bad boy" disqualifications, but as in all Reg D rules, the SEC's antifraud provisions apply. This leads most issuers to voluntarily make relevant disclosures to safeguard against later charges by disgruntled investors that they were not informed of material facts.

Alternate Exemptions

The enactment of Regulation D in 1982 simplified and facilitated the registration process for selling securities. That's a good reason for entrepreneurs to strongly consider Reg D, or state equivalents, for fundraising efforts.

There are several other rules and exemptions that are worth looking into for the same reason. They are found under the headings of Intrastate Offerings and Regulation A.

As pointed out in the last section, the principal advantage of an exemption from registration is that the buy-and-sell transactions can take place as soon as the parties decide to proceed. It eliminates the necessity of preparing and filing a prospectus with the SEC, and it saves legal costs, plus accounting and registration fees.

Exemptions under the Securities Act of 1933 ('33 Act) are listed as exempted securities and exempted transactions. They can save both time and money. The only drawback is they take a legal genius to interpret them. They're full of loopholes, and the courts have shown no qualms about ruling *against* the entrepreneur in their interpretations. Regardless, the end results should make them worth pursuing. But since the whole area of exemptions is so complex, the Ultrapreneur should not proceed without first seeking the advice of qualified legal counsel to determine the best form of exemption to apply for. Here's what the exemptions do:

Exempted Securities

Section 3(a) of the '33 Act exempts a number of securities because of the particulars of the issuer. For example, federal, state, and local governments are exempted so as not to hamper their ability to secure financing. Religious, charitable, educational, and nonprofit organizations are exempted. Also exempted are securities that do not present a substantial risk to the investor, such as short-term notes, drafts, bills of exchange, and insurance policies (except variable annuities).

Exempted Transactions

Section 4 of the '33 Act exempts certain transactions from the provisions of Section 5, which says, in effect, that a registration with the SEC must take place every time a security is sold. Exempted are transactions by any person other than an issuer (company), underwriter, or broker/dealer. This is aimed at ordinary daily stock and bond sales by any shareholder. For example, if Mr. Jones owns 100 shares of IBM, he does not have to register the transaction of selling it to his broker.

Section 4 also exempts transactions by an issuer not involving any public offering (the private sale exemption). This is an extremely complex area. It is meant to exempt the owner of a business who is selling his or her business to another person or a small number of people (fewer than 35).

And finally, Section 4 permits broker/dealers to trade for their own account or as brokers for others (retail customers) without registration.

Some transactions are allowable for brokers to make without going through the whole registration process, such as those covered in Rule 144, which allows a broker to sell privately held securities of a public company after they have been held for the required holding period. This covers the sale of restricted stock without the requirement of registration.

There are several particular exemptions worth noting.

Intrastate Offerings

This exemption falls under Section 3(a)(11) and Rule 147. It exempts certain offerings from registration requirements of the '33 Act. It refers to "Any security which is a part of an issue offered and sold only to persons resident within a single State or Territory, where the issuer of such security is a person resident and doing business within, or if a corporation, incorporated by and doing business within, such State or Territory."

The SEC makes clear that the intrastate exemption is "intended to apply only to issues genuinely local in character, which represent local financing by local industries, carried out through local investment." It puts complete responsibility on the company to ascertain the residency of each and every purchaser. It's specific in that the selling of a single share out of state during the distribution periods may result in the entire issue being considered a violation of the '33 Act. Good faith on the issuer's part that the purchaser is a resident is no defense when it comes to the company's liability.

Briefly, the interstate exemptions specify:

- The offerings are allowed in only one state.
- The issuer must be a resident of the state.
- The issuer does a majority of its business in the state.
- There are no dollar restrictions.
- Financial sophistication of investors is not required.
- There are no SEC filing requirements.

Lest there be any confusion, the issuer, if a person (sole proprietorship, partnership), or a company (incorporated), must be resident in the state in which the securities are being offered. This means that the principal office *must* be located in the state.

To further clarify, "doing business" in the state is interpreted as deriving at least 80 percent of the company's consolidated gross revenues within the state, with at least 80 percent of its consolidated assets located within the state, and intending, and in fact using, 80 percent of the net proceeds derived from its offering in the state.

No Dollar Restrictions. There are also *no* restrictions as to the total dollar amount of monies that can be raised or as to the individual amounts that can be subscribed for. And there are *no* restrictions as to the number of investors that can subscribe to the offering. However, it must be stressed, the rules are strict that every investor *must* be a resident of and maintain his or her principal residence in the state.

The original purchaser/resident investor must also be made aware that he or she may not resell the securities until the distribution is complete, and the securities, according to the SEC, "come to rest in the hands of the resident investors." What's more, a precedent has been established in the courts that all of the stock must stay in the original state for as long as 1 to 2 years, depending on the court. That means if Ms. Smith, the purchaser/resident of the stock, decides to move out of the state before the waiting period has passed, she legally cannot take the stock out of the state, as that would be construed as an interstate purchase rather than as intrastate purchase.

The Issuer Has Some "Must Do's." It is the responsibility of the issuer to (1) obtain a written statement from each purchaser confirming the purchaser's residence, and (2) place a legend on the certificate or other documents attesting that the securities have not been registered under the '33 Act. The legend must also set forth the limitations on resale (as presented in the preceding paragraph). If the issuer does not transfers its own securities, stop transfer instructions must be issued to the transfer agent, or the issuer must make proper notations to the effect in its own records.

It is most important that the issuer disclose in writing the limitations on resale and include the legend and notation requirements in connection with any offer (prospectus) or sales of the securities in question. Substitute certificates must carry the same information.

A Word of Assurance Is in Order. If the issuer can prove he or she acted with diligence on these matters, it's unlikely that the '33 Act would be interpreted harshly by the courts.

As far as financial sophistication is concerned, there is no requirement. The company (issuer) has *no* responsibility to ascertain that the purchaser of its securities is a savvy investor. There are *no* accredited or nonaccredited investor rules. Furthermore, the disclosure requirements are nonrestrictive, and the amount of disclosure is left strictly up to the individual issuer. Naturally, the standard provisions for fraud, misstatements, and the omission of material information *do* apply.

Referring to the above, an SEC filing is not required. The insurer must only comply with the individual states' securities rules and regulations.

Finally, because of the leniency for intrastate offerings, some financial promoters create *shells*. They then sit on them for a year or two, after which they try to sell them to Ultrapreneurs as public company shells. That could spell trouble! These shells, although they are public, are only public in one state. If the purchaser (Ultrapreneur) intends to broaden the securities shareholder base to other states or intends to conduct business in other states, a registration will have to be made with the SEC, which is time-consuming and can be very, very expensive.

Regulation A Offerings

Regulation A is seldom used, mainly because in some instances, depending on the dollar amount of the issue, it requires registration with the SEC. Regulation A is available to all issuers except investment companies or issuers of fractional undivided oil and gas interests or other mineral rights. It provides exemption from registration for up to $1 million in a 12-month period. Reg A also contains "bad boy" provisions, which prohibit "use of the exemption if the issuer, its underwriter, or any of the directors, officers, or principals have engaged in certain specified acts of misconduct."

Reg A has *no* restrictions on the qualifications of the investor (accredited or nonaccredited) or on the number of investors. Additionally, there are *no* restrictions on the resale of the securities, and an issuer can do some forms of advertising and general solicitation. An offering circular is required unless the total offering is less than $100,000, and the offering must be filed with a regional office of the SEC. This registration requires submission of two years of financial statements, but they do not need to be audited. However, under blue-sky laws, most states require audited financials.

Another reason Reg A is used infrequently is that one of its sections refers to *sterilized* stock. It deals primarily with the issuer (company) that has been in existence for less than one year prior to the offering, but has not realized a net income from operations. It also concerns an issuer that was organized for more than one year, but has had no net income for at least one of the last two years. It says, in effect, that all securities issued to promoters, directors, officers, underwriters, dealers, and security salespersons must be counted as part of the monies that constitute the offering. Otherwise the stocks must be placed in *captivity* (sterilized and not useable). It makes for too many unhappy people among the principal performers.

Avoiding Integration

Ultrapreneurs (issuers) using Regulation D or one of the alternative exemption methods of private financing are exempted from many SEC rules, but they can't always have their cake and eat it too. Some proposed public companies have attempted to use a private exemption *intrastate* and then made a public offering *interstate*. If the offerings are found to be a part of the same transaction, that is a definite no. They must be completely separate transactions.

An offering may be considered exempt in isolation, but it becomes nonexempt if *integration* is determined due to its being connected with other offerings. The SEC knows all the tricks. If there is even the remotest possibility that an exemption may be misconstrued because of an offering made at a later date, the transaction could be considered integrated. The best way to avoid this is to secure the advice of qualified legal counsel regarding integration and multistep financing plans. Or it could easily result in a lot of time, effort, money, and even the company down the drain.

A Final Reg D Note

As this book is going to press (Spring 1993), the SEC has proposed, and in some cases adopted, some new rules and regulations regarding both Reg A and Reg D. In some areas, the new rules are less restrictive than the basics discussed here. *However,* please note that many states' securities commissions are rejecting the federal rules and are choosing to adopt state blue-sky laws that are much more restrictive. Ultrapreneurs are strongly advised to check with qualified legal counsel on the fine points and most up-to-date rules and regulations as they may pertain to their particular project. You are assured that some form of a Regulation D type of investment vehicle is available for your moneyraising efforts. Use it—it could save your whole company.

Cashflow: It's Your Lifeblood

Cash is king for Ultrapreneurs. And cashflow is the bedrock of the kingdom. It's the lifeblood of an Ultragrowth company. A company without cash is no company. During the startup or concept stage, the founders usually trade off their time for cash. However, once the company is up and running, when full-time employees are hired, the Ultrapreneur has got to have cash to not only continue, but also to fuel the growth.

During the concept stage, it's usually the founders' personal cash or savings that enable them to write the business plan to obtain seed stage financing. Assuming they can then obtain the cash to execute the seed stage plan, their concern becomes conserving the cash to enable them to meet the objectives and benchmarks and still have enough cash while they pursue product development stage financing. This is a critical stage for almost all Ultragrowth companies. This development stage of financing, almost without exception, takes longer than anticipated; as many Ultrapreneurs learn, having a commitment is not the same as having the cash in hand. Several months commonly expire between signing an agreement and receiving the actual funds.

Rapid expansion has many cashflow needs, and in each of these there are cashflow traps. The most prominent, and the ones that can be systematically tracked, semi-influenced, and controlled, are inventory and receivables.

Inventory: You Have to Control It

Uncontrolled inventory really affects Ultragrowth. Scores of companies have been bitten big-time by this. It can come at you from two different angles. One is high growth rates on complicated products where the company has to carry large levels of various parts—all bought in large quantities so as to get discounted price breaks—to enable it to meet increasing customer demand. The second can happen when sales suddenly take a dive. The company ends up with large amounts of finished product on hand, no sales, and the cash is all invested in the ballooned inventory. This can also happen if the company's marketing program is dependent on it being a significant credit supplier to its customers by "floor planning" product, offering consignment, or extended credit terms. More than one company has found itself in the position of having to let key people go because it wasn't able to meet payrolls because its money was tied up in inventory. You can't eat or pay people with inventory. It's a high price to pay for failing to protect cash reserves for temporary glitches in sales.

Accounts Receivable: Control Them Also

A second great cash consumer is accounts receivable. A lot of Ultrapreneuring companies start out to be manufacturing or service companies and end up, much to their dismay, as banks. The stories are many; the tales of woe may vary in detail, but the substance is the same. The product or service is hot, everyone wants to buy, the Ultrapreneur wants to sell. Things go along smoothly for the first couple months, dealers buy and pay timely. The company is shipping increasing amounts of product or proving burgeoning amounts of service. All of a sudden, dealers' or customers' payments slow down. The first month or two, the company, in its Ultragrowth headset, doesn't notice. They're too caught up in the euphoria of their success, and too busy producing, shipping, or delivering. At the first sign of trouble, it's very hard to say no to customers who tell you how much they like your product, how if they just had the next shipment in they can turn it over immediately and send you your receivable payment. First thing you know, six months of this have gone by and the Ultrapreneur is blindsided by no cashflow. People have to be laid off, payables get extended, and rampant rumors start throughout the industry on how the entrepreneurial star is having money problems. This compounds the situation, in that formerly valued customers now determine to drag out their payments even longer on the chance that the company may not make it. Guess what? The Ultrapreneur doesn't make it. All because of cashflow.

Here Are Some Cashflow Pointers

Entrepreneurs tend to ignore cashflow where Ultrapreneurs prepare for it. They prepare by having a top accounting person on their team who puts superinventory, receivable, and cashflow management systems in place. This is backed up by the knowledge that Ultragrowth companies always need more money than they can generate internally. Inventory and receivable money has to come from outside sources. And the time to line up these sources is prior to a screaming need for them.

The Ultrapreneuring business plan should forecast this need. It should take into account when and how much extra debt cash is needed between probable equity financings. Financial management will start romancing these sources early on by supplying a continual stream of updated information which keeps these sources in the know. This way there's no surprises, there's a prebuilt familiarity with management and the company's operations, and no delays in obtaining the financing to continue to support Ultragrowth. These sources are familiar:

Professional venture capital (for subordinated interim debt)

Debtors (banks, SBA, individuals)

Credit companies (commercial)

Suppliers (for extended payment terms)

Customers (payments in advance)

Factors (high-cost loan programs)

Fixed-asset-based lenders (frees up operating cash)

Here's a Cashflow Tip.   This can be applied to almost any type of debt financing. It's called *skipped-payment loans.* This is especially useful for Ultrapreneurs who operate seasonal businesses. If you find you have difficulty making fixed loan payments 12 months of the year, many financing institutions will permit you to skip predesignated payments. In effect, this allows you to customize your payment schedule to cashflows.

The basic plan is ideal for companies in the construction industry. The company makes eight or nine monthly payments, skipping three or four months in the normally slow winter months. The company ends up paying more interest over an extended loan period, but it does help cashflow. An alternative is to double-up on some monthly payments when cashflow is highest. The point is, don't just accept traditional lending practices; be Ultrapreneurially innovative. You'll be surprised at the results.

Cashflow management is not just a key to successful Ultrapreneuring; it's a *must.* It's not just another part of the financial program; it's *critical.* It's not just a couple more pages in the financial projections; it's *integral* to the plan. It's not just a problem for the comptroller; it's *solution planning* by the Chief Financial Officer. The Ultrapreneur has to control and preserve the cashflow lifeline.

As We've Said—Use Both

Entrepreneurs often become shortsighted in their search for financing. Ultraprencurs, on the other hand, recognize that the secret is to consider all available resources. They recognize that there are two basic choices, debt and equity, and that most successful financings are completed by using both of them. Many of the available resources have been reviewed in these chapters, from the various *forms* of debt financing, including subordinated debt, to the many different *sources* of debt financing. Equity sources have been covered, with discussion on angels, venture capital, and a review of Regulation D and several alternatives. Ultrapreneurs recognize that the financing of their companies, if not a full-time occupation, is at minimum a full-time *pre*occupation. It requires the relentless pursuit of cashflow to survive till harvest time.

9

Making It Happen—
Ultrapreneurial Style

*Those who have supreme skill use strategy
to bend others without coming to conflict.*
SUN TZU

Financing obtained, the Ultrapreneur's challenge is making it happen—
simply, executing the business plan—flawlessly.

"Simply" is obviously an understatement, as is "flawlessly." There is also a
challenge in writing about making it happen. How does one go about
explaining an extremely complicated process in terms that can apply to the
variety of readers of this book? The subject is one of many books; however,
there are some points that are of particular importance to the Ultrapreneur
and they are covered in this chapter.

The Secrets Are Several

Planning is one. The Ultrapreneurial planning process needs to be taught
and passed on to become a part of the culture of the company. It's one of
the steps that's very important to Ultrapreneurial success. Many studies
have shown that most people don't plan, set goals (even personal), or establish objectives. Some reasons are listed in Figure 9-1.

The Ultrapreneur can't afford to have nonplanners on their team. They
need to know about team members' planning abilities early on by getting

193

Why People Don't Plan

Adopting a plan means establishing goals, determining priorities, making choices, and then making commitments. Some people just aren't capable of making commitments In their lives or in the lives of others. Consequently, they just refuse to plan, they let others plan for them, and then they react. In business, this is called management by crisis.

For other nonplanners, planning takes the fun and surprise out of life. They prefer the challenge of playing catch-up. It's a competitive world where they feel they excel best when under pressure to perform. This type of player may win a game, but loses the season.

Another lack-of-planning person may be that way because planning makes them nervous, creates tension and a fear of failure. Having to work under planned conditions causes mental and sometimes physical stress. These anxiety-inducing conditions, as a result of planning, just aren't worth it to these people.

Figure 9-1.

them into the planning process. If they show a reluctance to making plans, they also won't be able to assist in carrying them out. Nonplanners can't work for Ultrapreneurs. Ultrapreneurs plan, they insist their team members plan, and they insist that planning be pushed all the way down until it permeates the whole organization.

The Ultrapreneurial planning process is characterized first and foremost by flexibility. The flexibility comes into play when one considers that the plan has to be executed with a lot of common sense to allow for constant change. However, the change has to keep in mind the short- and longer-term goals of the Ultrapreneurial plan. More important, the established benchmarks still must be hit. It's called hitting target dates and performance objectives while maintaining flexibility.

A second secret to making it happen revolves around the old physics law that every action causes a reaction. These actions and reactive forces either steer or force the company toward success or failure, toward completing objectives called for in benchmarks, or missing them in timetables. The Ultrapreneurial challenge is to create *success forces* as opposed to failure activities—in other words, empowering management techniques.

The reason a team is established is to serve this purpose: to first realistically establish these targets for each management discipline and then track them religiously. They are moving targets, and there are many of them. In the beginning, they center around engineering, or systems for service companies. As production begins, the target may be suppliers and keeping them in line.

Administratively, it may be assuring that the paperwork flow doesn't develop a bottleneck stoppage. Some of these targets move slowly and need constant urging; others, which are often worth more, move fast, and are harder to hit. An example could be a newly discovered prospective customer who is about to make a purchase decision, and your engineering department has to determine if your existing product can be altered to fit their particular requirements. Further, manufacturing has to cost out the profitability, production has to determine if they can deliver, and marketing has to be sure your product design will fit the customer's needs. The fast-moving targets are obviously harder to hit. The challenge is constant change and the Ultrapreneurial team has to be prepared to take on increasingly tougher tasks as it is racking up Ultragrowth.

Breaking Out the Planning Process

Although in the planning process the Ultrapreneurial team has created a business plan, this is really the big-picture plan. It contains a few pages of the objectives and how they will be reached for each of the aspects of the company. But it doesn't show much detail. It doesn't break out specifics for each managed area. This information comes in detailed operating plans. These plans should be prepared by the individuals responsible, most likely vice presidents of respective areas like marketing, administration, production, or research.

Planning is the way that corporate goals set at higher levels become activities further down. As this planning process is pushed further down the organizational chart, it's helpful that the individuals involved in originating these departmental plans have a basic understanding of the planning process, purpose, and criteria involved. It's up to the Ultrapreneur to make this planning process happen by education and delegation.

Getting Clear on the Difference between Administrative and Operational Planning

The process of setting objectives is actually the starting point of planning. The objective-setting is determined and set forth in the company's business plan. Planning tends to be divided into two principal phases, administrative and operative. Administrative planning is concerned with determining bases of action, over a period of time, for the company and its various elements. It has greater futurity than operative planning as it deals with longer periods of one, two, or more years. Since the accuracy of foresight tends to vary inversely with the timespan covered, the administrative plan must be stated in more general terms, and it must be capable of modification if it is to be adaptable to changes in conditions. In other words, the Ultrapreneurial administration plan must be flexible.

Operative planning is concerned with determining bases of action to accomplish specific projects or undertakings. Operative plans deal with less futurity and they are ordinarily programmed within the time period covered by related administrative plans. Detailed operative plans are developed to support administrative plans. The Ultrapreneur is concerned with getting good operational plans developed by the people involved in executing them. This is part of creating a management system because the benchmarks contained in an operating plan automatically indicate timetables that require reporting and consequently imply accountability.

Operational Planning: Making Your Dreams Come True

Operational planning is a design for getting a person or a group from a particular point to some preestablished and clearly defined goal. It is the business of making desires and dreams come true. It involves deciding what goals are sought and then specifying the steps needed to reach them. Operational planning should be directly linked to control processes—to feedback, reevaluating the accuracy of the premise and assumptions supporting the plan. Planning boils down to sensing an opportunity and establishing the means to achieve it. It involves understanding the environment in which one operates and establishing the best way to get where you want to be. If you don't know where you're going, any path will get you there. If you don't plan, others will plan for you and their actions will determine your priorities.

The manager who wants to plan must first establish objectives and then specify the factors, forces, and efforts necessary for their accomplishment. Operational planning establishes the activities necessary to meet designated objectives.

The Advantages of Formal Operational Planning.   The most important contributions of formal operational planning are:

1. Creates a formal network of printed information that would not otherwise be available

2. Periodically forces operating managers to extend their time horizons and see the larger framework

3. Requires people to communicate about goals, strategic issues, and resource allocations

4. Systematically teaches managers about the future so they can better calibrate their short-term decisions

5. Creates an attitude about and a comfort factor concerning the future

6. Stimulates longer-term special studies that can have high impact for strategic decision making

7. Establishes a formal reporting system

It's Demanding Mental Work

Planning involves a lot of mental work. The Ultrapreneur recognizes that a person who is unwilling or incapable of performing this kind of work cannot fulfill his/her function satisfactorily. The planner must choose from among alternative courses of action which may be taken to achieve an objective. The raw material for mental work is managerial, technical, human, and company knowledge. Planning is essentially the intelligent synthesis of present knowledge and previous experience.

The Ultrapreneurial planner must possess knowledge, know-how, and facts to plan effectively. Knowledge refers to some basic body of principles, points of view, and other background information. Know-how refers to the body of facts and skills that one acquires from practical experience. Know-how cannot usually be acquired from books. The third ingredient, facts, are known conditions, and assumptions about unknown conditions. Some of these conditions are controllable, others uncontrollable. The operational planning principle becomes that the Ultrapreneur must get the facts, face the facts, and act as the facts dictate—not as they used to act, nor as others are acting, but as the facts *now* dictate.

The Seven Criteria of a Good Operational Plan

Once the knowledge, know-how, and facts are assembled, then an effective operational plan can be developed which will meet the following criteria:

1. The plan should state clearly the nature of the mission and its objectives. This helps those who are involved in executing the plan to understand, believe, accept, and support it.

2. The plan should provide measures of accomplishment in terms of quantity, quality, time, and expense. This assists in delegating responsibility and measuring results.

3. The plan should state the policies which should guide people in accomplishing the mission.

4. The plan should spell out what people or departments will be involved in accomplishing the mission.

5. The plan should indicate the time allowed for each phase of the activities.

6. The plan should specify the kind and amount of resources (money, people, items) allowable.

7. The plan should designate the leaders who will be held accountable for the accomplishments.

Why Plans Fail

Along with avoiding nonplanners, Ultrapreneurs making it happen need to have an understanding of why plans fail and what can be done to lessen the possibility of failure. What pitfalls contribute to failed plans? How can one work smarter in planning? There are some basic reasons why plans fail.

No Real or Realistic Goal.   This is caused by making vague goals or goals that are completely unreachable. Ultrapreneurial goals must be:

Specific with detailed objectives.

They must be measurable, with benchmarks everyone can understand.

They must have timeframes built-in to force accountability.

The participants in achieving the goals must agree that although it's a stretch, the goal is obtainable.

Lack of Commitment.   Commitment provides motivation; the people who are charged with implementing the goal must be committed to the plan used to achieve it. The best way to assure commitment is to get the participants involved in the plan. Guide them, but let them originate and substantiate the efforts needed to successfully execute it.

Failure to Anticipate Obstacles.   Every plan has to allow for changes, have some room for contingencies. This is especially true for Ultrapreneurial companies. No matter how carefully it is prepared, Murphy's Law is going to affect the best-laid plan in some way. Look for and discuss possible obstacles during the planning process. This creates an atmosphere of flexibility when carrying out the plan that makes the obstacles, when confronted, seem less devastating. They simply become hurdles to overcome with continuing enthusiasm.

Lack of Benchmarks and Reviews.   Plans that fail don't have concrete benchmarks and predetermined review points. This causes slips in achievement, and demoralizes those involved in implementing the plan because they feel no one cares until it's too late. This can't be allowed to happen in Ultrapreneurial companies. Benchmarks and continuing reviews are used to be sure these objectives are reached. They charge both the implementers and the overseers with responsibility. It's part of making it happen.

Failure to Be Flexible.   No plan is going to be obtained 100 percent. Just like allowing for obstacles, some flexibility must be maintained. Stubbornness in forcing adherence to all aspects of the original plan will assure that it won't be attained. Failing to revise goals when it is appropriate is ignoring reality; effective planning provides some resiliency to change both details and direction without scrapping the whole plan.

Planning is used to reduce uncertainty and to manage Ultrapreneurial risk. Working hard is inherent in Ultrapreneurship, and planning helps one work smarter. It's why Ultrapreneurs' plans are goal-oriented rather than activity-oriented; that's a secret of Ultrapreneurship and making it happen.

Psyching Up for Unrelenting Change: Yourself and Your Team

Ultrapreneurial planning often means change. Change requires a person to attempt new behaviors he or she doesn't already possess. This applies equally to Ultrapreneurs making it happen as well as to their teams. Almost inevitably, it means you are going to experience failure. Change causes problems and problems require solutions. Nothing can change until we do. When we change, our world will change—the answer is attitude. We live in an economy based on change; life means change. In our economy, anything that remains static is considered unhealthy. We are meant to grow with the changes/stresses because we have the built-in ability to adapt. Many people hate change and they resist it. To them it's disturbing, frightening, maybe even disastrous. Ultrapreneurs recognize this and consider the following factors when planning to implement change:

They affect people to help formulate the change.

They consider how the change will look to them.

They make changes slowly in small steps.

They recognize that two changes are four times as bad as one.

They provide lots of advance notice so those affected can get used to the idea slowly.

A Special Word to the Ultrapreneur/CEO Regarding Change

Ultrapreneurs themselves have some tough-change challenges in personally adapting for the changes of a growing company, but it's part of making it happen.

1. They have to develop a heightened emphasis on team building. Concentrate on building a confident, turned-on team while relinquishing some of their duties. They need to give people room to grow, to make mistakes and try again, both in and outside the company. They have to spend more time on the balancing of priorities, and focus on the management team by making assignments that lead to continued growth.

2. They have to develop greater skill in communications. With small companies, the process is simply passing the word to those around them; displayed emotions can be part of the message. As the company grows, the channels lengthen and the message must be clear, concise, and nonconflicting, but still purveying emotion. There is a greater need to assure sound feedback and two-way communication.

3. They have to develop a higher level of personal discipline, learning not to meddle with operations and decisions in areas they have delegated. The challenge is to be fair, be consistent, and avoid emotional outbursts.

In making it happen, the Ultrapreneur's concerns switch from being intimately involved and overseeing many details of the company to guiding, implementing, and orchestrating the operational side of the company's business plan. This requires a shift in the Ultrapreneurial mindset from doing everything oneself to empowering others. It means passing on planning skills, assuring smooth, positive changes, and assuring that the Ultrapreneurial garden is secured from natural hazards.

This shift in Ultrapreneurial thinking about planning and change requires that the Ultrapreneur deal with some broader issues like cycles, people phases, innovation, and adopting success forces.

Shaping Your Own Success Mindset

When an Ultrapreneurial company is up and running, it's proven that top management must shift some focus toward some more obscure areas. At first blush, these don't seem to have much pertinence to the daily operations of a company. However, these are some of the areas that do indeed make the difference between entrepreneurs and Ultrapreneurs. They're higher-level management issues and philosophies that cause and create value-added companies and contribute to off-balance-sheet assets. They can become the difference between success and the also-ran. Following are a number of success philosophies that Ultrapreneurs recognize and cultivate in the process of making the venture happen.

Staying Attuned to a Variety of Cycles

Everything in life is cyclical: nature, stock markets, consumer moods, economics, weather conditions, birth rates, crime, wars. The telling and foretelling of cyclical movements comes from keeping aware of broad patterns and phases. In Ultragrowth companies, especially in high-tech markets, the patterns are becoming harder to detect because cycle times are constantly decreasing. In the microcomputer market of 1978, it took six years to develop a product which then had a four-year sales span. In 1984, development was down to four years and product life was only two. In 1992, the figures were three years versus one-and-a-half. This shorting is not expected to decrease, and it applies to many high-tech products and related services. Everything rises and falls, often in regular patterns. Telling a cycle is often based on experience. Having enough experience, enough failures, and enough facts helps give Ultrapreneurs a feeling for cycles. For example, by the time most of us hear how everybody is making money on something, the cycle is already past its peak.

There Are Such Things as Passing Phases

Ultrapreneurs recognize that phases are akin to cycles in that if we are in-phase, just like if we catch a cycle, we will achieve success without much effort. If we're out-of-phase, the chance of failure is much greater. However, phases deal more with people than the cycle of things. The degree to which we are compatible with another person or a situation is how our specific set of biological relationships, at a specific moment or place in time, are in phase with that person or situation or event. This happens with Ultrapreneurs in dealing with team members, employees, and especially customers. Phases do not determine our fate, but rather they tell us the probability of compatibility with that person, situation, or event at that specific time. If you feel that the compatibility is out of phase, you still have an opportunity to work against or adjust to the probability and still achieve success. Ultrapreneurs stay mindful of phases. They recognize that many times, when things don't go as planned, it pays to keep cool and recognize that it may be just a phase that will pass.

Ego Control

Ultrapreneurs don't let their ego distort their good business sense. Ego is an important asset for Ultrapreneurs. It's a motivator that drives one to bigger and better things; it keeps you going and helps you keep others going in the tough times. The secret to good ego sense is to know when to put it aside and accept failure. A good example of ego gone astray is revenge. This is ego as a destructive force. Another good example of bad ego judgment is when a product doesn't sell or its market cycle has ended. Drop it. Ego goes with good sense, and Ultrapreneurs have to be especially sensitive to becoming attached to both beloved products and their egos.

The Assiduous
Cultivation of Humility

Truly successful Ultrapreneurs are genuinely humble. No matter how successful they become, they remain mindful of the fact that every person, regardless of station in life, is important. This is important for Ultrapreneurs to learn. There are countless examples of fast-growth companies that didn't make it to harvest with the entrepreneur still attached. Being a leader can be a heady experience at times. The early praises for getting a product or service into the marketplace are hard to keep in perspective. Fast growth that results in dozens or perhaps hundreds of employees in the first couple of years will gain a company a lot of public recognition and accolades. Ultrapreneurs keep these praises in perspective, and recognize that for them, the main objective—the harvest—is still to come. Employees and customers appreciate humility on the part on their leaders.

Committing to Excellence

When Ultrapreneurs are faced with accepting mediocre work, they don't. They reject it and spend the time and money to produce the best possible results. They don't strive for perfection, because perfection is frustration personified and is very rarely achieved. Instead, they strive for excellence—every time. Ultrapreneurs adopt an excellence-over-average attitude. When you do this, you're tipping the scale toward greater success.

To Give Up or Not to Give Up

An Ultrapreneurial saying is, "Never give up until you have no choice." Ultrapreneurs muster all the persistence they can, and don't give up until they've given it everything they're capable of giving at the time. The Ultrapreneurial world is full of traps, disappointments, and failures. These are tests of one's drive for success. If you can withstand these pitfalls and not give up, Ultrapreneurial success soon will follow. The thin line between never giving up and letting your ego distort your good business sense can be found in one simple two-pronged question: "Do I feel there is still a chance for success *and* is it worth it?" If the answer is "no," you're satisfying ego; if "yes," don't give up yet.

Taking Control of Success Forces

Along with recognizing success philosophies and building a success mindset, Ultrapreneurs also recognize some forces that effect success. These are additional keys to making Ultragrowth happen and separating Ultrapreneurs from run-of-the-mill entrepreneurs. The basic assumption is that for every action there is a reaction. These forces, positive or negative, can steer or force you toward either success or failure. They are:

Always Be Honest

This is the strongest and most powerful Ultrapreneurial force. There is a strong failure force associated with dishonesty. Each time you are honest and conduct yourself with honesty, a success force will drive you to greater success. Honesty is relative. What is honest to you may not be honest to someone else. It is judged strictly in the eyes of the beholder. Dishonesty creates a failure force that often manifests itself in other ways—often not apparent to the outside observer. Honesty has to be worked at and used as a guiding philosophy. You'll be amazed at how powerful it is; if you'll remember from Chapter 3, it's a primary characteristic of the Ultrapreneur. You can't make things happen without being honest.

Cherish Your Failures and Benefit from Them

We learn from our failures. Some Ultrapreneurs feel that if they pile up enough failures, success becomes a sure bet. Failures give us the reassurance and knowledge to try most anything. If we fail, it will create a force for future success. It is an Ultrapreneurial trait to take action, because to not take action is a bigger disgrace than failing. The key to failure is to bounce back. Not many people are willing to give failure a second opportunity. They fail once and it's all over. Ultrapreneurs attempt things in life with the attitude that if you fail, you should consider it a success force that will later

help you succeed. To fail and bounce back requires resiliency, commitment, and self-confidence—again, all Ultrapreneurial characteristics.

Relish Your Problems

Every problem has in it a hidden opportunity, often so powerful that it
dwarfs the problem. The Ultrapreneurial style is not to ignore problems or
unrealistically try to "positive think" them out of existence, but to say, "I
know I have a problem, but I also know there is a hidden opportunity. What
is it, and where do I find it?" Here's how to find the opportunity:

1. See it as a situation, an opportunity, a challenge.
2. Clearly define it in writing.
3. Set down the probable causes that trigger it.
4. Identify all possible solutions with no prejudgment. Determine what's
   ideal before what's possible. Think and talk without being negative.
5. Stay solution-focused, not problem-focused.
6. Choose one or more solutions and make a decision.
   a. Decide when a decision will be made.
   b. Decide specific responsibility on what's to be done.
   c. Determine logical steps. Who's to do what, to what standard, using
   what resources, under what timeframes?

   Ultrapreneurs relish problems because it gives them a making-it-happen
challenge to find an opportunity.

Concentrate Your Powers

Ultrapreneurs learn to concentrate on one area. They develop one product
or one service before splitting off on tangential products or services. Tan-
gents cause failure. By concentrating, you can learn from your mistakes; as
you learn, your productivity goes up. Diffusing focus diminishes efforts and
causes new learning curves, new mistakes, which then creates a new set of
failure conditions. You also divert attention from your area of prime effectiveness. Ultrapreneurs carefully decide how many things they can concentrate on and discipline themselves not to stray.

Do It Differently

Every element you copy is a failure force, but every time you innovate, it is
a success force. Ultrapreneurial innovators are persons who do things others think can't be done or who do things few people have done before. For

many Ultrapreneurs, innovation might be as simple as putting the same thing together in a unique way. This may be the way a product is manufactured or it may be the way a service is marketed. Regardless, innovation enhances Ultrapreneurial breakthroughs.

Success Pressures

Ultrapreneurs recognize that every success has a compensating pressure. If they develop a successful product, the marketplace puts on a lot of pressure to repeat the performance. Here's an example based on experience. When you make a lot of money, you're moved to go out and buy an expensive car. The consequent success pressure is spending a lot of time and attention worrying about or trying to prevent parking-lot dings and scratches. Often, success pressures can't be anticipated. Just be prepared to expect a pressure that may take away from the luster of your success.

Innovate or Expirate

Making things happen requires a constant focus on innovation. Ultragrowth companies have to keep new products coming on line. The Ultrapreneurs main challenge in the making-it-happen stage is to be sure that innovation is ongoing lest the Ultragrowth pattern come to a screeching halt. Companies without a sexy, promising future, built around the mystery of new products or services coming on-stream, don't make attractive harvest candidates. Innovation becomes the value-added leverage for harvestable companies.

Canon: A Case in Point

Canon, under the direction of its president, Ryuzaburo Kaku, has gained a superior reputation for product innovation. Since the mid-seventies they have introduced new cameras, copiers, fax machines, electric typewriters, laser beam printers, medical equipment, micrographics, semiconductor production equipment, and a lot more.

This has happened because Kaku purposely established a management system that encourages and supports innovation. Canon's three broad product groups—business machines, cameras, and optical products—are supported by three separate systems. These systems interlink and serve all product groups. One is the Canon Development System, charged with doing research into and the creation of new products and technology. Second is the Canon Production System, charged with achieving the best quality and utilization of all the Canon manufacturing facilities. Third is the Canon Marketing System, which is responsible for operating "a scientific and systematic marketing plan to provide personalized service to every Canon customer."

Although the Canon management system sounds entrepreneurial, remember the company's sales exceed $8 billion annually. These results, in a multibillion company, are continued because of a basic success philosophy that decisions are founded on:

1. Being sure that Canon has the needed physical resources (financial, human, logistical, and technological) to carry out innovation

2. These resources are being arranged in an organizational format that encourages their use

3. Constantly coaching and preaching to everyone in the company that innovation is Canon's lifeblood

If sales of a particular product or service have started to level off, are passing their peak, something should already be happening to solve this. Ultrapreneurs must pay a lot of attention to renewing, improving, extending, innovating, and remarketing existing product lines. They keep mindful of the time lags involved in new product or service development. If it takes two years to develop or innovate something new and the sales life cycle is only eighteen months, someone better concentrate on shortening the development time or else get a lot of new projects going simultaneously.

Ultrapreneurial innovators encourage, create innovative atmospheres, get personally involved, ask lots of questions, and probe and prod for innovative results.

Ultrapreneurial Edicts

Successful Ultrapreneurs must develop a bible of making-it-happen edicts, proclamations of command, decrees to live by. More specific than a mission statement, they need to be applicable to many different parts of the organization. Some are only applicable to specific management areas, while others apply broadly. They become vital recommendations and guides for management and employees. Many become absolutely essential to Ultragrowth. Reading through the edicts that follow is like walking down the line of a cafeteria—a lot of them look good, but you will have to pick and choose the ones that fit your appetite. Some are like appetizers in that they apply at the startup stages. While others make a main course, edicts have to be built up to. And finally, you'll find the desserts, little tidbits of sweetness. In between, there's a soup course, a few vegetables, some interesting relishes and your choice of salads. Have a sip of wine and *bon appetit!*

Management by Objective

It's simple: You focus on an end result and try to make it happen. You determine what you're after and set out to get it. For Ultrapreneurs, the big objective is the harvest. But a lot has to happen—identify the crop, find the ground, plow the soil, plant the crop, fertilize, repair the fence to keep the stray animals out, apply the pesticides, weed the plot, irrigate, and pray a lot. It's a long, tough row to hoe from idea conception to harvest and there are a lot of rocks in the way. That's why the Ultrapreneur needs to have a continuing stream of objectives. He or she needs to learn to focus all available resources on accomplishing several specific goals or operational objectives, within stated time periods.

There is a terrible tendency on the part of entrepreneurs to scatter resources, to take on too many tasks. Early-stage companies have limited resources and the winners are those that focus on a competitive niche and pursue it narrowmindedly. This narrow focus results in the company gaining a greater sensitivity to opportunities and then enables it to react quickly since its attentions and resources are not diverted toward numerous other activities. Line up your objectives and manage your operations to achieve them.

Alternatives

There are several alternatives to management by objective. Generally, they don't work for Ultrapreneurs because they focus on day-to-day objectives instead of the longer term, with the idea that everything will work out all right. However, in some cases or areas, they may prove the right choice in making it happen.

Managing by Hope.　Hope operates on the basis that certainties are hard to find, that the best path to pursue is all paths. This is a form of reacting as opposed to being proactive. It works for some broad-based initial research or when initially looking at methods for distribution. The caution is to watch for paralysis by analysis where all the overwhelming variables lead to total indecision.

Managing by Crisis.　Crisis has long typified the entrepreneur. It's especially typical when the team is mostly composed of engineering types. They are usually good problem solvers and, when confronted by a crisis, they bring a lot of energy and innovative solution forming abilities to the cause. Think about how much time, creative effort, and dollar expense can be gained if the attention is focused on identifying potential problems and establishing alternatives instead of reacting to another crisis.

Managing by Subjectives. This is the mystery approach to where the company is headed. It's presumed the boss knows, but it's not shared with the rest of the staff. It works for very simple enterprises but is a definite "no-no" for Ultrapreneurs. High-quality people aren't attracted nor, if by chance they join, will they stay with this type of organization. People by nature want to know where they are going and enjoy contributing to how to get there.

Management by Extrapolation. This works on the basis that today is, and tomorrow will be, about how it was yesterday. All that really needs to be done today is to figure out how to do the same thing tomorrow with a little more efficiency. This is a common attitude for mature companies, even today, but it no longer works. Although it may have some applications for routine tasks, it is better to shift one's attention to strategic planning for tomorrow.

Expand Carefully
from a Profit Mindset

Optimism is an inherent characteristic of the Ultrapreneur, but it can also be detrimental. It takes a careful balance in one's thinking that all things can be accomplished with an understanding that all things can't be done simultaneously. The tendency is to embark on an all-encompassing mission, to try to develop a product or service that answers many needs, and develop them all at the same time. Successful Ultrapreneurs recognize that they have to focus on a particular area, get it properly developed and marketed, and—bottom line—do it profitably. Once this is well on its way, then they can move forward into other areas or market applications. Each step must be grounded on profitability, on being able to ultimately stand on its own; the sooner in the cycle, the better. Profits don't just happen. Like sales, they have to be made to happen.

The Ultrapreneur's job in making it happen is to move from the old to the new, to do a single thing exceptionally well, to learn to do it consistently and profitably.

Hire for Tomorrow

Ultragrowth has a particular people challenge. It's creating an environment in which people can grow with the company. The challenge is the choice between hiring for today's job versus tomorrow's position. If you hire for today, tomorrow's additional responsibilities may be more than the person can grow into. If you hire for tomorrow, you'll pay a premium for an overqualified person who may not have enough challenge to keep them interested today.

Try to determine during initial interviews if the applicant is willing to let go of the old and rise to greater responsibility and the challenges of Ultragrowth. Determine if they can buy off on pushing responsibility down and encouraging accountability and reporting of information back up. That's the only way one can monitor a situation and provide guidance when needed. This means you have to have information systems in place ahead of growth. The hiring of the right people, showing them and granting them opportunity to grow, and establishing better information systems for proper control, allows the Ultrapreneur to take occasional breaks to integrate their thinking about next month with what needs to be accomplished long-range. In an Ultragrowth situation, this task is complicated by the fact that everything is happening at a much faster pace. But it's absolutely necessary, albeit difficult, to take your mind off immediate problems and focus on the future. A failure of Ultrapreneurial vision inevitably leads to an underperforming team.

The Ultrapreneur will also find that their daily job descriptions change very rapidly, all the time. They have to learn to find the right people, determine attainable yet people-stretching goals (that include measures of performance), and then back off and let them do their jobs. This should be happening at all hiring levels of the company: people letting go of old jobs and reaching for new ones.

Gain Eyes, Arms, Ears, and Legs

And you do so by delegating. For Ultrapreneurs, this can be their biggest single growth challenge. Letting go of responsibility and authority as the company ripens is very difficult. They have to learn that delegating is not a skill but an attitude. When you push responsibility outward and downward, you give up something. But you can count on the fact that two more responsibilities will replace each one you give up. And they will prove more challenging. One way to ease into the delegating attitude is to expand the parameters of job descriptions to make change occur. The only way people can grow is if you let them take risks. The only way the Ultragrowth company can keep on the fast track is to practice delegating, to achieve results through others. This needs to be bred into the company culture right from the start so that there is an evergrowing core of talent available to respond to the increasing challenges of making it happen.

Lead People; Manage Things

Ultrapreneurs recognize that people live up or down to the expectations their leaders set for them as well as by the examples of the leaders themselves. Just as what we see in others is a reflection of ourselves (mirroring), what others see in us is what they emulate.

An interesting and sometimes revealing hiring exercise asks the following questions.

If you could create the perfect job for yourself, what would it be? The person's answer tells you if they have any idea what they want and, just as important, if you can give it to them.

If you had all the money you need, what is the biggest thing you would buy? Their answer tells you about the size of their financial dreams. If the potential of your opportunity is only $50,000 per year and this person's dreams require $300,000 per year, you may not have a match.

Ask them to write down, in front of you, 21 things they are committed to. First of all, if they are not committed to other things, they're not going to be committed to you or their new job. Another point brought out by this question is surrounded by the old adage, "If you want something done, find someone who is busy." For the Ultrapreneur, the saying should be "someone who is busy and committed."

Ultrapreneurs lead by stretching people, by giving them responsibility for things they think they want to do, but are unsure that they are ready to do. Unless the Ultrapreneur's team grows, the Ultrapreneur will not. Being able to grow yourself assumes that you have grown enough to let people make mistakes without you getting angry and resentful. It's tough to do many times, and those tough times don't last long, but tough people do. To make it happen, be a leader of people and have them manage the things.

Leadership

Leadership is the heart and soul of management. What you lead and manage is people. Leadership is the ability to inspire other people to work together as a team, following your lead, in order to attain a common goal. Ultrapreneurs believe in one-team management leadership, where all team members are committed to moving as fast as possible toward a single, agreed-upon set of objectives. Their leadership is exercised as the ability to lead and inspire others and is more instinctual that premeditated. It is acquired through the experiences of one's everyday life.

You Can't Fight Reality

Ultrapreneurs don't fight realities; they innovate and determine ways to capitalize on them and use them to their advantage in making it happen.

After World War II, America emerged as the wealthiest and only unscathed industrial power in the world. Since then we have lived off the fat of the land, paying the highest wages in the world, while cutting the demands of productivity from our workforce. Additionally, we allowed our basic industrial facilities to become technologically obsolete. As a people, compared to other countries, we became slack, complacent, self-centered, and self-indulgent. The economies that grew fastest between 1965 and 1990 were in the Pacific Rim. The Pac Rim countries have been moving into high-tech manufacturing with unbounded enthusiasm. Japan's progress is well documented. Hong Kong produces textiles and lots of clothes which are not only less expensive but equal if not better in quality to ours. Korea builds oceangoing ships that we can never equal in price or quality. Western Europe surpasses us in a lot of basic smokestack types of manufacturing and has proven time and time again that they are no slouches in research in many areas. Now they are gaining a whole new Eastern Europe workforce, albeit at great expense and investment, that is eager to make up for decades of suppression.

How do these realities affect Ultrapreneurs? By their very existence, in that not only should one carefully consider opportunities in which they may be competing head to head, but also in that one should look to the efficiencies of these countries and seek to enter into strategic partnerships in some way to take advantage of combined strengths.

Criterion One

When all is said and done, the company, the Ultrapreneur, and the team is judged by one criterion, "performance." Lost and gone are the short-term struggles and the long-term battles. Forgotten are the days-into-nights-into-days of labor. Dismissed are the hand-wrenching sessions over who gets paid this time and the agonizing hiring and firing decisions. What remains are the results, the record of the company and its performance. How did it compare to the rest of the marketplace? How did it perform in its economic environment? What was its performance over the long haul, not just the last quarter? How did its growth and accomplishment over a protracted period of time measure up in an everchanging atmosphere? Collectively, these questions are "performance" and that's what Ultrapreneurs make happen.

Keep Your Eye on the Pot

Ever try to cook a gourmet meal over an open campfire? It's a culinary challenge to say the least. It holds a likeness to Ultrapreneuring in that there are a lot of uncontrollable elements involved: the dryness of the wood, the wind in the campsite, the intensity of the fire, sometimes the distance from the heat source. Toss in a recipe for which you may not have all the proper ingredients, which means you have to add your own, resulting in innovation. It means add a little here, watch it cook, check it again, taste-test it for improvements, add a little more. Check and possibly replenish the fire, taste it again, correct it. Whatever you do, keep your eye on it. It's kind of like Ultrapreneuring—some science, some art, no immutable laws, no predictable machinery. But what you do have is people that, even with their faults and frailties, provide the essence of a fine enterprise, which, when properly prepared, results in an extraordinary accomplishment.

What You Got When You Got
What You Didn't Expect

It's experience! This is the process of discovering, with the result that you learn something new. It should grow, if properly cultivated, into cumulative capability. You have to venture forth and seek it, reach for it. You have to search your environment, stretch your mind, come up with something better, try a new way, create a different way of doing things. That's called creative experience. Even failures count as long as they're added in a positive way to your storehouse of knowledge. Experience is what you get when you don't get what you expect. It's also called Ultrapreneurship.

The Only Real Mistake
You Can Make

One of the fundamental faults with entrepreneurs (as opposed to Ultrapreneurs) is that they are losing their zest for adventure, for taking risks, for doing something that no one has done before. The reason behind this is that corporate America has taught us the mistaken belief that professional business managers are supposed to be so sure of themselves that they never make a professional mistake. In school, you get an A only if you score 90 to 95 percent. But in business, you can get an A with 80 to 85 percent. More important than the score is the attitude when making a decision. It should be imaginative and creative and based upon an adequate knowledge of the facts—substantiated facts. Learn to probe for unshakable facts. They are hard to come by because many times the so-called facts are colored by the bias of the person presenting them. Ultrapreneurs try to get their facts from a variety of sources, strip away the biases, including their own, and try to get a true picture of what is involved. When you can see the picture clearly, the decision is usually clear and easy. Facts are power—they are crucial to good management. The facts make the decision for you. Then the only real mistake is not making a decision.

Management *Must* Manage

Must is the operative word, the active word in the credo. Management is a living force, the force that gets things done to acceptable standards, high standards. But it must *manage*. It doesn't mean solving every problem, reaching every goal, being an outstanding success every time. No sports team wins all their games, but you have to be good enough to win most of them. In business, you have to be better than your competitors; how much better depends on the standards you set. But you must manage to achieve results. If you can't get those results all the time, that's acceptable too. Then you change your environment. Sell the business and get into something else. You change. That is management. What you don't do is go on accepting inadequate results and explaining them away. You *must* manage to make it happen.

Monitor and Respond

Many an entrepreneur has gotten into deep trouble with their company because they ignored a very important point. Amid all the pressures of operating their company, they forgot about one of their most important assets, their customers. New technology, foreign competition, and new pricing strategies suddenly put a dent in their growth plans. Often, the surprise could have been avoided if they had stayed in touch with their customers, talked with them, questioned them, found out their needs, asked what's new. It requires that top management stay eyeball to eyeball with customers instead of pushing that contact farther downstream. It requires that the Ultrapreneur commit some time, all the time, to interrelating with the companies' customers. Superb customer service is built around the idea of long-term partnerships with people. These partnerships are enhanced if the Ultrapreneur cultivates these relationships. By monitoring the customer's needs, the company is in a much better position to respond in making it happen.

Test: Early, Often, Carefully, and Habitually

Entrepreneurs are infamous for faulty product launches; however, Ultrapreneurs test. They test early, often, carefully, and realistically. They recognize that despite the time and trouble, reality-testing of their product or service is the only way to go.

Alpha Testing. The first tests are called *alpha tests*. These tests take place in your plant or office and definitely behind closed doors. They include a number of tests, as appropriate, to be sure things work and to check the innovation factor.

Beta Testing.   The second-level tests are called *beta tests*. They are conducted outside the plant or office and preferably in an ultimate user environment. Put your creation into the hands of a potential customer, show them how to use it, let them use it, and then watch them, query them, and listen to their reaction to your solution.

If you're using a focus group, which is common especially with consumer products, you should decide ahead of time what you want to learn. Consider their reactions to the following points:

Its usefulness?

Does it do what it's supposed to do?

Is it easy to operate?

Are the instructions adequate and clear?

How does it look to them?

Their thoughts about the pricing?

General packaging and product appearance?

Does the name capture their attention?

After beta tests, you'll most likely need to change your product or service solution; at least modify it. Once debugged, beta test again, and preferably expand the test base. This accomplished, with further refinements incorporated, don't forget to revise your business, marketing, and operational plans to reflect your testing results.

Limited Production Testing.   At this point, you're ready for yet another test. This one is called *limited production testing*. At this stage, your chief test is of the production system. The system is encompassing and includes:

How good is the team? Are they adequately trained? Can they work well together?

What mass production problems can be anticipated?

Are suppliers adequate and reliable?

Are raw materials available and assured?

What quality controls need to be put into place?

Ultrapreneurs, despite temptations, don't shortcut testing. The debugging of products or services as well as production procedures is time-consuming. However, it's a drop in the bucket compared to recalls, bad first impressions, and botched product introductions. Ultrapreneurs reality-test while making it happen.

Success and Unsuccess

If one spends some time reviewing the many published reports and documents, surveys and obituaries of successful and unsuccessful businesses, some interesting and thought-provoking points arise. A list of failure causes can easily guide the Ultrapreneur to many areas they should avoid as well as highlight points to concentrate on when making it happen.

A List of Causes of Failure

One-person management

Lack of internal communication

Lack of technical know-how by management

Squabbles among top management

Absentee management

Uncertainty of objectives

Lack of diversification

Inadequate records

Elaborate but unusable records

Too much capital investment

Excessive payroll

Inadequate sales representation

Sales to insolvent customers

Poor sales records

Ineffective bidding

Poorly managed subcontracting

Poor market research

Neglected tax liability

Excessive expansion costs

Excessive borrowing

Four other items continually stand out.

1. Successful companies have good financial records and make full use of them. Unsuccessful companies don't have good records.
2. Successful companies emphasize sales with top executives participating. Unsuccessful companies regard selling as a nuisance.
3. Successful companies consciously work on research and development. Few unsuccessful ones do the same.
4. All successful companies actively work on administration, have clear lines of authority, and make decisions without a lot of fuss. Unsuccessful companies are very inept at administration.

This old making-it-happen adage sums it up: "management, management, management."

Market Share Idealism

There is an absolute ideal pattern to capturing a major market share position in a new industry for Ultragrowth companies. When the industry is new and still small, it's important and very possible to obtain a significant share without having to be a large company. As the industry grows, the company grows and maintains its market share while still maintaining high profits. This is ideal from both the companies' and the venture capitalists' point of view, because Ultragrowth creates a profitable application for capital to expand the company's capacity to handle increasing business.

A company with larger market share gets more practice in performing its business and should be able to develop a higher level of competence. It also enjoys economics of scale—quantity discounts on materials, spreading of advertising and marketing costs, higher justification for greater tooling and automation investments, and more research and development. Combined, these result in lower unit costs, allowing lower prices, and consequently outselling competition to gain still more market share. And the cycle should continue with introduction of additional generations of product. This is the ideal Ultragrowth market share strategy.

Marketing Variables

It is standard reasoning that an Ultrapreneurial team needs to assess its proposed marketplace when initially determining a product or service around which to build a company. The initial planning will have taken into consideration many variables affecting the development, production, introduction, and maintenance of the product or service. They will have considered the five variables under their control—price, product, place, promotion, and people.

When the company is up and running, and many times prior to this event, another group of variables come into play. These are not within the control of the market strategist but, on an ongoing basis, need to be accounted for in a well-defined marketing strategy. These uncontrollable marketing variables include the economy, values, climate, environment, politics, and cultural and social trends.

As times and these uncontrollable variables change and evolve, we witness changes in the scope of the marketing activities of business in response to the changes, size, and variety of the markets. The United States markets have not only expanded internationally, but also intranationally. The American cultural landscape has broadened to incorporate buyers, products, and service representatives of more and more ethnic groups, age groups, sexual orientation groups, and both sexes in ever-increasing numbers. A brief review of some of the products and services developed, introduced, and maintained in the marketplace helps to understanding the need to strategically anticipate the inclusion of these factions in Ultrapreneurial market planning.

As women have entered the workforce, and so increased their buying power, there have been some notable changes: a major growth in the child-care industry, a renewed private sector movement into education, the toy industry expanding into new markets as well as large stand-alone operations, diversification of the female clothing industry into maternity and business segments.

Dual-career couples have created new markets for the expanding food industry into microwaveable everything: packaged ready-to-eat desserts, salads, snacks; a burgeoning catering industry providing food from parties to breakfast in bed; retail and wholesale outlets with food items alongside trendy footwear, motor oil, greeting cards, management books, and dinners to go. Dry cleaners, home-cleaning services, lawn care, and home maintenance are appealing to those homeowners occupied elsewhere, including the new fitness and recreational centers.

It's impossible to list all the ways the cultural diversity and its recognition by business have expanded marketplaces. Point is, the Ultrapreneur attempts to not only keep track of the effect in their marketplace but also to capture and capitalize on the everchanging trends as part of making it happen.

Marketing is a planning/strategy-based process attempting to satisfy the needs and wants of a constituency through a competitive advantage at a profit. The key is to satisfy the needs and wants of a constituency. If someone doesn't want or need a product, all the marketing in the world will not make the company successful.

Define the problem as your potential users see it. What problem(s) does it (are you) solving? Do people really need or want to know what this problem is? What do your users wish they could do . . . and how are they solving this problem now? What are they willing to pay to solve this problem?

The old saying, "Necessity is the mother of invention," is true—if you can find a large number of users with the same necessity, you have a market in which to make it happen.

Making It Happen— Summarized (The Keys)

Ultrapreneurs make it happen by being prepared to anticipate constant change—by continually adopting their business plans for the changes that are dictated by the realities of their marketplace, customers, and team.

Making it happen, Ultrapreneurial style, can be summarized by addressing two primary pressures, those from outside and those from within the organization.

Outside Pressures

Outside pressures mainly emanate from a customer perspective. They're natural pressures resulting from Ultragrowth and a company that is gaining more and more visibility.

The Ultrapreneur has to be responsive to the outside forces that affect and impact your customer base. Sometimes they're subtle things like a decrease in foreign interest rates that allows a foreign competitor to be able to reduce their sales price. At other times they're not so subtle, like a major technological breakthrough that completely destroys the company's technology edge. Maintaining responsiveness takes staying close to the customers and pushing customer contact. These customer perspective awareness signals in an Ultragrowth situation come from the top, by communication and by actions on the part of the key executives.

It can't be just outside sources like market research. Market research is not a substitute for knowing your market, for physically going out and looking for yourself to validate and invalidate questions to be sure you don't become a victim of your own prejudices. Remember, you can't research something that doesn't exist. Twenty years ago if someone asked you to invest $5000 for a machine to do your payroll, your reply would have been, "I don't have a problem doing payroll." But since the computer has come on the market, we all use it to compute payroll.

You cannot market with something that doesn't exist. But your customer will tell you what their problems are if you ask them. Then you can respond to outside customer pressures with solutions.

Inside Pressures

Inside pressures come from a variety of sources and deal with both the increasing size and the complexity that is generated by various problems and crises.

Inside pressure can be reduced by building a culture: a culture built on flexibility, cooperation, and appropriate competitiveness. This allows your company to be adaptable to the changing and evolving mix of customers, production, marketing, and distribution requirements being placed on it. All organizations, small or large, military or civilian, reflect the personality and character of the person who leads them. These leaders establish an organization's culture. The culture is built by an ever-expanding circle encompassing communication, participation, monitoring, and responding.

Building Communication Culture.   The Ultrapreneurial team needs to guard against communication becoming a one-way street. It's easy in the heavy-duty rush of day-to-day events to hear and see only what's comfortable. Subordinates naturally shy away from being harbingers of potential bad news. You need to build internal lines of communication that ensure that information flows up as easily as it does down. Outside communication should also be encouraged from members of your Board of Directors and Advisors. They can help pose hard questions and bring realities into focus.

Building Participation Culture.   Participation in day-to-day activities is one of the attractions of small companies. But it gets harder to maintain that hands-on attention as the company grows and the distance expands between the decision makers and employees or customers. It's important that as people are promoted, and new hires are made, one of their job qualifications becomes their ability to communicate. People do respond to structure and formal organizational charts. A person's boss is their primary reference point in their world of work. If that person is weak or vacillating, the signal gets through. The boss needs to be informed and communicative on the company's objectives, able to describe how each person fits into the scheme of the company's plans and how they contribute to the whole. Participation is how you encourage adaptive, enthusiastic, and supportive workforces—employees that don't say, "It's not in my job description," but instead say, "I want to do this"; you reply "go for it." Participation is how you gain a culture of trust and loyalty.

Building Monitoring Culture. Monitoring is an Ultrapreneuring skill that can be learned, taught, and refined. It is a skill in the understanding of relationships and events which is essential to executing strategies, plans, and programs. It should be built into the Ultragrowth culture to increase productivity improvement through people, to encourage the operational autonomy that results in stimulating entrepreneurship.

As with all culture-building activities, proper monitoring begins at the top with the main Ultrapreneur. You need to establish superior reporting systems that allow you to track and examine key operational data. It also requires that this process of establishing monitoring habits gets instilled in all levels of a company's operations. This is how the culture is instituted, encouraged, and confirmed. Proper monitoring creates a bias toward action.

Building Responding Culture.   An Ultrapreneur's single biggest challenge is letting go of responsibility *and* authority as the company grows. *Delegation* is the operational word. Delegating is not a skill as much as it is an attitude. You need to give up authority and responsibility by pushing it downward and outward. You gain eyes, ears, arms, legs, and ideas by doing so. Your people grow stronger, more responsive, and sharper with time and encouragement.

By delegating properly, you achieve responsiveness and get a communication return—a response in transmitting and sharing of ideas, opinions, and critiques on the work being done, and the progress being made toward the established goals. This is a lifeline process of the company. Interchanges about tasks at hand promote an understanding of the culture of the company.

The Ultrapreneur Dances

Making it happen is never simple, but like the whole entrepreneuring process, it is a step at a time. For the Ultrapreneur, it is akin to dancing, many steps at a time in a critical sequence, further complicated by having to be the lead dancer in the chorus, as well as the choreographer, executive producer, ticket taker, usher, set designer, and sometimes also the janitor—a challenging set of tasks to say the least. But the reward for successfully confronting the challenges is the Ultrapreneurial harvest.

10

The Ultrapreneurial Harvest

We can do no great things, only small things with great love.   MOTHER TERESA

Every grower, be they a tender of a flower box, a backyard gardener, or owner of thousands of acres, looks forward to the harvest. Realizing the fruits of their efforts is their goal. For many, the reward is not monetary; it's simply the beauty of the bloom or the satisfaction that they had a direct input into the taste of a salad. For commercial growers, this harvest process is their exit for that season's toil. Ultrapreneurs are commercial growers and mindful of the harvest from the first day they plant the seed for their enterprise.

They choose their teammates, determine their markets, and secure their financing based on the timing and payoff of their harvest. How long will it take to grow the company to the point where they can realize a substantial profit, and how much profit will they make when they do so? The Ultrapreneur knows the answers when they start, how they are going to cash out. They have a good estimate as to when that will be and they focus on developing their company to fit into the existing operations of a targeted buyer or some other predetermined harvest strategy.

Is the Exit Important?

Simply stated, exit strategy is what separates the minor league players from the pros. It's the difference between making a livable wage for the owner of

221

a company and providing an abnormal return for the Ultrapreneurial team and their investors. It takes a mindset that is harvest-focused.

The primary exit strategies for harvest are explored in this chapter. These include the following:

Absentee ownership. Getting the company to the stage that it simply runs itself. The trick is to cause it to be a "cash cow," spinning off lots of excess dollars. This allows ample payment to faithful employees, a solid stream of internal reinvestment dollars, and money left over for new Ultrapreneurial investment.

Management buyout. A way to recognize financial liquidity for the investors and the operating principals as well as pass the wand to fresh blood coming into the company. Commonly, this is accomplished over an extended period of time.

Outright sale. Probably the most common. This can take many forms including cash, stock, earn-outs, and combinations of same. Ideally, it would be an outright cash sale and the principals can move on. Frequently, it's limited cash upfront with some stock and more cash as time goes on. Hopefully, it doesn't also include long-term management contracts and noncompetitive agreements, for the Ultrapreneur is anxious to move on to the next project.

Employee Stock Option Plans (ESOPs). These are a form of management buyouts where the employees are offered the opportunity to continually increase their share of ownership while the investors are simultaneously cashed out. It has become a popular method of transferring ownership, but is *not* the preferable method for Ultrapreneurs.

Mergers/acquisitions. This is most common with closely held firms; usually the cashed-out principals remain under long-term employment agreements so as to assist in assuring their ultimate reward. However, if the current financial market temperament is growth via acquisition (the opposite of mergers), and the acquiring company is hell-bent to create a conglomerate, they may just acquire your company and move their own managers into the operations or combine it with an existing subsidiary. This is a very desirable harvest for the Ultrapreneur.

Going public. Long the dream of Ultrapreneurs, often held as the epitome of entrepreneurial success, it takes the right financial marketing climate, and the team has to be committed to staying with the deal for a reasonable time period. On the other hand, it's almost the only way to achieve outrageous financial rewards. A detailed study is presented in my book, *Cashing Out—The Entrepreneur's Guide to Going Public* (Harper Business, 1991).

The toughest part of exiting is getting all the exit players to agree on the deal and the timing. Harvest windows often aren't there very long and most require a preset determination as to the method, pricing, and timing.

Even when agreement is unanimous, there are a lot of pitfalls. But that's why we started to begin with. Sellers' remorse be damned. Firm up your ideas, set your goals, construct a plan, execute it flawlessly, and be sure your harvest is timed for the fall season so you can spend the winter where it's warm.

Pricing and Terms

When the Ultrapreneur is looking to harvest their company, two big factors come into play—pricing and terms. *Pricing* is the actual total amount of the deal, most times based on a valuation of the company and what's it worth. *Terms* are the amounts, methods, and timing of the payout. There is an old adage that becomes the Ultrapreneur's credo whenever they get into discussions on pricing and terms. It is, "You name the price and I'll set the terms." Or it can be stated in the reverse, "You name the terms and I'll set the price."

Ultrapreneurs understand pricing and terms. Using them creatively is a place where Ultrapreneurs excel. Although many of the items in this harvest discussion pertain to buying and selling businesses, they are good exercises in Ultrapreneurial creative financial thinking. Ultrapreneurs may acquire additional companies to add to or enhance their primary company as they grow to the harvest stage. Acquisitions add value, and Ultrapreneurs are ever-conscious about increasing the true and perceived value of their enterprise. Ofttimes, acquisitions are made just prior or even simultaneous to a harvest.

Pricing

Determining the price is seldom simple and is often complex. Above all, it is never easy. Whether buyer or seller, the most outstanding point to remember is that there are a lot of ways to determine it; you should always use a combination in making a final determination. (Some pricing and valuation "ratios" were provided in Chapter 4.)

Karl Vesper, in his book *New Venture Strategies*,[1] pointed out seventeen pricing methods which he breaks into seven categories.

Net Worth Methods

1. Book value
2. Adjusted book value (goodwill added)

---

[1] Karl H. Vesper, *New Venture Strategies*, Prentice-Hall, 1980, p. 269.

Asset Methods

3. Liquidation value (auctioneer estimates)

4. Fair market value (professional appraisal)

5. Replacement value (go shopping)

Income Methods

6. Historic earnings (maybe weighted) times a multiple

7. Future earnings, present owner, times a multiple

8. Future earnings, new owner, times a multiple

Cashflow Methods (New Owner)

9. Payment-serving capacity (for payback on cash deal)

10. Discounted cashflow (assume eventual resale)

11. Adjusted cashflow (include salaries, perks, fringes)

Market Methods

12. Last trading price (if there was one)

13. Competitive current bids (or what they are likely to be)

14. Comparable company prices (whatever they may be)

15. Special formulas in some industries

Heuristic Methods

16. Intuitive value to buyer (including a job, independence, other personal perks, satisfactions)

17. Seller's preconception of price (buyer can yield on this and recover on terms)

Why look at all these methods? Usually the best way to cut a deal is to accept the seller's price and work on making a successful deal by designing acceptable terms. However, the buyer needs to be satisfied with the price of the deal, as well as determine if the asking price is reasonable. It's common for the buyer to use several pricing methods for ammunition in negotiating either price or terms. This is why it's best to use several methods and combine them in determining a final price, for both the seller and the buyer.

The Ultrapreneur needs to be familiar with pricing *prior* to ever beginning their project. Part of the planning process is determining the harvest point and price. Using the various guides provided throughout this book will assist the Ultrapreneur in successfully starting and operating their company. Now is the time to review pricing methods so that you have a good grasp on the negotiating points and various pricing methods which will be used when confronting the harvest negotiations. Not all the methods described herein will be used or are even applicable for every project; however, one should find that at least six or eight will be applicable to their specific deal. A brief description of each method follows to assist in determining which is right for your deal.

Methods Descriptions

The following describes the various methods used in pricing.

Net Worth Methods. *Net Worth or Book Value* is the quickest method to determine a price. It's simply reviewing a company's balance sheet and finding its listed net worth (assets minus liabilities). An advantage to the buyer is that many assets may have been depreciated to below-market value (common for private companies); if the buyer can negotiate a sale based on book value, they may be making an undervalued purchase.

In reality, the chances of making a book-value purchase are slim. More common when looking at net worth methods is that *adjusted book value* will be used to more fairly price a deal. Adjusted book value is simply adding some mutually agreed-upon price to the book value which is attributed to goodwill. It may in fact include allowances for such intangible items as customers lists, long-term employee value, location, time in business, and certain proprietary processes used in the business. The rationale is that these items cost a lot of time and dollars to assemble which aren't reflected directly on the company's asset side of the balance sheet. A common ratio used to determine adjusted book value is to add three times the annual earnings to the actual book value after deducting normal owner/managers' salaries.

Asset Methods. For distressed companies, one often hears the term "fire-sale" value. This in effect is *liquidation value* of the assets. Under this method, one determines price by figuring out how much the company is worth if everything that's a part of the company is sold off quickly. Accounts receivable are sold to a factor. Inventory is "quick-sold" to customers, competitors, or scrap dealers. Plant and fixtures may go to auction or private deals made with competitors.

A step up from liquidation value, and a method commonly used in smaller private transactions, is *fair market value*. Here, one retains professional appraisers, or the parties mutually agree from published price information on the current value (fair market) of the hard assets. *Replace-*

ment value is also akin to fair market value with the buyer's underlying question being, "Can I buy this somewhere else for less cost?" Some intangibles come into play such as the true value for patterns, custom tooling, research, and design.

Income Methods. The next category is income methods, reviewed from the income statement as opposed to the balance sheet; the first method here is based on *historic earnings*. The premise is that a company's value can be based on its past earnings, say, over three to five years or more. The second method is *future earnings under a new owner.* Here, rather than rely on the fact that the company has made *x* number of dollars each year over the last five years, the assumption becomes that a new owner will be able to increase earnings by bringing in new management techniques. All three income methods are translated into a price by multiplying them by a price/earnings ratio (PE). PE ratios can be found for all types of businesses; the most common sources are the ratios listed everyday in newspapers listing the New York Stock Exchange, the American Stock Exchange, or the NASDAQ (National Association of Securities Dealers Automated Quotations) for over-the-counter stocks. Looking at both high and low PE ratios and comparing them with the prospective company's results is a good crosscheck on pricing.

Cashflow Methods. The next set of methods, *cashflow methods,* requires factoring the terms into the deal. The concern here is how much money the company can make to justify the price being paid. Three subfactors need to be considered:

1. How much money is being paid in a downpayment (to figure cost of funds or return on investment—ROI)?
2. How much money is needed to cover the debt service?
3. How much money is needed for operating capital?

Don't forget that the latter can also be impacted by a seasonal business. The first method here is the *payment servicing capacity* applied as noted above or on an all-cash deal. The price must be one that the company's profits and cashflow can pay back or pay off for interest *and* for principal as well as generate some reserves for unknowns.

If the entrepreneur is planning on reselling the business at some time in the future, it's common to use a *discounted cash flow* calculation where one computes the value of the sale price based on the future value of the company at its resale. This calculation is used with an interest rate figure of choice, or better yet, several different interest figures, depending on one's prediction of which direction future interest rates are going. It requires the use of a calculator or discount table. The higher the entrepreneur estimates the risk of the deal, the higher the interest figure that should be used, which in turn lowers the price.

The third cashflow method is the *adjusted cashflow*. This method is not used too often by Ultrapreneurs, as the prime consideration is the salaries and perks included in the deal, i.e., company car, travel, entertainment, and the like. These are tax deductions through the company which benefit the buyer, and the Ultrapreneur is much more concerned in leveraging and enhancing total corporate value than collecting perks.

Market Methods.   When looking at market methods, the focus is on what value others may place on the company or deal. The first method here, for a publicly traded company, is the *last trading price* listed in its most recent stock quotation. If the company is private, it may be the last price the company sold for, with current condition adjustments, or the price at which a comparable company recently sold. If there are other bidders or interested buyers/sellers, a method is the *current competitive bid*. Third, the *comparable company price* is simply what other similar companies have sold for. And last, *special formula* deals which are frequently found for service companies. In these cases, there are numerous precedents for the particular industry. These types of companies turn over on a fairly routine basis and it's difficult to negotiate too far off the industry norms. The best source for these formulas is a reputable business broker or a banker. In all of these market methods, remember that terms can have a lot of bearing on the total price paid or offered.

Heuristic Methods.   The last of the methods deals with heuristic methods, or "it's anybody's guess what motivates the price." The first one, *intuitive value,* is somewhat what feels right but may also have some justifiable grounds. For the buyer, it might be an intuitive feeling assigned to the risk involved. For the seller, it may be that they have always dreamed that their company would be worth *x* dollars when they sold. Again, this type of a deal can be successfully concluded if the terms are worked out to everyone's satisfaction. In some cases, it is the *seller's preconception of price* that has to be dealt with—again, maybe *x* number of dollars or *x* dollars per month. One never knows what personal thoughts enter into buyer or seller conceptions; the adage of "you name the price and I'll set the terms" is the Ultrapreneur's way of dealing with these type of transactions.

The key to pricing is to use as many of the different methods as possible when analyzing a deal. The different methods will give the Ultrapreneurs a solid range of prices from which they are then prepared to negotiate the terms.

Terms

Where the concern in studying pricing was oriented toward the determination of what is to be bought and at what price, the study of terms is how the deal is actually structured. Although there are many considerations when looking at terms, there are five which lend themselves to the greatest degree of Ultrapreneurial creativity. They are:

1. Cash downpayment
2. Installment payments
3. Guarantees of payment
4. Payment with stock
5. Use of options

Cash Downpayments.   At first blush, it wouldn't seem that much creativity could be applied to cash downpayments. You either pay or receive cash, or you don't. For a harvest, Ultrapreneurs aren't usually concerned with how a buyer gets cash. However, if the buyer is short on cash, the Ultrapreneur may wish to share some of their cash-obtaining secrets to help the deal along. For the Ultrapreneur, the creativity comes from knowing how one generates the cash. For Ultrapreneurial acquisitions it commonly would come from company funds, personal funds, family or friends, borrowing, recruiting other partners, and the like. But the Ultrapreneur in a harvest acquisition mode might use what today is commonly thought of as a leveraged buyout: simply using the assets of the proposed purchase as collateral for the downpayment borrowed from a lending source and then using cashflow to service the debt behind the balance of the transaction. Ultrapreneurs make acquisitions to enhance company value for their own harvest.

A further example could be when an Ultrapreneur has an opportunity to make a purchase which has undervalued assets (such as machinery, excess inventory, or even real estate) that they will not be needing in the ultimate company operations. The key is to find a buyer for the unused assets, and pre-arrange for a simultaneous transaction where the unused-asset buyer pays cash on the day of the primary transaction closing; those monies are then used to fund the cash downpayment. Another example could be where the Ultrapreneur arranges to sell a prospective company's receivables to a factor and then uses that money for the cash downpayment. Ultrapreneurs are innovative when seeking cash for their acquisitions or in arranging harvests.

Installment Payments.   This term area is also pretty straightforward. The buyer arranges to pay the seller a fixed amount over a specified period of time. Ultrapreneurial flexibility can be written into these types of term agreements, such as adding balloon payments at the end of the time period which make up for lesser monthly payments. Terms might also be monthly payments for the first year, or just the interest only and then interest and principal payments for the balance of the term. Payments can be scheduled to coincide with the seasonality of a business or with bonus payments contingent on the successful completion of certain contracts. An Ultrapreneurial form of time payments laps over into the next category of guarantees of payment. This could take the form of a consulting payment to the Ultrapreneur seller which may have more favorable tax consequences.

Guarantees of Payment. The consulting agreement mentioned above is one form of guarantee of payment. Another Ultrapreneurial approach could be the payment of royalties. This type of term is also used as a "sweetener" in the deal in that the Ultrapreneurial seller might be persuaded to take a lower initial price and then be paid a continuing royalty that would, over time, result in a total higher payout. The Ultrapreneur who is in an acquisition mode has a bonus here in that this form of a term means the payments are made from future earnings of the company over the extended time period. Ofttimes, royalty payments can be structured to be paid only when the company reaches some predetermined sales goals, annually or collectively. They can also be constructed so that they only apply to a certain product and have no effect on second generations of the product line.

A further type of guarantee can be when the Ultrapreneur brings in a cosigner to an acquisition. This cosigner adds a level of comfort to the seller, and the Ultrapreneur can obtain the cosigner's cooperation by issuing a percentage of the acquired company or combined companies' stock. The cosigner gets some new potentially profitable equity without much risk, and the Ultrapreneur gets the deal without scrambling for more cash or tying up valuable equity (which is saved for the next deal).

Stock as Payment. Using stock as payment is frequently referred to as "funny money," since the true value of the stock as a cash item may not be known until some time in the future. However, for the Ultrapreneur, it's a valuable "deal-doing tool." You can make a deal that includes some stock which then promises, because of the new deal, to be worth even more in the future. The seller gets full payment based on today's valuation with the upside that the stock will be worth more in the future. Consequently, the seller receives a bonus price for the total transaction. The Ultrapreneur obviously preserves hard cash or future cashflow. This type of transaction is more prevalent when the buyer is a publicly traded company, but can have a lot of attractiveness to sellers if the company's intention is to go public in the near future.

Options. The objective of an option is to give the buyer an opportunity to put the total deal together. The Ultrapreneur may need some extra time to get some money in place, they may need some extra time to close a companion deal, they may need to identify additional equity sources, or they may wish to pretest the proposed company's product salability in their organization. Options are a highly versatile tool for Ultrapreneurs who are putting deals together. They can expand both the buyers' and sellers' choices.

Other Considerations

Price and terms are the primary negotiating points in either buys, sells, or the Ultrapreneurial harvest. However, a lot of other items need to be factored in to be sure the deal works to everyone's best and lasting advantage.

Tax considerations should always be prominent in all dealings. The laws change with such frequency that it's difficult to make any concrete, specific recommendations in a book. As an example, as this book is being written, Congress is again (as it has for years) talking about a reduction in the capital gains tax. This is a very important tax ruling that affects Ultrapreneurs regardless of the ruling itself. Best said, Ultrapreneurs never make strategic buy or harvest transactions without superior, current tax and accounting counsel.

The obvious other primary consideration in all Ultrapreneurial dealings is to have highly capable legal counsel. The Ultrapreneur's feelings toward legal counsel is to use them to prevent trouble as opposed to using them to get out of trouble. Generally, the Ultrapreneur is best served to negotiate their deals prior to bringing legal counsel into the scene. You should always try to get the basic price and terms determined prior to engaging legal help. Attorneys prefer that the deal is struck before they are involved, because they realize it saves a lot of money and headaches in trying to continually revise agreements. In many cases, the Ultrapreneur may wish to "brief" their legal counsel before they start intensive negotiations just to be sure their intended path is down the right road. This also helps in keeping counsel appraised as talks progress, in that they are up to speed when they're needed and keep the Ultrapreneur on the right path.

Harvest Choices

The harvest mindset has required the Ultrapreneur to create real value added in their business. Unless this is done, the Ultrapreneur is a failure. Unless a company is developed which has value to someone other than the Ultrapreneur, the Ultrapreneurial mission hasn't been accomplished. The company has to make some major contributions in several forms:

In technological advances

In job creation

In returns to investors

In solid future value creation

In concrete benefits to society

Building and harvesting a company results in a recycling of talent, money, and knowledge that in turn spurs on the Ultrapreneurial cycle.

With a basic understanding of pricing and terms, the backbone of cutting harvest deals, we can take a more in-depth look at the Ultrapreneurial choices in a harvest plan. As mentioned earlier, these include absentee ownership, management buyouts, outright sales, ESOPs, mergers/acquisitions, and going public.

Absentee Ownership

At first blush, creating a company that carries on under absentee ownership wouldn't seem to fit our Ultrapreneurial game plan. However, if the company is a "cash cow," one in which the operating efficiencies, coupled with high profit margins, permit the company to generate a high level of excess cash, it can quite easily fit the Ultrapreneur's harvest strategy. The Ultrapreneur simply uses the excess cash to develop additional enterprises. In some cases these may be independent of the original company; in others, they may be spinoffs or divisions. These spinoffs can be incubated in the original company until they are capable of standing alone.

Often this point is reached after an alpha test on a product or service concept. The advantage, then, is that the product or service has built an underlying strength that enables the Ultrapreneur to obtain launch capital at more attractive terms than if capital has to be raised to complete the initial development. Initial development financing tends to take considerable equity and dilutes the Ultrapreneur's position. If this dilution can be prevented by accessing internally generated funds, the Ultrapreneur also retains more control and the opportunity of even greater potential. This type of situation is ideal when exploiting products or services that have cross-industry applications.

If the product is one that has other industry applications and can be developed through alpha testing, this is an ideal time to seek and negotiate a strategic partnership. The partnership may be a much larger company (which feels more secure in knowing that the technology really works and is proven in a different marketplace) that provides beta tests, financial help, and marketing/distribution. For the Ultrapreneur, this creates a very acceptable harvest for the spinoff company. What's more, this can be a very fast-track type of deal, in that development time is minimized since this is simply a technology adaptation from the original enterprise and the largest chore is usually marketing. Spinoffs can be harvested in two years or less.

The Ultrapreneur who creates an absentee ownership company which has a lot of excess cashflow, is positioned to then create multiple spinoff harvests. It's not a bad way to go and definitely leverages both dollars and talent, kind of like having your cake and eating it too.

Management Buyouts

There are several different ways to look at the harvest strategy of management buyouts. One is where the Ultrapreneur is the purchaser and buying out other investor interests or, on the other hand, where the Ultrapreneur is bought out by a number of the management team members. The financing mechanism used is similar in both cases.

During the 1980s, the common name for management buyouts was *leveraged buyouts,* or LBOs. In fact, they in essence became one of the darlings of Wall Street as they were rolled into the junk bond dealings. These were usually cases where the top level of management of the company arranged to buy out their division of a larger company with the financing provided by junk bonds.

In simple terms, a buyer group, usually representing some part of management, arranges a loan that is secured by the assets of the company, to buy out the principal shareholders. In Ultrapreneurial cases, these shareholders could be the Ultrapreneur, the Ultrapreneurial team, a venture capital firm, or other investors who provided the primary financing to the company. The buyer group could also be the Ultrapreneur buying out the primary investors, or it could be the second level of management that buys out the Ultrapreneurial team, or part of the team, with the balance remaining with the ongoing company.

Here's How Financing Works.   Regardless of who the buyers are, the financing arrangement is our concern. In smaller companies, the typical arrangement is that the buyers provide some amount of equity, and the balance of the purchase dollars are borrowed from a traditional lending source (commercial bank) which secures the loan by laying claim to all of the company's assets. Frequently, this is additionally collateralized by the personal signature guarantees of the buyers. The intention is that the ongoing profits of the company will be sufficient to service both the interest and the debt repayment.

In many of the 1980s LBOs, the equity portion became minimal, frequently less than five percent of the total purchase price. Today, as it was prior to junk bonds, ten to twenty percent is a more normal initial equity percentage.

The positive or Ultrapreneurial harvest in management buyouts is that the original investors recapture their initial investment with a large capital gain that is provided by the value added to the company during its development. The advantage to the buyers is that they can gain a substantial equity stake in the company which in most cases they helped to grow. Eventually, they also would seek to harvest their interest which has further increased in value due to the leverage provided by debt in the buyout.

There Are Also Some Negatives.   The negative aspects of a buyout is what may happen should the buyout company experience a major downturn in its markets or some other misfortune wherein it is not profitable enough to service the highly leveraged debt. The buyers could stand to lose not only the company, but also the equity they provided to accomplish the buyout. Generally, the Ultrapreneurial seller's desire is to receive full payment at the time of the buyout so they are removed from further risk. On some occasions, they may "carry back" some portion of the debt, usually as subordinated to the primary lender, which means that they too would lose should the replacement team be unable to cause the company to continue profitably.

Buyouts are an acceptable harvest for Ultrapreneurial endeavors. The Ultrapreneur and investor group gets cashed out to pursue a life of Riley or other Ultrapreneurial interests. The buyers get to continue to manage a company they know well with an opportunity to gain their harvest rewards at a later date.

Outright Sales

Many Ultrapreneurs dream about the outright sale, especially if they're two-thirds of the way to their harvest objective and everything seems to be going against them—long hours, big problems, seemingly unobtainable solutions, just plain bad nightmares. But then, early one morning they have the pleasant recurring dream of the big payday. Right there before their very eyes, some very intelligent soul is handing them a cashier's check with a whole lot of zeros on it and bidding them bon voyage as the Ultrapreneur sets sail for a year's cruise around the world. Ah, such a dream.

But dreams do come true in the form of outright sales, unfortunately not usually as depicted above. All cash upfront and the Ultrapreneur walking away seldom happens. However, as we learned, there are a lot of ways to cut a deal.

Most successful Ultrapreneurial cash-out sales have some strings attached. They frequently are sales to larger companies, many times companies that are publicly traded. Consequently, a lot of sales are combinations of cash and publicly traded stock. Besides, no matter what the tax laws are at the time of a sale, it's almost prohibitive from a tax standpoint for an Ultrapreneur or the team to take all cash upfront. Stock for stock exchanges can be structured so that the immediate tax consequences are lessened and the Ultrapreneur can then sell the acquirer's stock at times that are more tax convenient to them.

A problem with cash and stock sales is that the Ultrapreneur is subject to the unpredictability of the stock market itself, not to mention the ongoing whims of the performance of the larger company that did the acquiring.

Additionally, there are many, many, sad stories of sales made in heaven that turned into pure hell when the Ultrapreneur agreed to stay on in an active or semiactive role. The EDS (Electronic Data Services) and General Motors story is world famous for the friction that resulted between EDS founder Ross Perot and GM Chairman Roger Smith and the GM board of directors. Perot received financial comeuppance but not before a lot of blood was spilled. Even then, Perot lost a dream of creating the world's leading computer services firm on the coattails of GM to perhaps even outdistance IBM.

Continuing consulting agreements between the buyer and the Ultrapreneurial team need to be carefully constructed. Each executive who agrees to stay on needs to have a clear understanding of their new role. Many times, operations under a larger corporate structure vary considerably from the basic freewheeling style of an Ultrapreneurial enterprise. Fat management contracts lose a lot of appeal when the subject has to adjust to the day-to-day reality of big corporate quarterly operating pressures.

Outright sales can be an ideal harvest if they can be tailored to fit the goals of all the parties involved. They take a lot of soul searching on the part of the Ultrapreneurs and the team members but offer handsome rewards to all investors.

ESOPs

Employee Stock Option Plans (ESOPs), also know as employee stock ownership plans, are a kind of way of selling the company. The process enables the employees to purchase equity interests in the form of the company's stock from the Ultrapreneur or founding investors. This can be a gradual process that enables the Ultrapreneur to gain liquidity. The employees frequently gain a higher level of ownership motivation. ESOPs gained a lot of favorable publicity in the 1980s and are expected to become even more prominent during this decade.

These types of plans are very complex and take a watchful management eye. They can be very burdensome to administer and require continuing legal and accounting input. However, for the Ultrapreneur who wishes to gain a continuing liquidity stream, is okay with giving up predetermined continuing amounts of stock control, and is comfortable with having their employees knowledgeable about the financial information about the company, they can have a fruitful harvest.

Mergers and Acquisitions

The names are almost synonymous, but the differences in an Ultrapreneurial harvest can be great from an Ultrapreneurial point of view. A *merger* is where their company is merged into another, usually larger firm, ofttimes to offset strengths and weaknesses. An *acquisition* is where the larger firm outright acquires the Ultrapreneurial company as a smaller division. The reasoning behind both is that it's quicker and almost always less expensive to acquire an existing company than to start it from scratch. On a practical basis, the two blend into the same animal. Let's explore some of the problems.

Watch Out for These Problems.   In either a merger or an acquisition, some common problems surface. In many cases, these problems don't come to the forefront until some time after the transaction is completed. They are oriented around the companies' culture mix and the integration of people, products, and pricing.

While during the negotiations of a transaction the Ultrapreneurs are justifiably concerned with the pricing, structure, and terms of the deal, they should also have a concern about the nonfinancial areas involved.

People Decisions Are Emotional.   Employees in both the acquiring and acquired companies feel and express their feelings about M&A (merger and acquisition) transactions. Many times these are negative, with fears of job loss, small kingdom breakups, and trepidation about unknown management. Upper management and Ultrapreneurs can guide the emotional track for both the acquiring and target companies' employees.

The focus, as soon as practical in the transaction process, should be on reassuring and explaining the benefits of the transaction. They should discuss how the combined management and staff will be utilized, what if any downsizing will take place, the effects of any labor contracts, the attempt to justify the educational and cultural differences of management style, and they should place a clear emphasis on the opportunities that lie ahead for all parties concerned.

Product Integration Becomes Critical.   Product integration decisions are determined by a multitude of factors. Included are research and development strengths, manufacturing methods, selling procedures, distribution channels, product or service pricing structure, product life cycles, and many more. People are involved in each of these functions, and consideration should be given to the interrelationships of these people. Again, will the two cultures mix to gain new levels of accomplishment? Should some employees be removed or transferred prior to the transaction because they will impede the success of the combination? If so, whose responsibility is this both in talking with the affected person and perhaps transition or placement costs?

Transaction Pricing Affects People.   Pricing of an M&A involves the consideration of a number of valuations, assessments, structuring, terms, and negotiating the deal. All of these issues are tied directly into effects on people and the products or services the combined companies will offer. Can economies of scale be realized that will allow greater expenditures for research and development that in turn may require increases in marketing budgets? Can the same selling and distribution channels be utilized for both companies and new products? What happens to the management teams, both upper and middle? In short, will the price paid for the deal economically and emotionally factor into a compatible structure for the transaction?

Mergers and acquisitions don't automatically lead to higher growth or better combined entities. It takes careful strategic planning to accomplish the merging of people, products, and pricing. Ultrapreneurs give just as much consideration to these people, product, and pricing factors as they do the valuations and pricing of the deal. They recognize that feelings and emotions are involved, and they're sensitive to the people issues in mergers and acquisitions.

Going Public

When it comes to the subject of going public as a harvest strategy for Ultrapreneurs, I have to admit to a strong bias. I've been involved in taking companies public since 1970 when I was an officer and director of a company that I was instrumental in taking public. Since that time, I have been involved in over 50 public offerings. I have an intimate knowledge of the OTC market as a player, broker, trader, corporate finance officer, and syndicator. Additionally, I've been a public company founder (on more than several occasions), as well as an officer, director, and president (even Chairman of the Board), and I have invested in hundreds of companies, both as a private and a public investor. Finally, I was the lead author of the book, *Cashing Out—The Entrepreneur's Guide to Going Public.* With over two decades of hands-on experience, I feel I have gained a thorough knowledge of the business cycles, government actions and reactions, and an understanding of the internal politics and how all the various players that are central to the process interrelate when going public. Considering these biases, I state: *I feel the going public process is the ultimate harvest reward for the Ultrapreneur.*

What Is "Going Public"?   Basically, going public is the process in which a business owned by one or several individuals is converted into a business owned by many. It involves the offering of part ownership of the company to the general public through the sale of equity or debt securities—commonly considered selling stock. It means that one can easily buy or sell the company's stock through a stock exchange or in the over-the-counter (OTC) market. For the Ultrapreneurs and their team members and investors, it means liquidity of their investment, usually at very high multiples over their initial investment outlay. But, that's what we've been considering since page one—the harvest.

Although the subject is too complex to cover in this chapter, there are some points that are of particular concern or interest to the harvest-minded Ultrapreneur.

Advantages and Disadvantages

Advantages.   There are two fundamental reasons for going public. One for the sake of the company, and the other to the founder's advantage.

For the Sake of the Company.   Capital is the "wealth used in trade." It is the money invested in a company that allows it to:

- fund operations
- purchase equipment necessary for production
- increase inventories of both raw and finished goods
- support growing receivables
- expand ongoing operations
- support the company's administration
- further research
- develop the next generation of product or service
- retire prior debt
- increase market share

Contained within each and every one of these capital purposes is often the objective for going public, to support and sustain the growth of the company. The public investors hope their added investment will enhance the company's possibility for successful growth and thereby increase the value of their share of the company. Other company advantages include added prestige among customers, suppliers, and business associates; enhanced ability to finance because of improved debt-to-equity ratios; less dilution as the stock price goes up at higher P/E multiples; and other intangible advantages.

To the Founder's Advantage.   Bottom line, the founder's advantage is dollars. Simply, there are very few methods that result in the leverage of investment dollars to the extreme that being a founder in an Initial Public Offering (IPO) offers. Millionaires and multimillionaires have been created time and time again. The percentage return on a founding investment can be phenomenal. Typically, a publicly traded stock sells at 10 to 15 times its earnings. This is the price-to-earnings, or P/E, ratio. In a small initial public offering, this ratio may be as high as 40 to 50 times the company's annual earnings!

Since it's common practice for Ultrapreneurs and their team members to have a significant portion of their personal wealth tied up in their company, the IPO allows them the opportunity to liquefy some of this investment. In many cases, they have made loans, postponed salaries, and cosigned for financial obligations. These can be repaid and/or cleared up with an IPO.

Finally, having marketable stock gives the founders the financial liquidity advantage of selling stock on a timely tax-advantaged basis.

Disadvantages. The disadvantages can be grouped under three categories:

1. Disclosure/accountability
2. Control or loss of control
3. Expenses

Disclosure. From an operational standpoint, the company must disclose a lot of information that it would normally prefer to keep internal. This can include such items as marketing methods, amounts of markup, supplier and distributer names, sales by area and specific product line, and more. From a founder personal basis, the company must disclose a lot of information that pertains to the people involved in the company including the number of shares they own and how much money they make, both salaries and bonuses plus expense or perks reimbursements. From an accounting standpoint, the company must disclose detailed financial information via audited financial statements.

Accountability. This is a form of confession by the company to the public. Disclosure must include common ownership between the company and any suppliers or sales agents, and any unusual transactions between the company and its employees, especially its officers and directors; all this disclosure continues every quarter for the life of the company—thus continuing accountability. The forms are many and varied and they must be filed with various governmental bodies which make them public information, continually.

Control or Loss of Control. The emphasis is really on loss of control. The Company, because of having gone public, now has many more shareholders. Management has to report to these shareholders. They have to be responsive to them in the form of individuals, brokers, and analysts. This takes a lot of time for the CEO and CFO—time they can't control because it's a job that, like it or not, must be done. Being public causes management to think twice about the timing and effect on the stock price when considering acquisitions, mergers, and both short- and long-term internal planning. Control can also be affected by who owns how many shares of the company. In most cases, the financial founders will still hold voting control; however, there may be cases where pure majority ownership has been diluted below fifty percent. Good communication between management and the shareholders should obliterate this voting control problem.

Expenses. Few people realize how expensive it is to take a company public or the continuing expense of operating a publicly held company. The costs are very high. It's not the least bit out of line that the initial costs exceed fifteen percent of the total dollars raised and twenty percent-plus is not unusual for small offerings. On an ongoing basis, the costs are considerably higher than for a private company, primarily because of the SEC reporting requirements and the extra shareholder communications expense.

But It's Worth It.   As our society continues its evolution from an industrial/manufacturing foundation to a service/information base, we will find that the decade of the nineties will produce an increasing number of Ultrapreneurial stars. These enterprising company owners are going to become richer faster and take more people with them than ever before. Why? Because our society has become more global and consequently more complex, we have become more aware of the problems raised by this increasing diversity. The challenges we will be facing are great. Once again, the doors of opportunity will open to those industrious individuals ready to jump in with appropriate and timely solutions. The spark that brings these issues to flame is capital, and going public is the flint upon which these capital reserves are struck. Going public is the ultimate Ultrapreneurial harvest.

It's Harvest Time

If you consult a dictionary for the nonagricultural definitions of the word *harvest,* you come across such phrases as:

The time or season of gathering

The results or consequences of any action

To receive the benefits of an action

The product of any labor

To gain, win, or acquire

The Ultrapreneur likes the sounds of these words: gathering, results, benefits, product, *win*. It's why they get into the game—to identify the plot of ground, carefully choose the seed, the time of planting, the type of fertilizer, the proper amount of water, and anticipate the harvest.

As professionals, Ultrapreneurs develop a knowledge base about pricing and terms. They establish a familiarity with the various choices of cashing out at harvest time and focus on only those that fit their growth strategy. They do everything within their control to be sure they arrive at the harvest table with only the best they can produce.

Epilogue

An epilogue can be a short speech—spoken directly to the reader—after the conclusion of the main body of work. Often it deals with the future of the subject matter.

In this case, I want to make some points about the past that could have a lot of relevance in your future. Regardless of whether you get directly involved, I can guarantee you that you have been and will continue to be influenced by this Ultrapreneurial opportunity. It has been one of the most influential events in our society for the past few decades, and will continue for even more. It has created not only numerous Ultrapreneurial companies but also whole new Ultragrowth industries. It has directly affected your life as well as all of society around you, and it will continue to do so. In whole, it's what makes Ultrapreneuring so much fun.

Capture Your Opportunity
with the Baby Boomers

There are two primary points to be made here. First is to justify my claims, and secondly to give you some food for thought—to provide some seeds for you to plant and bring to harvest.

We've been overwhelmed with stories, books, articles, TV shows, and movies about baby boomers—virtually bombarded with the information that they are an influence on society. My desire is to condense a lot of information in a few brief paragraphs; it's up to you to find the nuggets that fit your style.

Almost one-third of all Americans—76 million people—were born between 1946 and 1964. We know of them as the "baby boomers," a generational mass that has dominated American culture for four decades. Their concerns, needs, and obsessions have been the dominant force of many Ultrapreneurial efforts. Witness the following:

Boomers moved the baby food business from 270 million jars in 1940 to over 1.5 *billion* jars a year by 1953. For them, we created sugar-coated cereals, Saturday morning cartoon shows, and countless TV toys.

Dr. Spock, as the medical guru for millions of moms, became the leading pediatrician in the country, who unknowingly provided the method of treatment for many childhood injuries and illnesses. In the mid '50s—1957 in fact—our local school districts built more elementary schools than in any one year before or since. We even had double sessions in schools which carried forward to the high school baby boomer period. The high school population doubled and we built more high schools in America in 1967 than in any year before or since.

Boomers created the market for hula hoops, skateboards, Slinkies, Frisbees, and the list goes on. We've had television shows that have catered to the baby boomers from "The Mouseketeers," "Captain Kangaroo," "My Three Sons," and "Father Knows Best," to the recent "thirtysomething."

Each of these had commercial sponsors whose products were often created just to serve the boomer audience of the time. In the late '50s, this resulted in teenage girls purchasing one-fifth of all cosmetics and of teenage boys buying $120 million a year in hair oil, mouthwash, and deodorant. By 1964, teenagers spent over $12 billion by themselves, and their parents spent another $13 billion on them.

Boomers created the fastfood industry and then went to college. The college student population tripled between 1965 and 1975 from 3.2 million to 9 million. New colleges opened, a total of 743. This same group caused the profits from Zig-Zag roll-your-own cigarette papers to rise by 25 percent every year for a decade. The Gap clothing stores went from founding in 1969 to a 165-store chain with annual revenues of almost $1 billion in just seven years. That's a lot of boomer jeans.

In the seventies, the boomers' attention turned to concerns over personal identity, lifestyle, and earning a living. What became "in" was *I'm OK—You're OK, Your Erroneous Zones,* and *What Color Is Your Parachute?* Also in was est, Lifespring, Silva Mind Control, and Transcendental Meditation. During the eighties, the in publications were the *Wall Street Journal, Esquire, Money, Forbes,* and *Fortune,* as well as books titled *In Search of Excellence, Megatrends, Iacocca,* and *Trump.*

When a few thousand, even a few hundred thousand, people across the United States share an opinion, read a book, or buy a product, that's interesting, maybe even a trend. But when 76 million people do so, it's a revolution. When baby boomers arrive at any stage of life, the issues of concern to them become the dominant social, political, and marketplace obsessions of the time.

As the boomers continue to grow up and out, this generation is destined to be the one force that most profoundly influences our lives. As boomers grow, America grows.

Would-be Ultrapreneurs, pay attention!

Final Thoughts

Through this book, we have traveled a significant distance together. My intent has been to furnish for you and instill in you the basis for becoming an Ultrapreneur—to try to pass on to you not experience, but knowledge. You'll find, as you make your own Ultrapreneuring journey, that this book has furnished you with a vast amount of information, too much to grasp in one reading. However, your base familiarity with its contents will allow you to use it as a continuing desk guide and reference source.

Building an Ultrapreneurial company is a dynamic process. It takes a continuing, unrelenting, and committed attempt to create value. You must strive to achieve new insights, encourage innovation, and pursue excellence—excellence in your product or service, excellence in your management team, and excellence in your customer results.

The rewards are achievable; they're significant. They can feel good—both in your pocket and in your heart. I hope that after you accomplish it yourself, you will share your experience and expertise with others. Teach them, mentor them, use your organizational skills and leadership gifts to help and encourage others. Pass your tenacity on to those who can benefit from it.

My Ultrapreneur's wish to you is that this book has helped you gain the confidence you need to plant the seed, cultivate the crop, and gain your Ultrapreneurial harvest.

Index

About the Author

James B. Arkebauer (Denver, Colorado) is the founder of Venture Associates Ltd., an investment banking and consulting firm. He has been an entrepreneur for over 25 years, and his experience in corporate finance includes all phases of this discipline. He has been involved in risk analysis and evaluation of many new technologies, assembled management teams, and structured and implemented equity and debt financing for both private and public companies. He is a Co-Founder/Chairman of the Rockies Venture Club, one of the country's leading groups in the support of entrepreneurs, a frequent lecturer, and the author of *OTC Financial Public Relations* and *Cashing Out: The Entrepreneur's Guide to Going Public.*